JUNCTION TRUE

WRITTEN BY
RAY FAWKES

ILLUSTRATED BY
VINCE LOCKE

PUBLISHED BY TOP SHELF PRODUCTIONS
PO BOX 1282
MARIETTA, GA 30061-1282 USA.

EDITOR-IN-CHIEF: CHRIS STAROS.

TOP SHELF PRODUCTIONS IS AN IMPRINT OF IDW PUBLISHING, A DIVISION OF IDEA AND DESIGN WORKS, LLC. OFFICES: 2765 TRUXTUN ROAD, SAN DIEGO, CA 92106.

DESIGNED BY CHRIS ROSS.
LETTERED BY ROBBIE ROBBINS WITH CHRIS ROSS.
PUBLICITY AND MARKETING BY LEIGH WALTON (LEIGH@TOPSHELFCOMIX.COM).
EDITED BY CHRIS STAROS WITH LEIGH WALTON AND ZAC BOONE.

ISBN 978-1-891830-99-0

PRINTED IN HONG KONG.

18 17 16 15 5 4 3 2 1

"FOR SHANNON"
-R.F.

"FOR ETHAN, JONATHAN AND THOMAS"
-V.L.

CHAPTER ONE

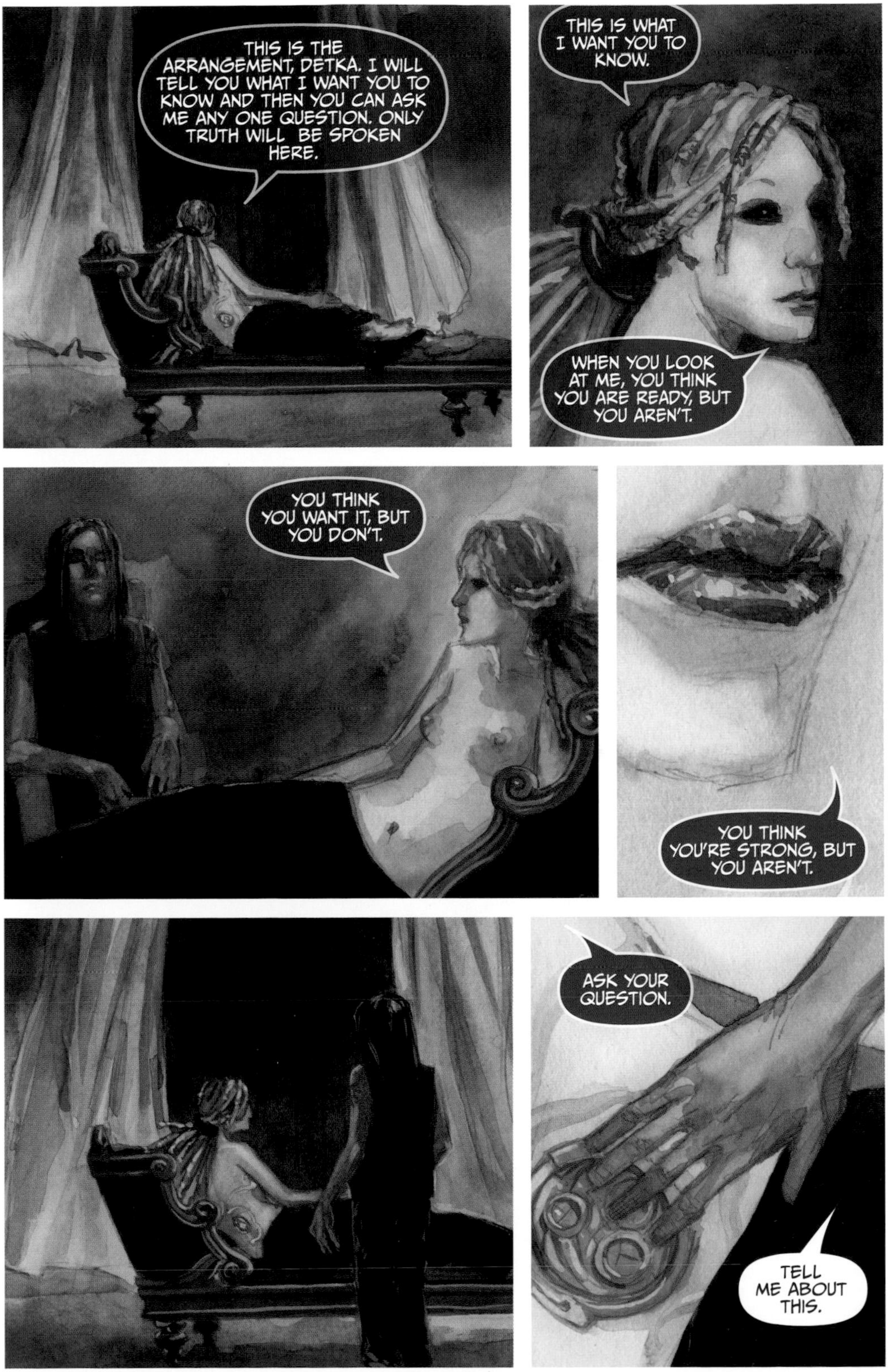
THIS IS THE ARRANGEMENT, DETKA. I WILL TELL YOU WHAT I WANT YOU TO KNOW AND THEN YOU CAN ASK ME ANY ONE QUESTION. ONLY TRUTH WILL BE SPOKEN HERE.
THIS IS WHAT I WANT YOU TO KNOW.
WHEN YOU LOOK AT ME, YOU THINK YOU ARE READY, BUT YOU AREN'T.
YOU THINK YOU WANT IT, BUT YOU DON'T.
YOU THINK YOU'RE STRONG, BUT YOU AREN'T.
ASK YOUR QUESTION.
TELL ME ABOUT THIS.

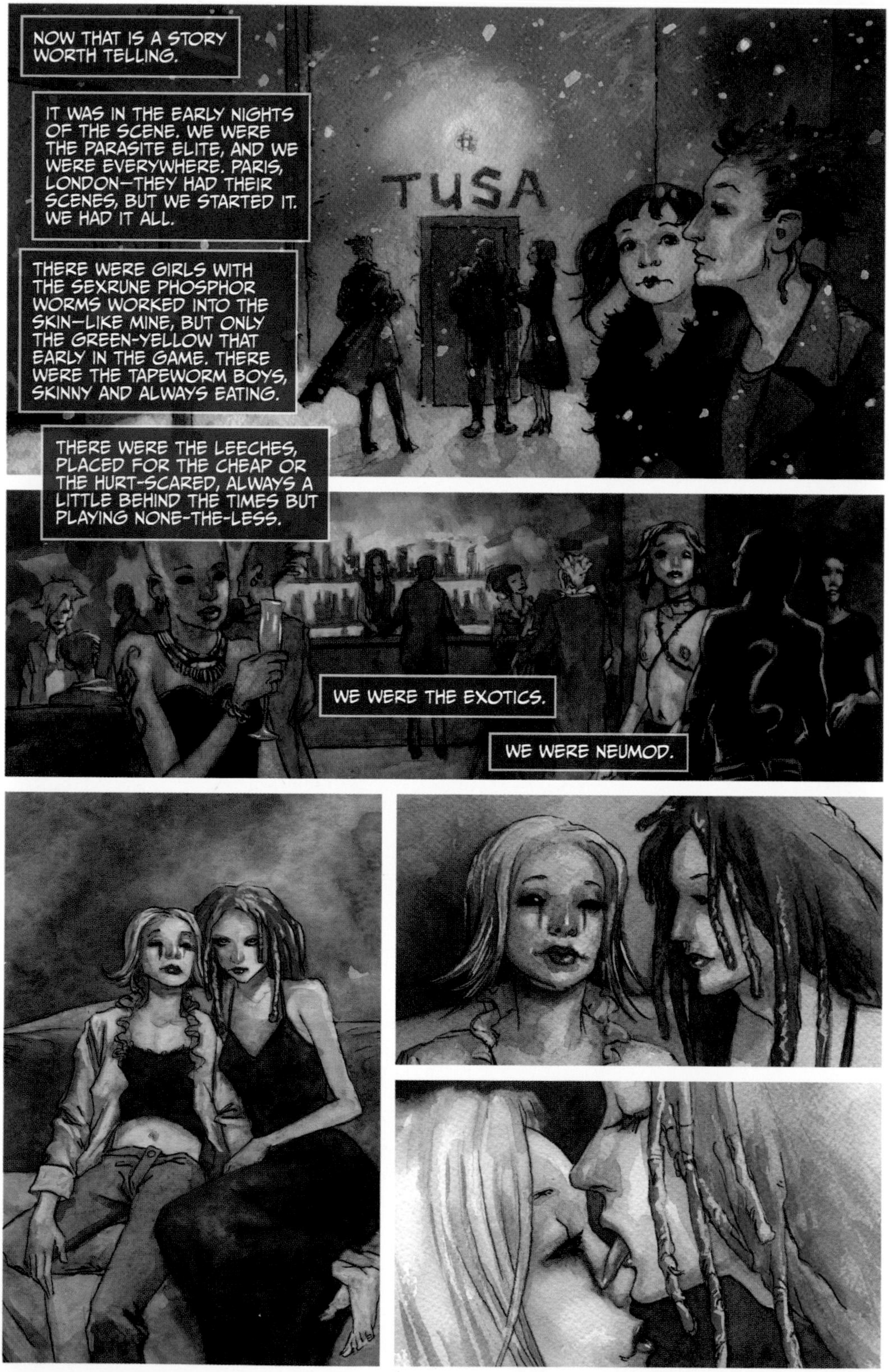
NOW THAT IS A STORY WORTH TELLING.
IT WAS IN THE EARLY NIGHTS OF THE SCENE. WE WERE THE PARASITE ELITE, AND WE WERE EVERYWHERE. PARIS, LONDON—THEY HAD THEIR SCENES, BUT WE STARTED IT. WE HAD IT ALL.
TUSA
THERE WERE GIRLS WITH THE SEXRUNE PHOSPHOR WORMS WORKED INTO THE SKIN—LIKE MINE, BUT ONLY THE GREEN-YELLOW THAT EARLY IN THE GAME. THERE WERE THE TAPEWORM BOYS, SKINNY AND ALWAYS EATING.
THERE WERE THE LEECHES, PLACED FOR THE CHEAP OR THE HURT-SCARED, ALWAYS A LITTLE BEHIND THE TIMES BUT PLAYING NONE-THE-LESS.
WE WERE THE EXOTICS.
WE WERE NEUMOD.

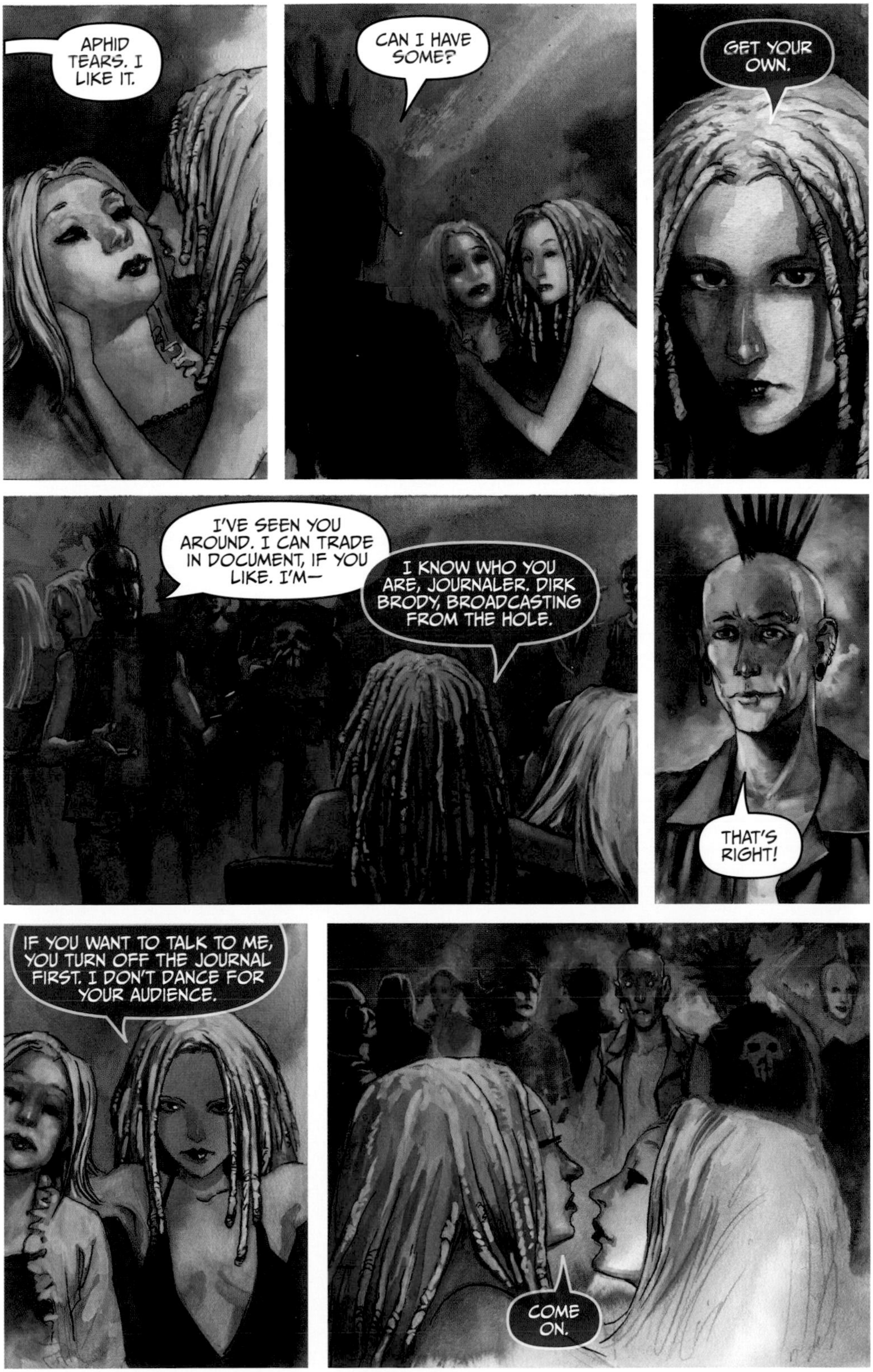
APHID TEARS. I LIKE IT.
CAN I HAVE SOME?
GET YOUR OWN.
I'VE SEEN YOU AROUND. I CAN TRADE IN DOCUMENT, IF YOU LIKE. I'M—
I KNOW WHO YOU ARE, JOURNALER. DIRK BRODY, BROADCASTING FROM THE HOLE.
THAT'S RIGHT!
IF YOU WANT TO TALK TO ME, YOU TURN OFF THE JOURNAL FIRST. I DON'T DANCE FOR YOUR AUDIENCE.
COME ON.

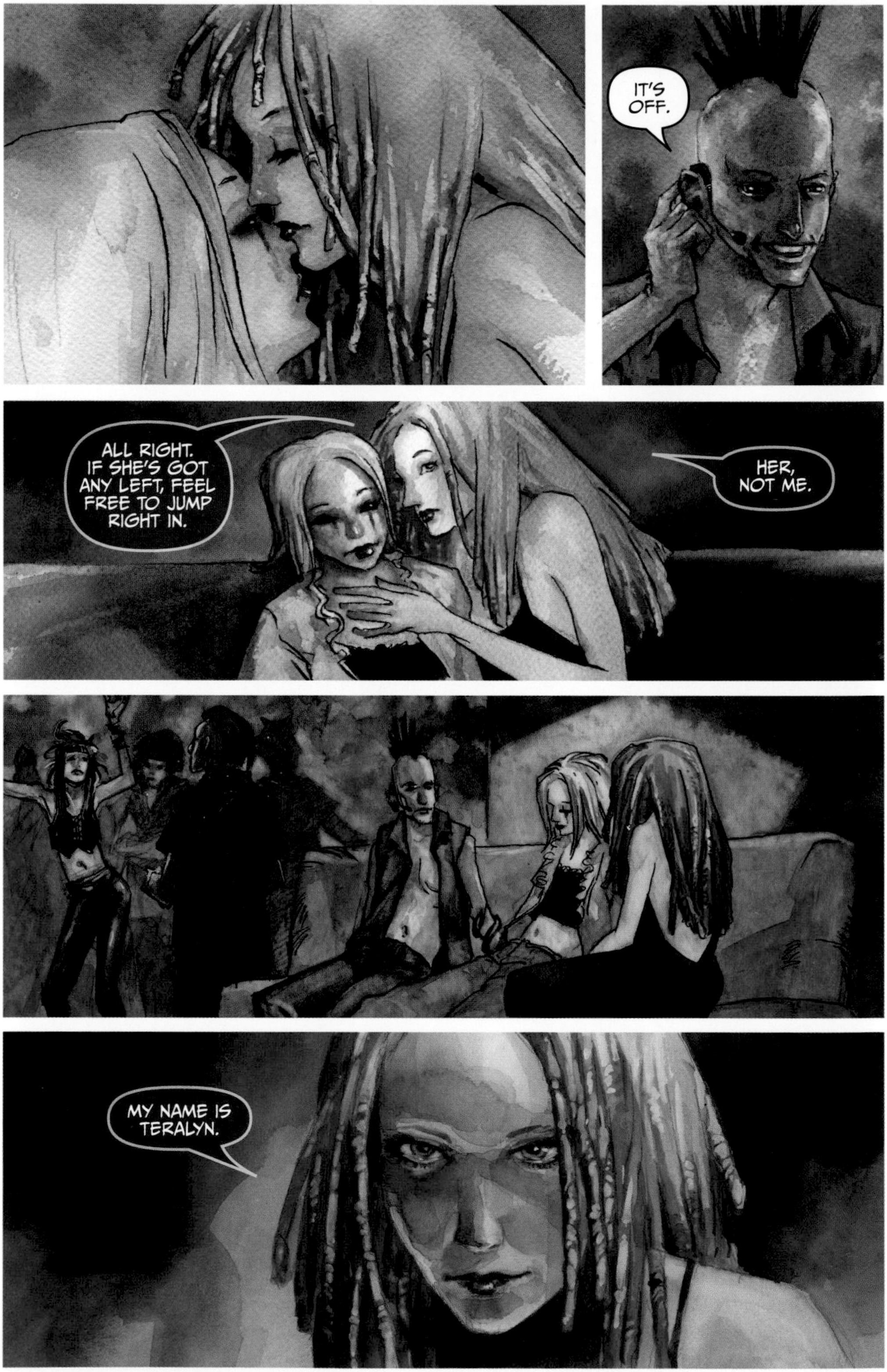
IT'S OFF.
ALL RIGHT. IF SHE'S GOT ANY LEFT, FEEL FREE TO JUMP RIGHT IN.
HER, NOT ME.
MY NAME IS TERALYN.

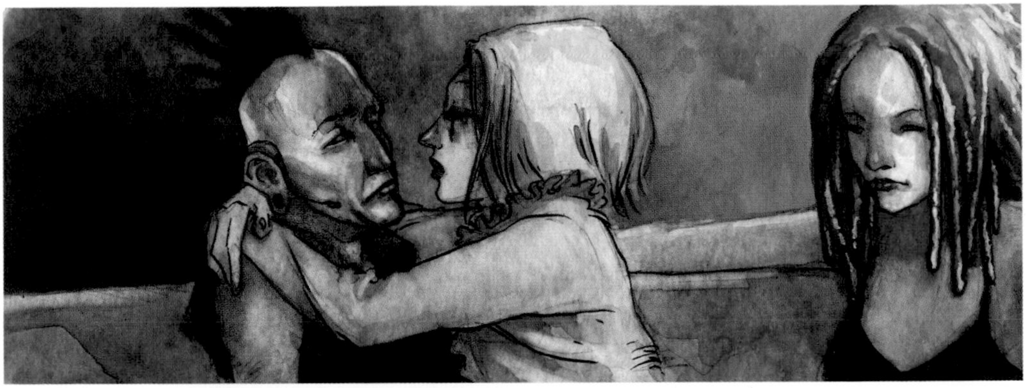

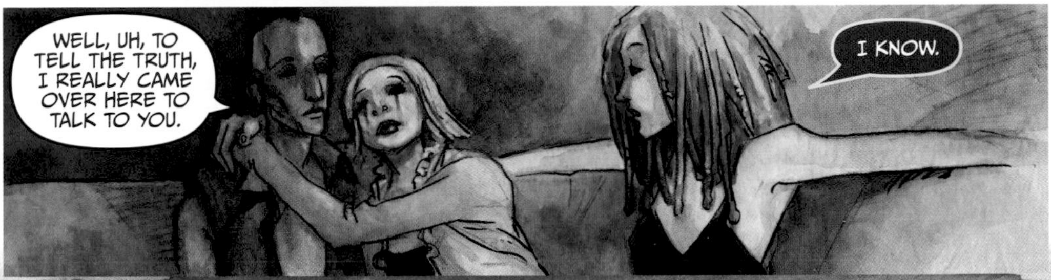
WELL, UH, TO TELL THE TRUTH, I REALLY CAME OVER HERE TO TALK TO YOU.
I KNOW.

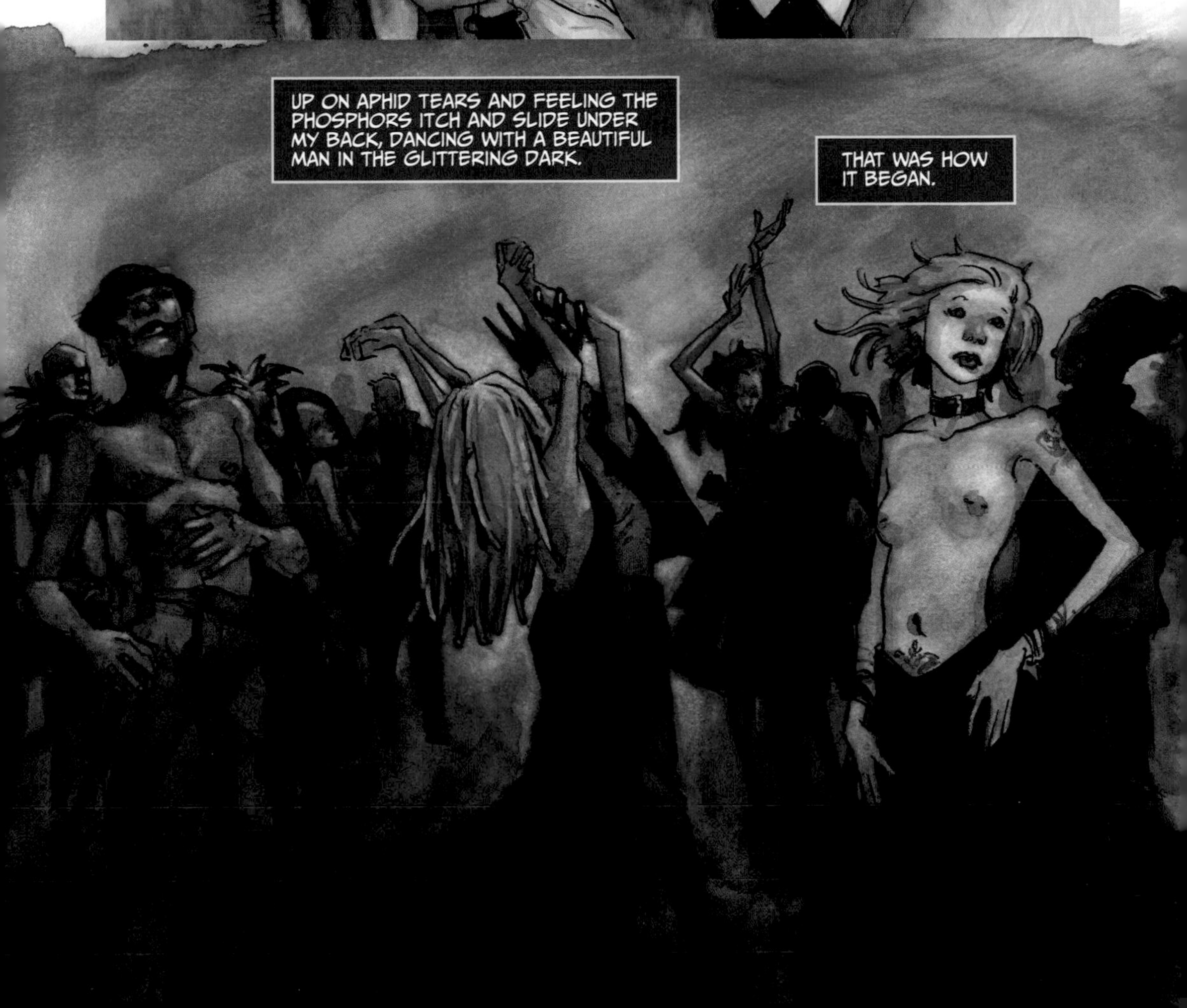
UP ON APHID TEARS AND FEELING THE PHOSPHORS ITCH AND SLIDE UNDER MY BACK, DANCING WITH A BEAUTIFUL MAN IN THE GLITTERING DARK.
THAT WAS HOW IT BEGAN.

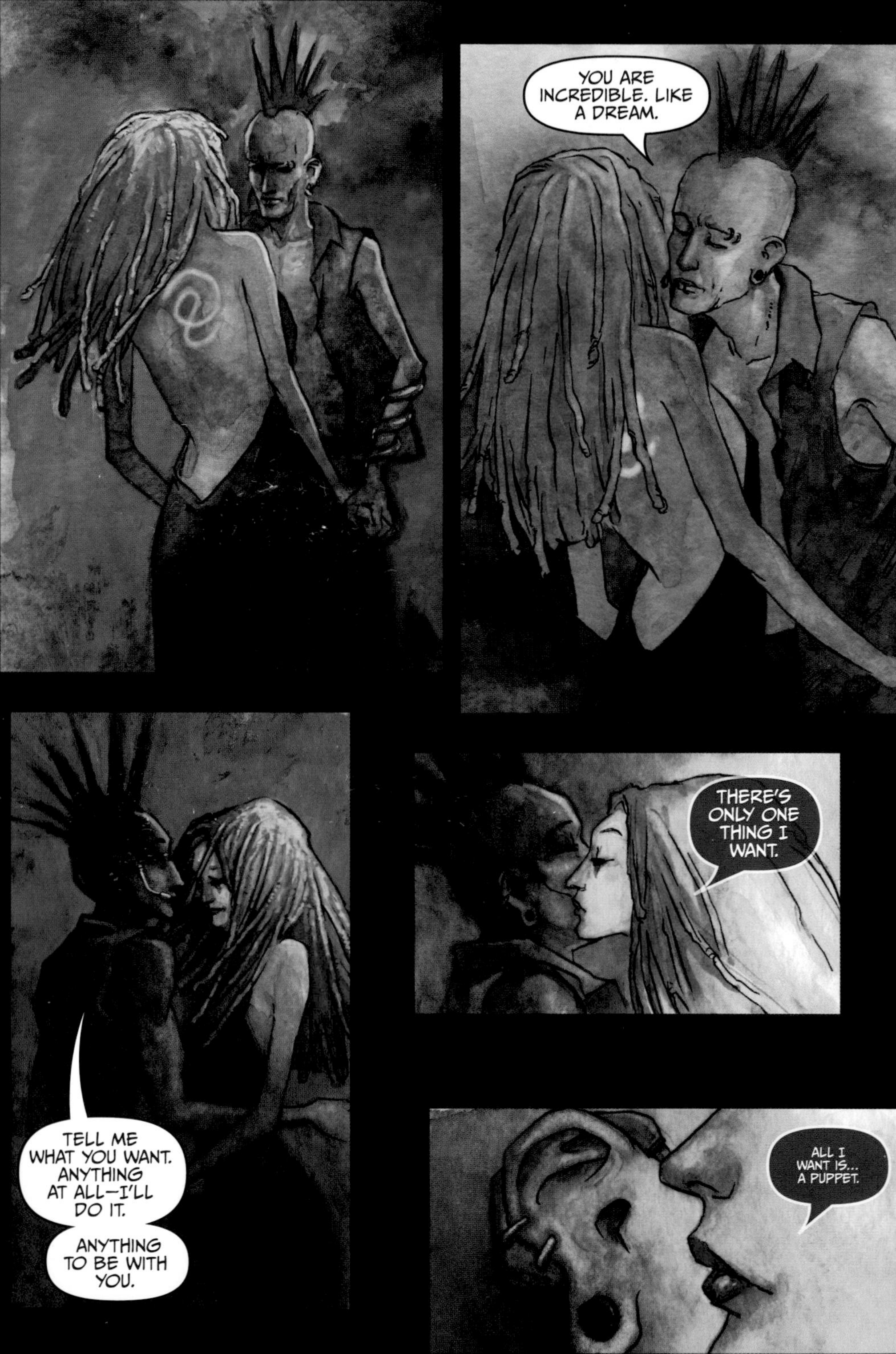
YOU ARE INCREDIBLE. LIKE A DREAM.
TELL ME WHAT YOU WANT. ANYTHING AT ALL—I'LL DO IT.
ANYTHING TO BE WITH YOU.
THERE'S ONLY ONE THING I WANT.
ALL I WANT IS... A PUPPET.

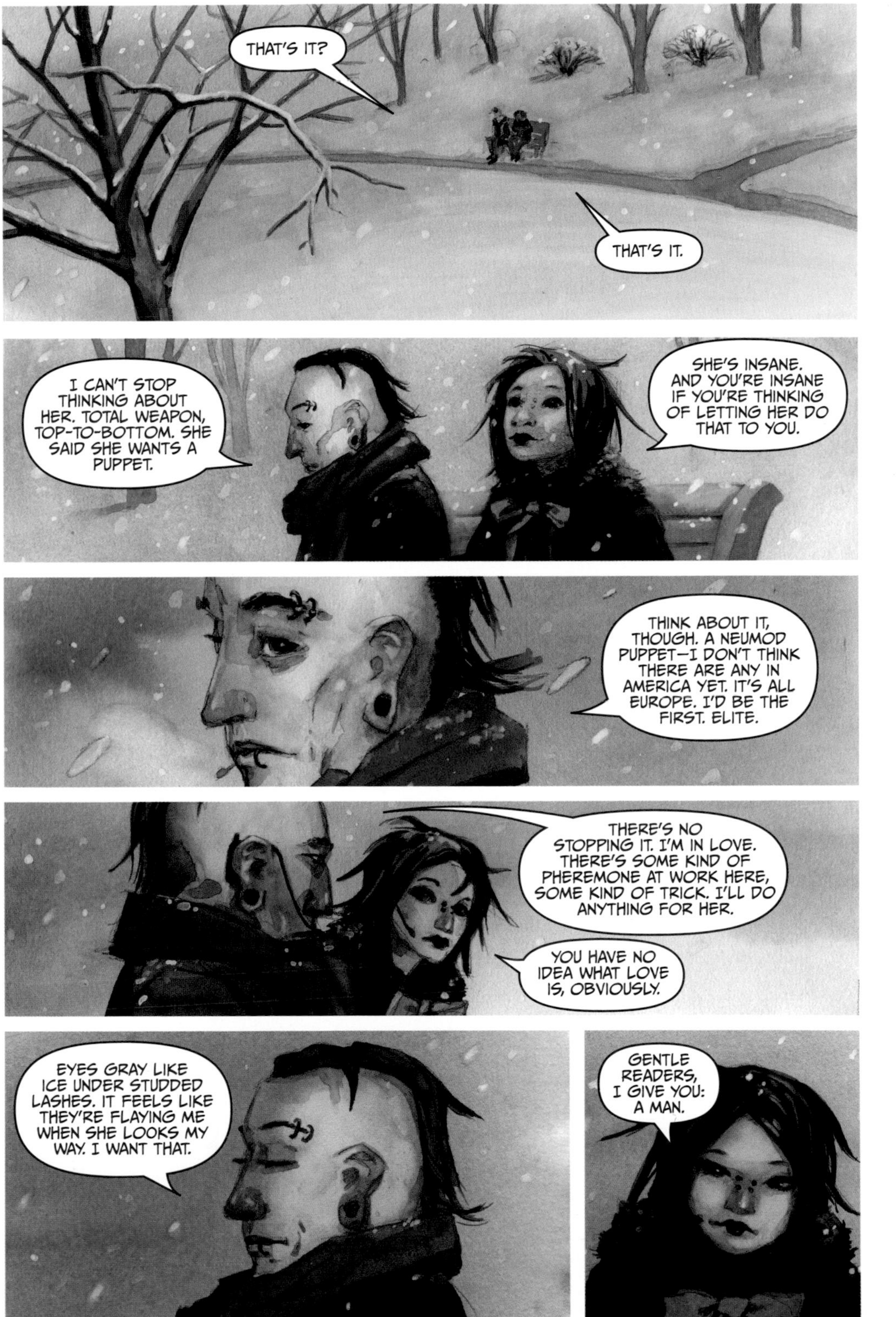
THAT'S IT?
THAT'S IT.
I CAN'T STOP THINKING ABOUT HER. TOTAL WEAPON, TOP-TO-BOTTOM. SHE SAID SHE WANTS A PUPPET.
SHE'S INSANE. AND YOU'RE INSANE IF YOU'RE THINKING OF LETTING HER DO THAT TO YOU.
THINK ABOUT IT, THOUGH. A NEUMOD PUPPET—I DON'T THINK THERE ARE ANY IN AMERICA YET. IT'S ALL EUROPE. I'D BE THE FIRST. ELITE.
THERE'S NO STOPPING IT. I'M IN LOVE. THERE'S SOME KIND OF PHEREMONE AT WORK HERE, SOME KIND OF TRICK. I'LL DO ANYTHING FOR HER.
YOU HAVE NO IDEA WHAT LOVE IS, OBVIOUSLY.
EYES GRAY LIKE ICE UNDER STUDDED LASHES. IT FEELS LIKE THEY'RE FLAYING ME WHEN SHE LOOKS MY WAY. I WANT THAT.
GENTLE READERS, I GIVE YOU: A MAN.

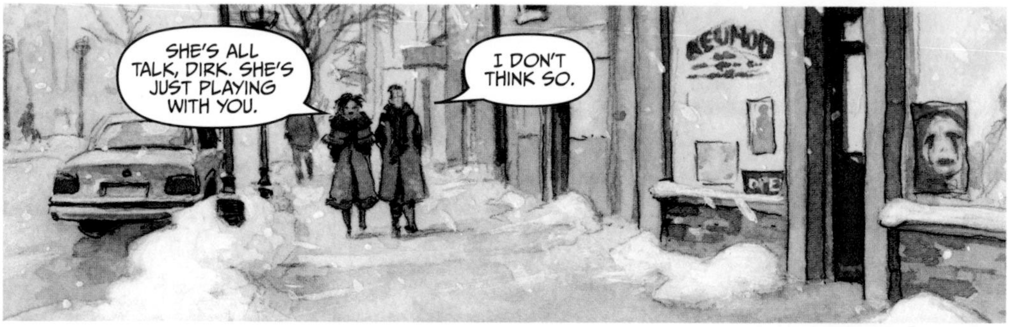
SHE'S ALL TALK, DIRK. SHE'S JUST PLAYING WITH YOU.
I DON'T THINK SO.
NEUMOD
OPE

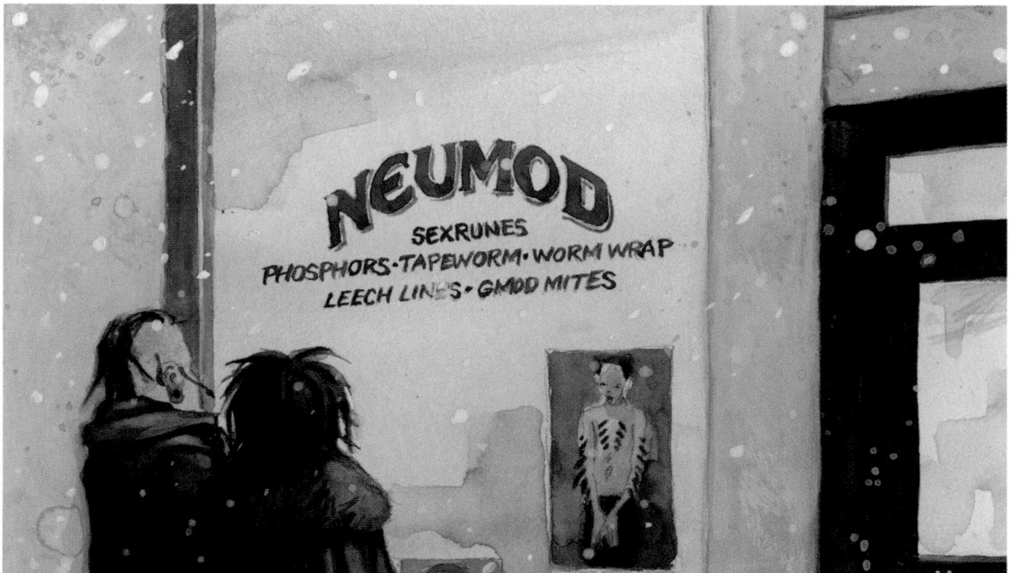
NEUMOD
SEXRUNES
PHOSPHORS·TAPEWORM·WORM WRAP
LEECH LINES·GMOD MITES
OPEN

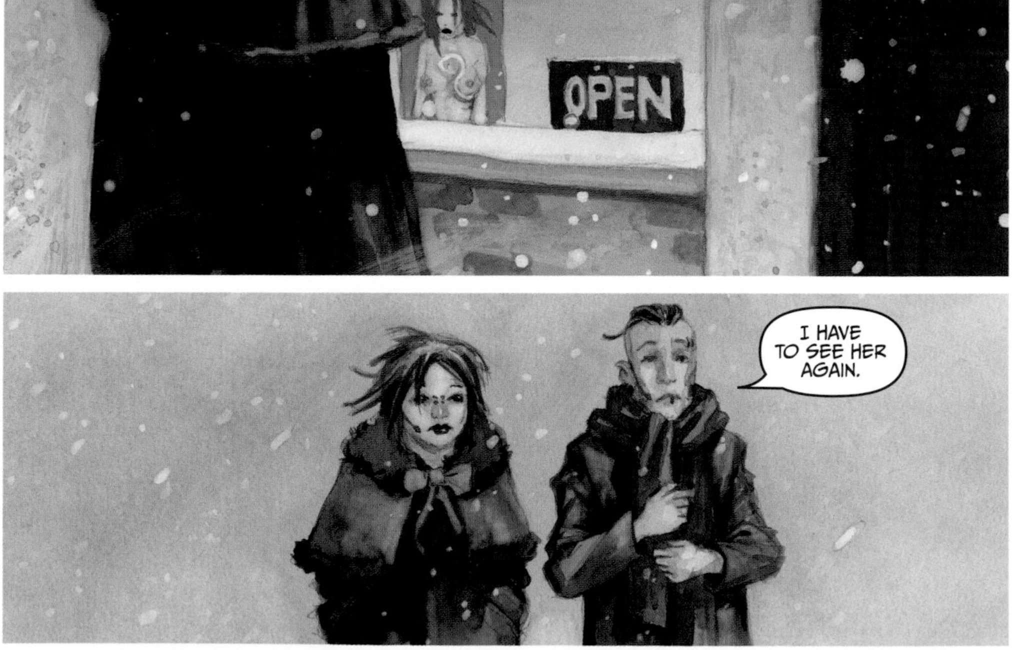
I HAVE TO SEE HER AGAIN.

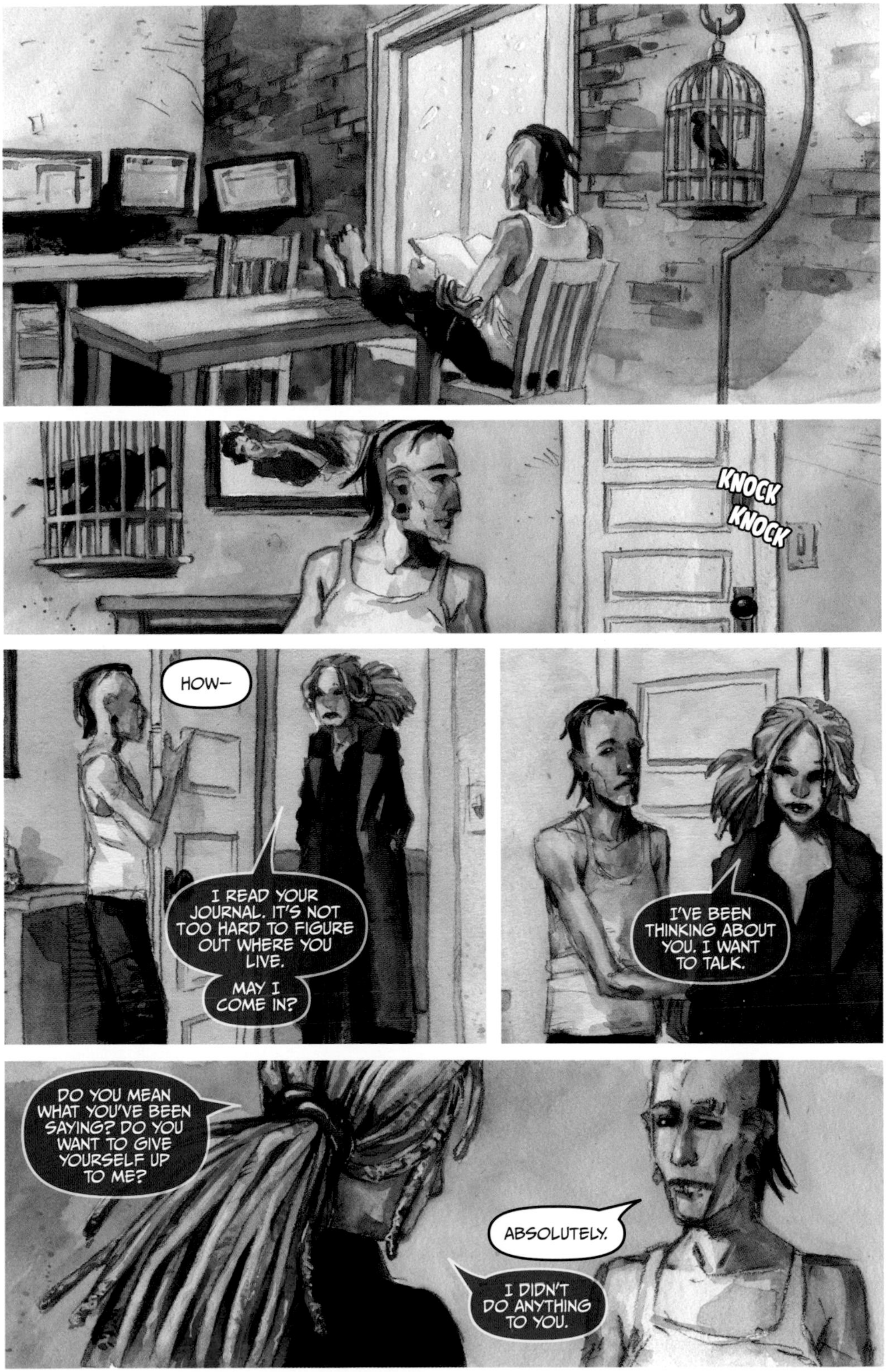
KNOCK
KNOCK
HOW–
I READ YOUR JOURNAL. IT'S NOT TOO HARD TO FIGURE OUT WHERE YOU LIVE.
MAY I COME IN?
I'VE BEEN THINKING ABOUT YOU. I WANT TO TALK.
DO YOU MEAN WHAT YOU'VE BEEN SAYING? DO YOU WANT TO GIVE YOURSELF UP TO ME?
ABSOLUTELY.
I DIDN'T DO ANYTHING TO YOU.

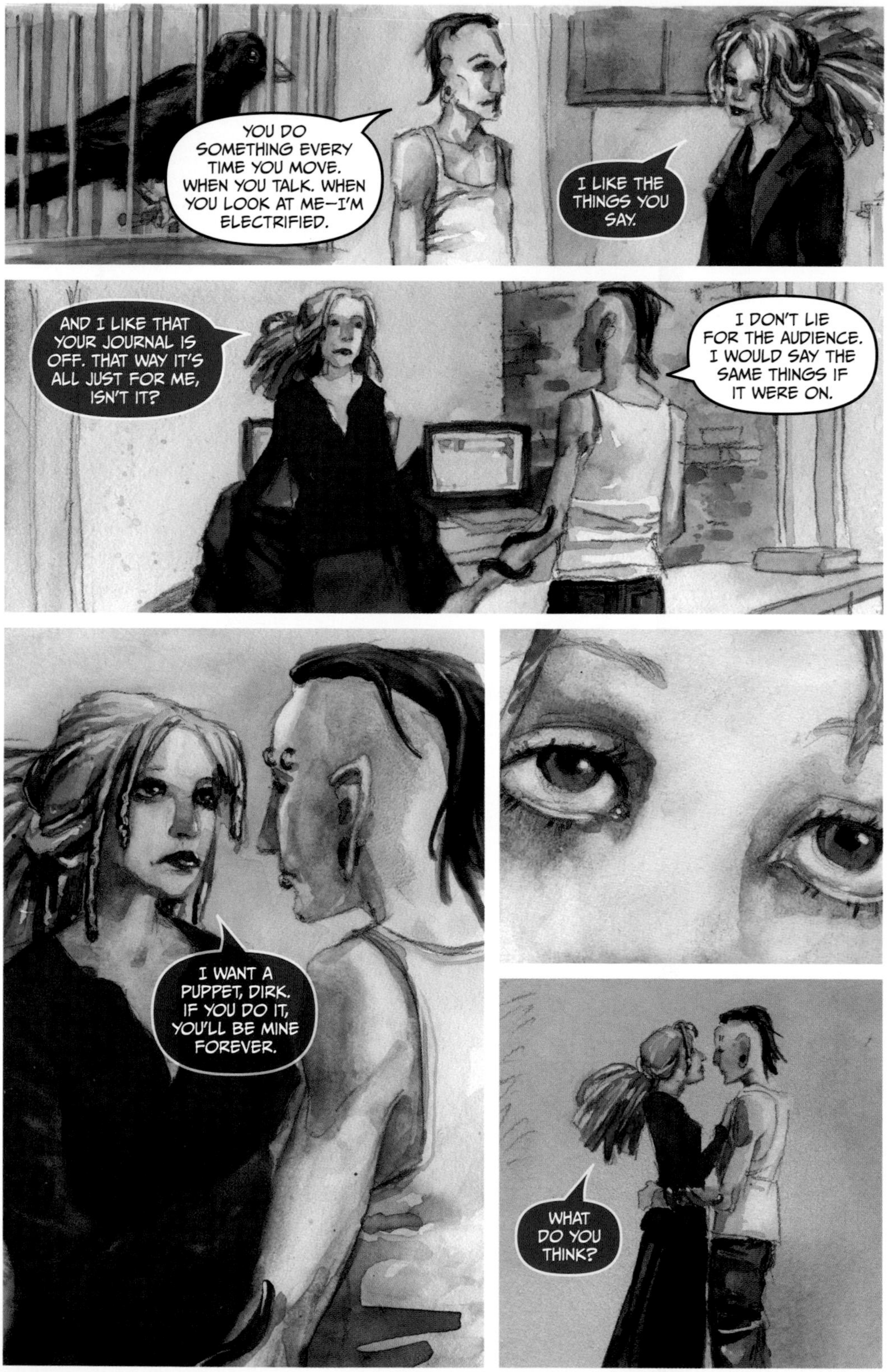
YOU DO SOMETHING EVERY TIME YOU MOVE. WHEN YOU TALK. WHEN YOU LOOK AT ME—I'M ELECTRIFIED.
I LIKE THE THINGS YOU SAY.
AND I LIKE THAT YOUR JOURNAL IS OFF. THAT WAY IT'S ALL JUST FOR ME, ISN'T IT?
I DON'T LIE FOR THE AUDIENCE. I WOULD SAY THE SAME THINGS IF IT WERE ON.
I WANT A PUPPET, DIRK. IF YOU DO IT, YOU'LL BE MINE FOREVER.
WHAT DO YOU THINK?

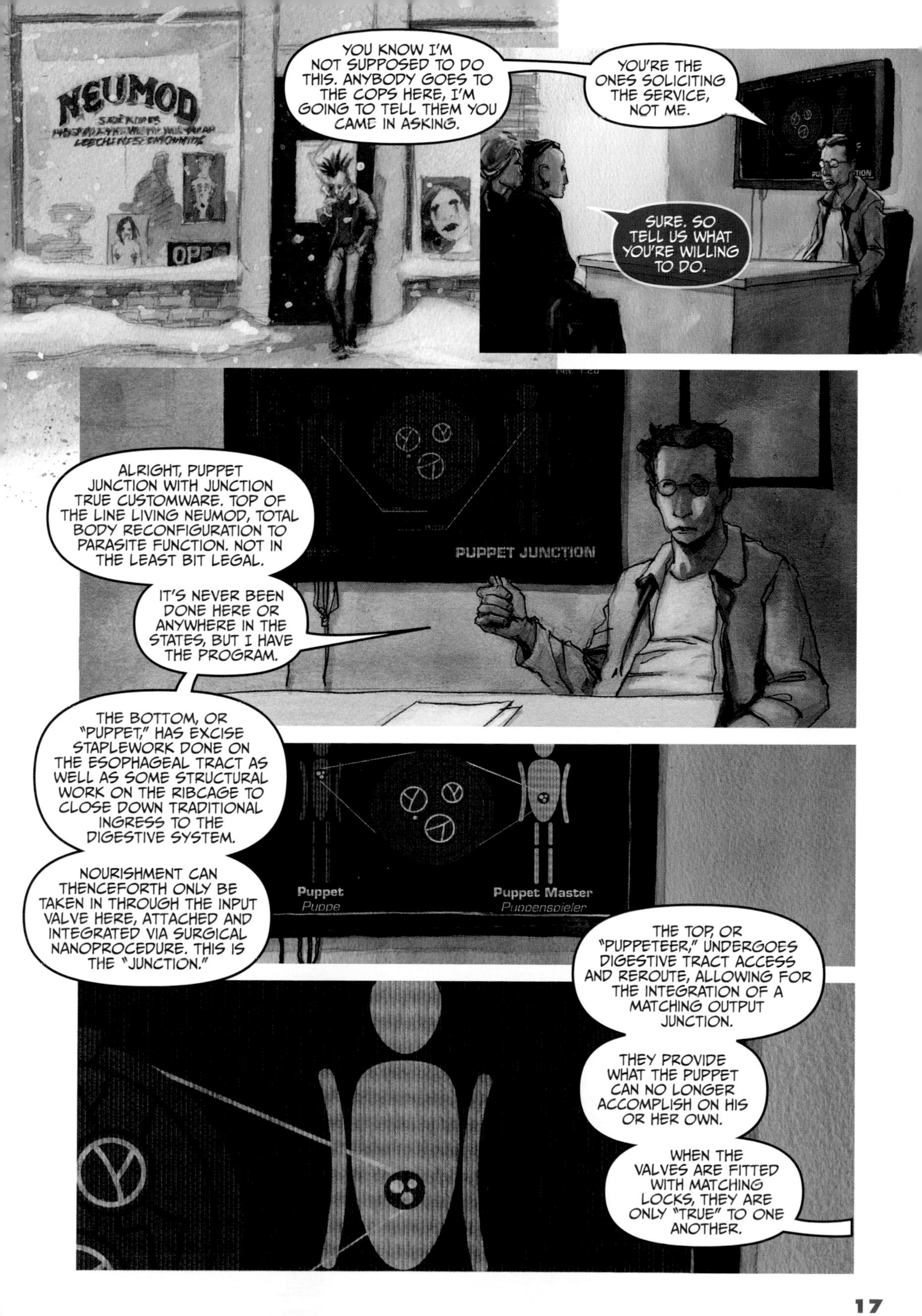
NEUMOD
YOU KNOW I'M NOT SUPPOSED TO DO THIS. ANYBODY GOES TO THE COPS HERE, I'M GOING TO TELL THEM YOU CAME IN ASKING.
YOU'RE THE ONES SOLICITING THE SERVICE, NOT ME.
SURE. SO TELL US WHAT YOU'RE WILLING TO DO.
ALRIGHT, PUPPET JUNCTION WITH JUNCTION TRUE CUSTOMWARE. TOP OF THE LINE LIVING NEUMOD, TOTAL BODY RECONFIGURATION TO PARASITE FUNCTION. NOT IN THE LEAST BIT LEGAL.
PUPPET JUNCTION
IT'S NEVER BEEN DONE HERE OR ANYWHERE IN THE STATES, BUT I HAVE THE PROGRAM.
THE BOTTOM, OR "PUPPET," HAS EXCISE STAPLEWORK DONE ON THE ESOPHAGEAL TRACT AS WELL AS SOME STRUCTURAL WORK ON THE RIBCAGE TO CLOSE DOWN TRADITIONAL INGRESS TO THE DIGESTIVE SYSTEM.
NOURISHMENT CAN THENCEFORTH ONLY BE TAKEN IN THROUGH THE INPUT VALVE HERE, ATTACHED AND INTEGRATED VIA SURGICAL NANOPROCEDURE. THIS IS THE "JUNCTION."
Puppet
Puppe
Puppet Master
Puppenspieler
THE TOP, OR "PUPPETEER," UNDERGOES DIGESTIVE TRACT ACCESS AND REROUTE, ALLOWING FOR THE INTEGRATION OF A MATCHING OUTPUT JUNCTION.
THEY PROVIDE WHAT THE PUPPET CAN NO LONGER ACCOMPLISH ON HIS OR HER OWN.
WHEN THE VALVES ARE FITTED WITH MATCHING LOCKS, THEY ARE ONLY "TRUE" TO ONE ANOTHER.

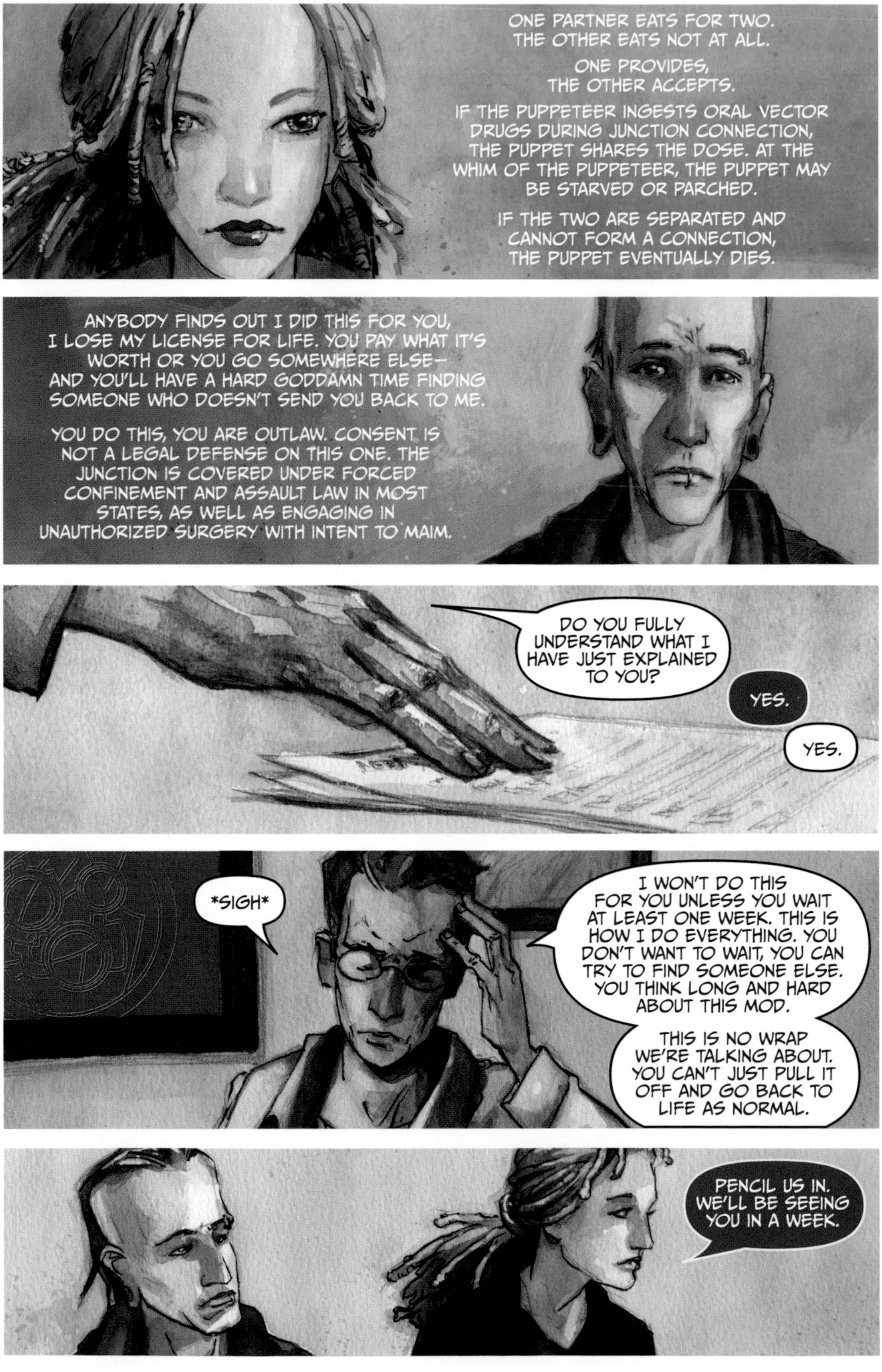
ONE PARTNER EATS FOR TWO. THE OTHER EATS NOT AT ALL.
ONE PROVIDES, THE OTHER ACCEPTS.
IF THE PUPPETEER INGESTS ORAL VECTOR DRUGS DURING JUNCTION CONNECTION, THE PUPPET SHARES THE DOSE. AT THE WHIM OF THE PUPPETEER, THE PUPPET MAY BE STARVED OR PARCHED.
IF THE TWO ARE SEPARATED AND CANNOT FORM A CONNECTION, THE PUPPET EVENTUALLY DIES.
ANYBODY FINDS OUT I DID THIS FOR YOU, I LOSE MY LICENSE FOR LIFE. YOU PAY WHAT IT'S WORTH OR YOU GO SOMEWHERE ELSE— AND YOU'LL HAVE A HARD GODDAMN TIME FINDING SOMEONE WHO DOESN'T SEND YOU BACK TO ME.
YOU DO THIS, YOU ARE OUTLAW. CONSENT IS NOT A LEGAL DEFENSE ON THIS ONE. THE JUNCTION IS COVERED UNDER FORCED CONFINEMENT AND ASSAULT LAW IN MOST STATES, AS WELL AS ENGAGING IN UNAUTHORIZED SURGERY WITH INTENT TO MAIM.
DO YOU FULLY UNDERSTAND WHAT I HAVE JUST EXPLAINED TO YOU?
YES.
YES.
SIGH
I WON'T DO THIS FOR YOU UNLESS YOU WAIT AT LEAST ONE WEEK. THIS IS HOW I DO EVERYTHING. YOU DON'T WANT TO WAIT, YOU CAN TRY TO FIND SOMEONE ELSE. YOU THINK LONG AND HARD ABOUT THIS MOD.
THIS IS NO WRAP WE'RE TALKING ABOUT. YOU CAN'T JUST PULL IT OFF AND GO BACK TO LIFE AS NORMAL.
PENCIL US IN. WE'LL BE SEEING YOU IN A WEEK.

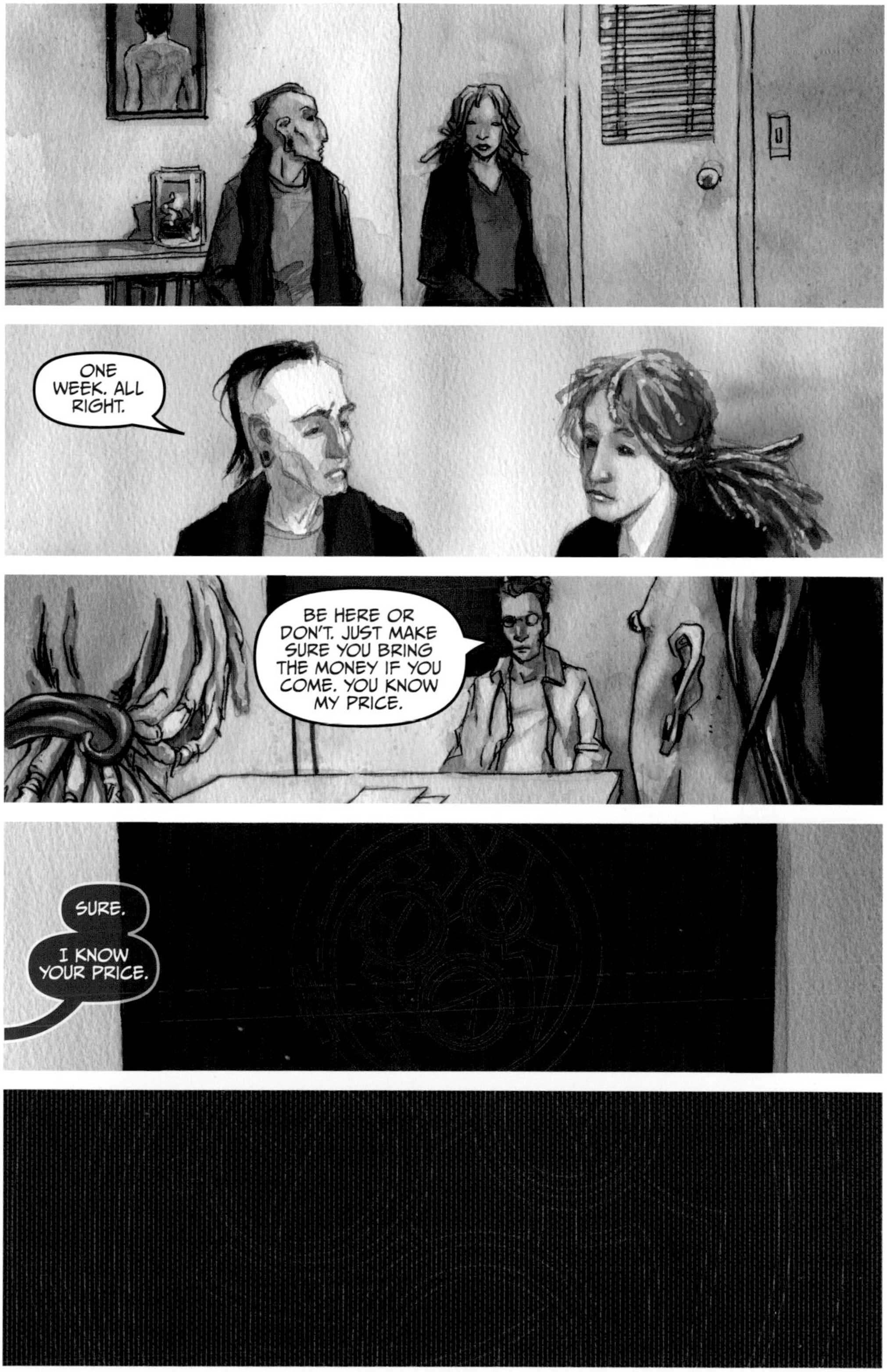
ONE WEEK. ALL RIGHT.
BE HERE OR DON'T. JUST MAKE SURE YOU BRING THE MONEY IF YOU COME. YOU KNOW MY PRICE.
SURE.
I KNOW YOUR PRICE.

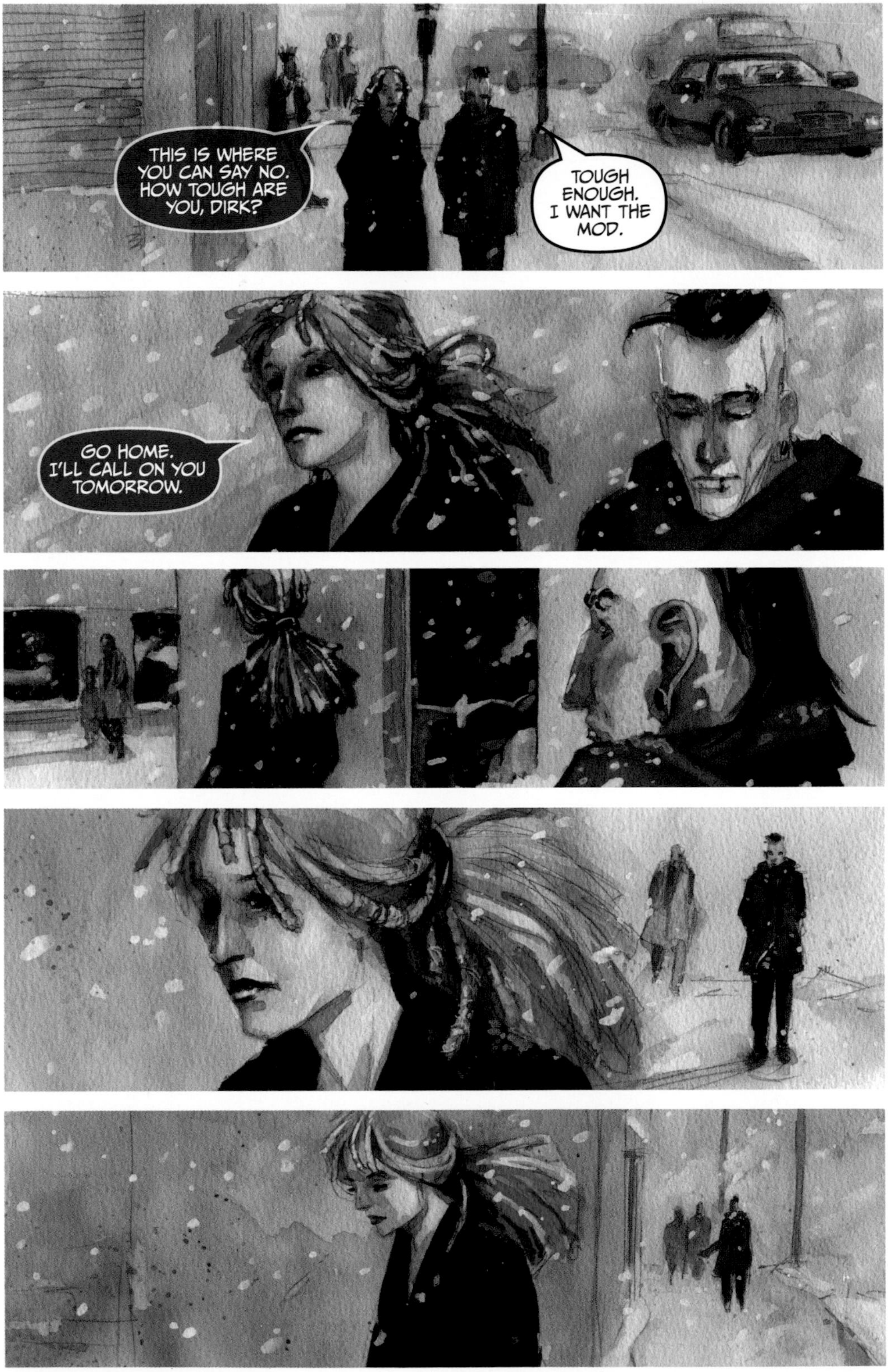
THIS IS WHERE YOU CAN SAY NO. HOW TOUGH ARE YOU, DIRK?
TOUGH ENOUGH. I WANT THE MOD.
GO HOME. I'LL CALL ON YOU TOMORROW.

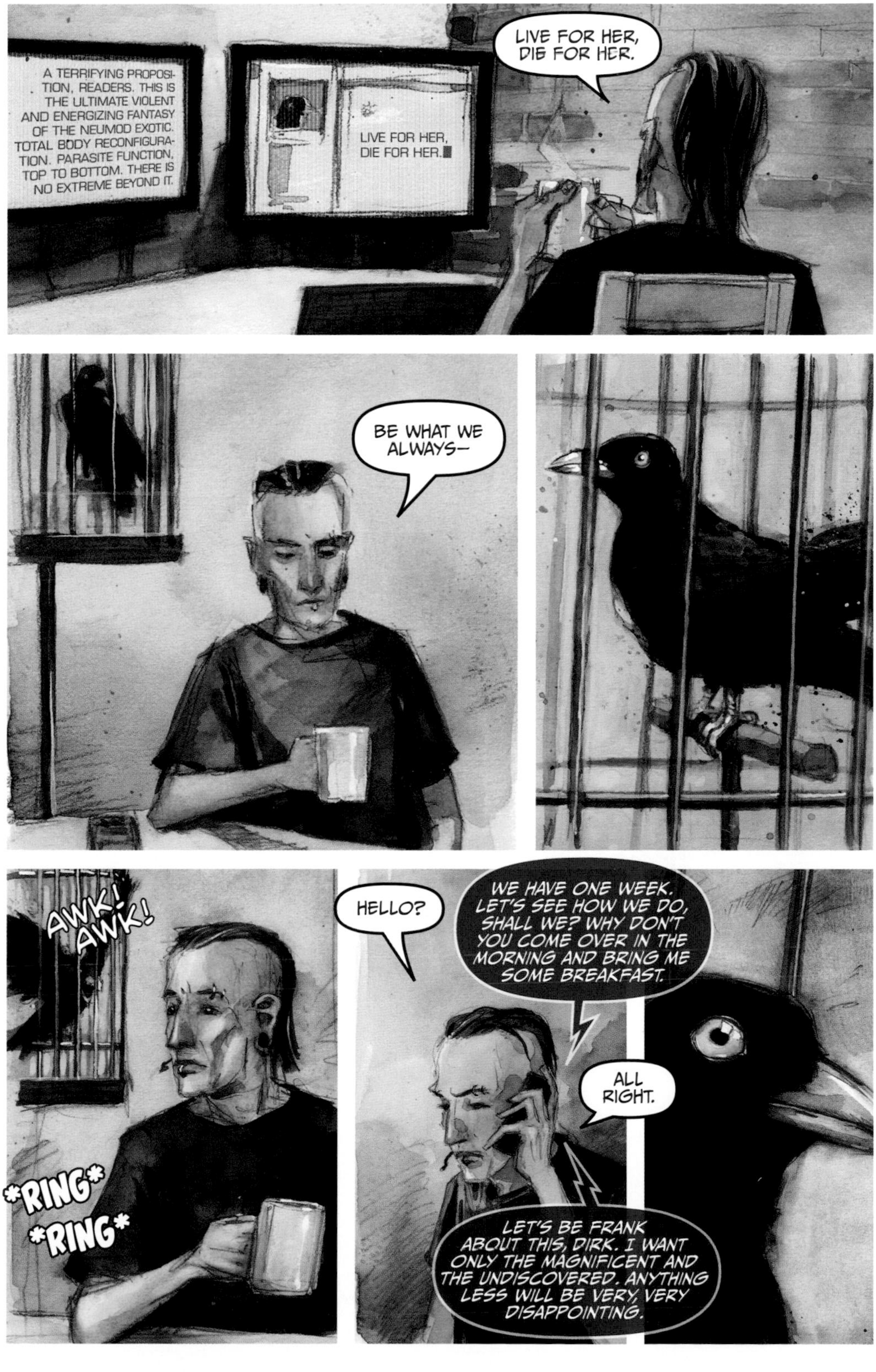
A TERRIFYING PROPOSITION, READERS. THIS IS THE ULTIMATE VIOLENT AND ENERGIZING FANTASY OF THE NEUMOD EXOTIC. TOTAL BODY RECONFIGURATION. PARASITE FUNCTION, TOP TO BOTTOM. THERE IS NO EXTREME BEYOND IT.
LIVE FOR HER, DIE FOR HER.
LIVE FOR HER, DIE FOR HER.
BE WHAT WE ALWAYS—
AWK! AWK!
RING *RING*
HELLO?
WE HAVE ONE WEEK. LET'S SEE HOW WE DO, SHALL WE? WHY DON'T YOU COME OVER IN THE MORNING AND BRING ME SOME BREAKFAST.
ALL RIGHT.
LET'S BE FRANK ABOUT THIS, DIRK. I WANT ONLY THE MAGNIFICENT AND THE UNDISCOVERED. ANYTHING LESS WILL BE VERY, VERY DISAPPOINTING.

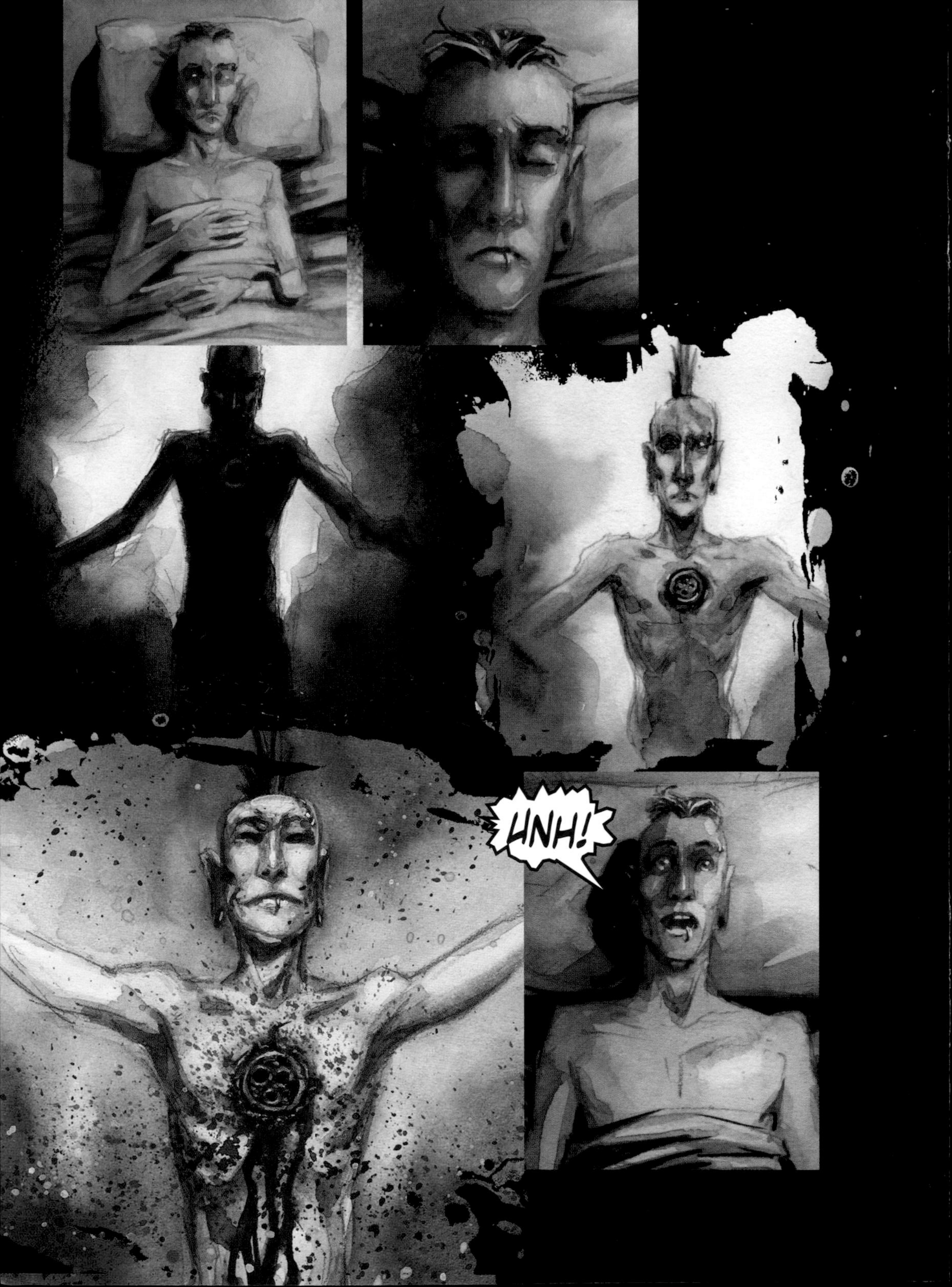
UNH!

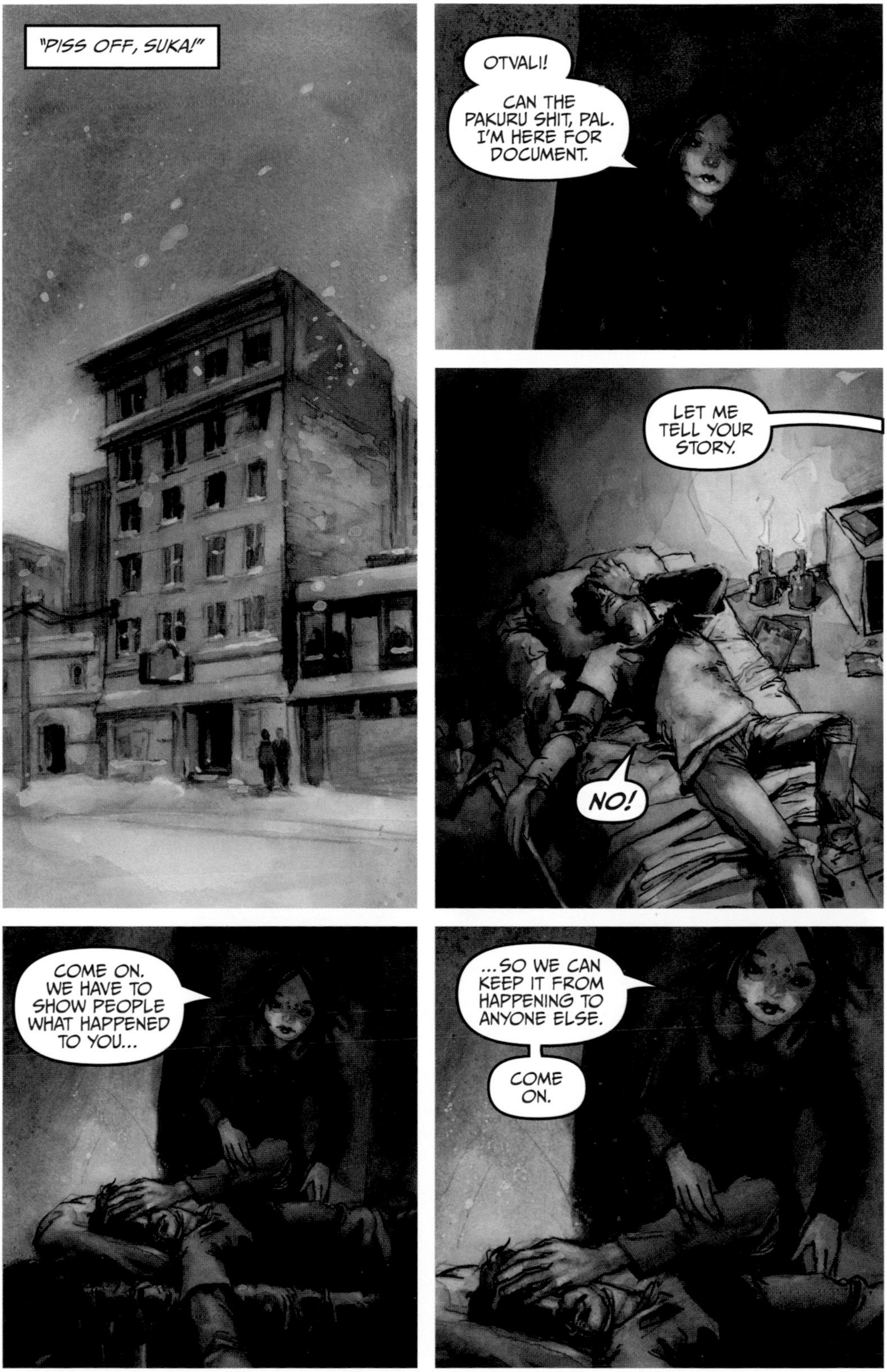
"PISS OFF, SUKA!"
OTVALI!
CAN THE PAKURU SHIT, PAL. I'M HERE FOR DOCUMENT.
LET ME TELL YOUR STORY.
NO!
COME ON. WE HAVE TO SHOW PEOPLE WHAT HAPPENED TO YOU...
...SO WE CAN KEEP IT FROM HAPPENING TO ANYONE ELSE.
COME ON.

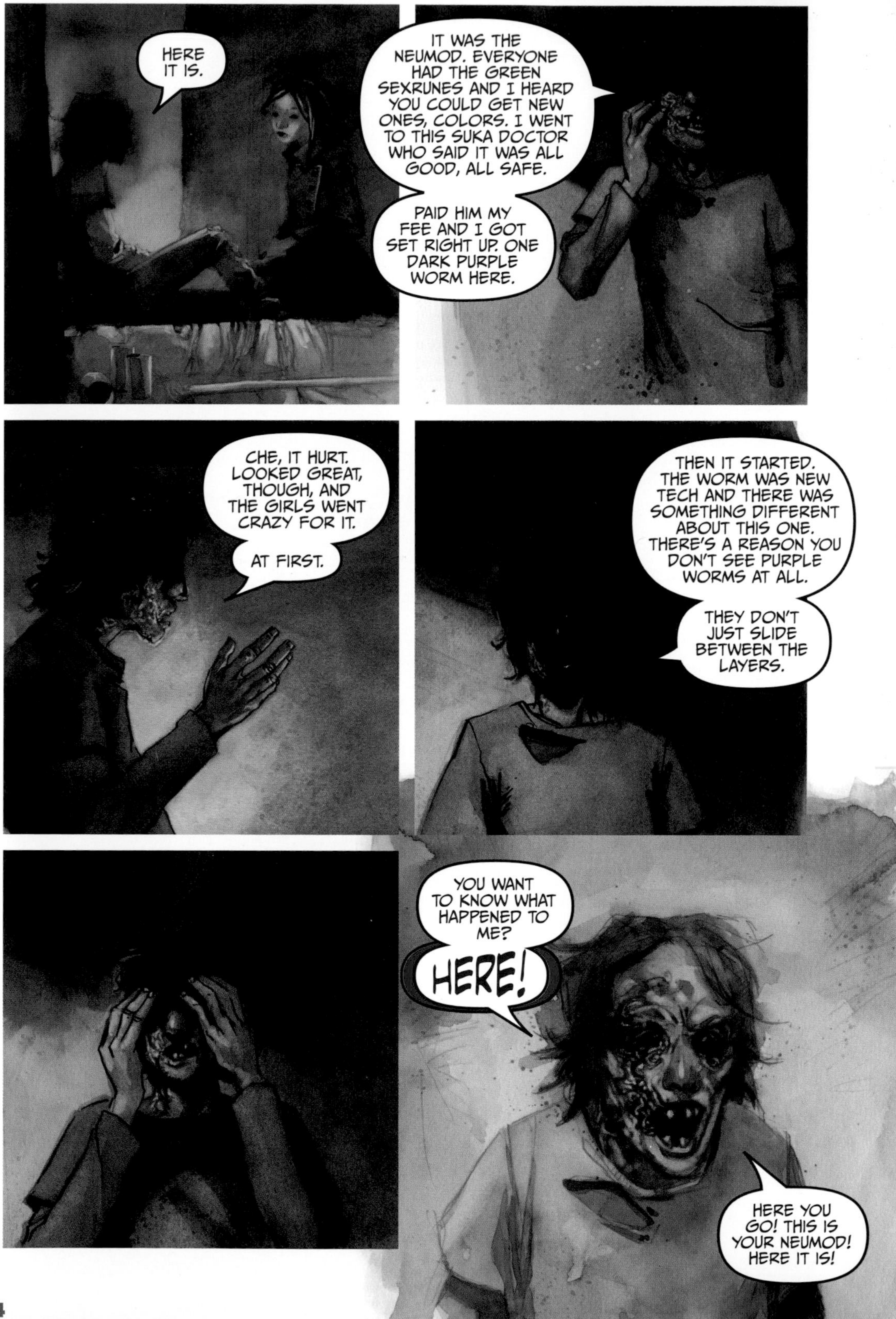
HERE IT IS.
IT WAS THE NEUMOD. EVERYONE HAD THE GREEN SEXRUNES AND I HEARD YOU COULD GET NEW ONES, COLORS. I WENT TO THIS SUKA DOCTOR WHO SAID IT WAS ALL GOOD, ALL SAFE.
PAID HIM MY FEE AND I GOT SET RIGHT UP. ONE DARK PURPLE WORM HERE.
CHE, IT HURT. LOOKED GREAT, THOUGH, AND THE GIRLS WENT CRAZY FOR IT.
AT FIRST.
THEN IT STARTED. THE WORM WAS NEW TECH AND THERE WAS SOMETHING DIFFERENT ABOUT THIS ONE. THERE'S A REASON YOU DON'T SEE PURPLE WORMS AT ALL.
THEY DON'T JUST SLIDE BETWEEN THE LAYERS.
YOU WANT TO KNOW WHAT HAPPENED TO ME?
HERE!
HERE YOU GO! THIS IS YOUR NEUMOD! HERE IT IS!

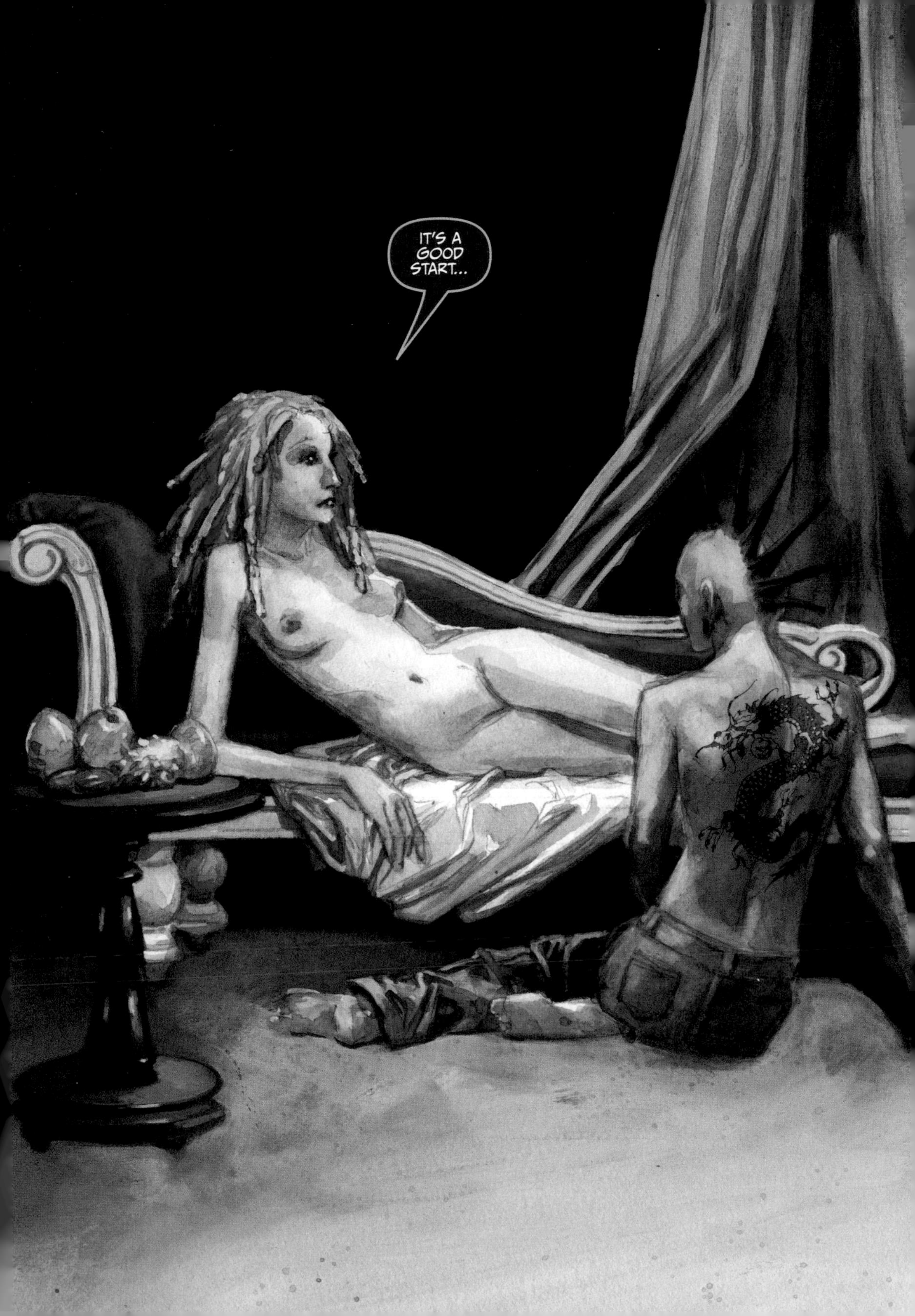
IT'S A GOOD START...

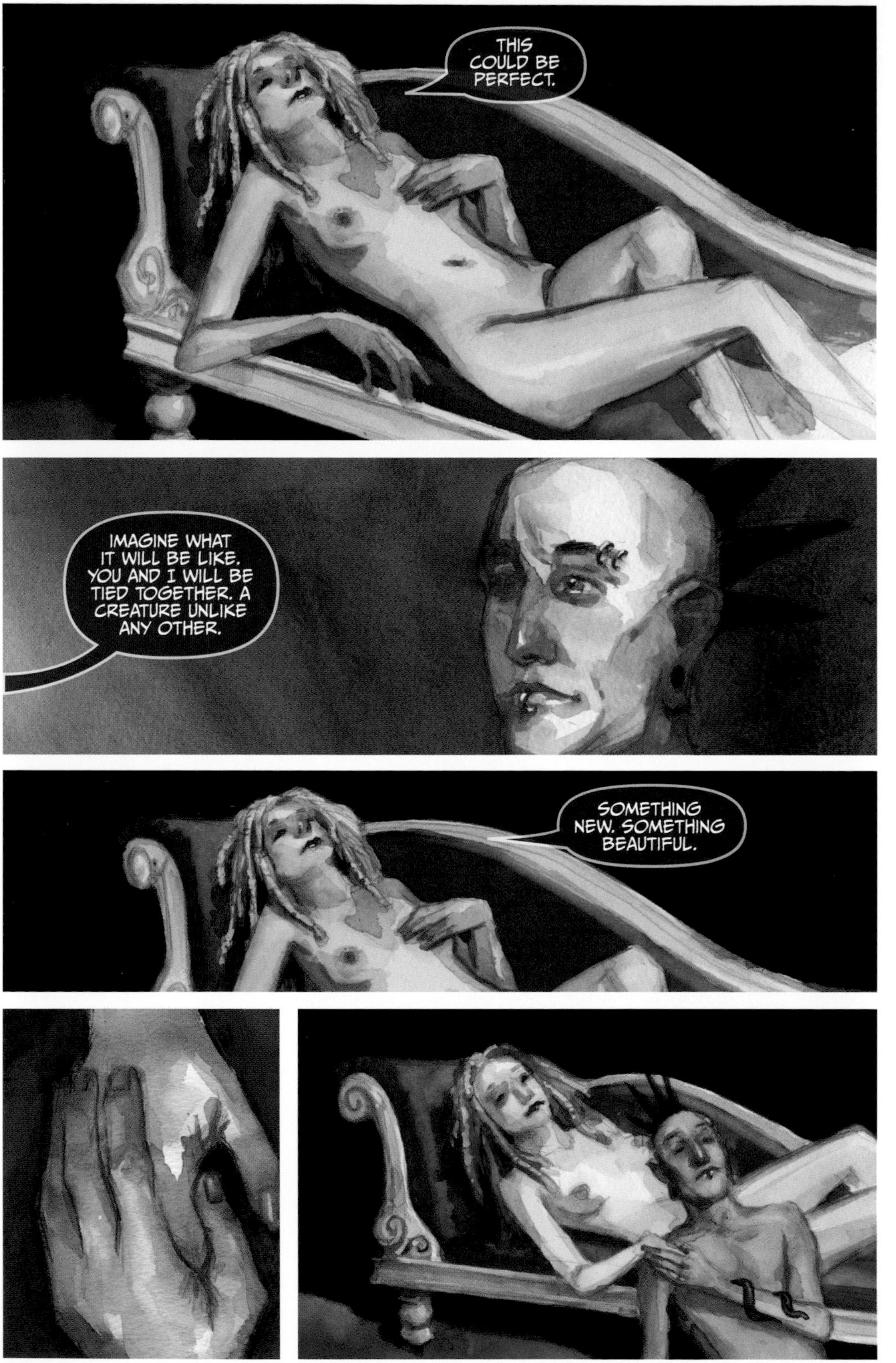
THIS COULD BE PERFECT.
IMAGINE WHAT IT WILL BE LIKE. YOU AND I WILL BE TIED TOGETHER. A CREATURE UNLIKE ANY OTHER.
SOMETHING NEW. SOMETHING BEAUTIFUL.

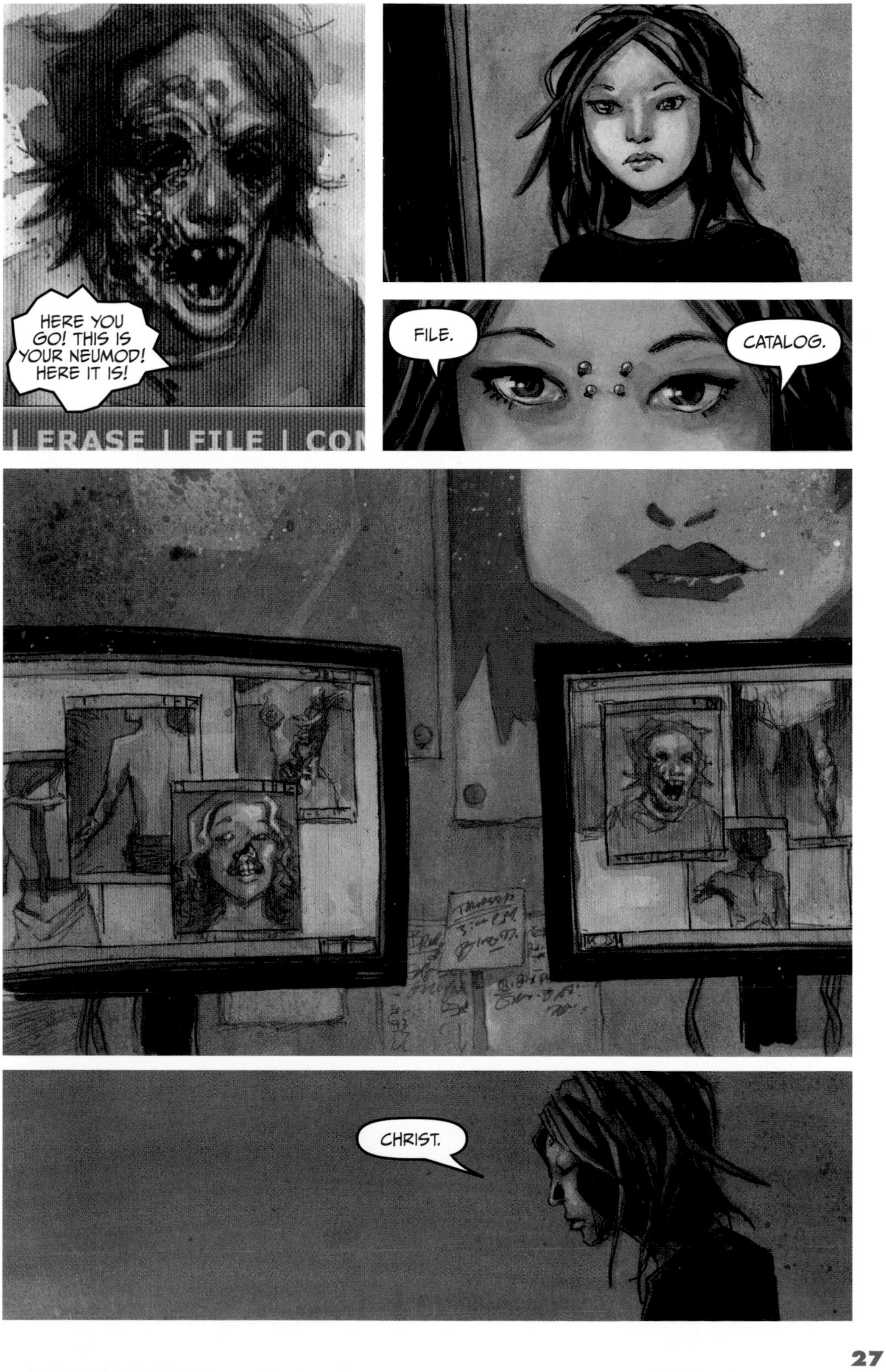
HERE YOU GO! THIS IS YOUR NEUMOD! HERE IT IS!
| ERASE | FILE | COM
FILE.
CATALOG.
CHRIST.

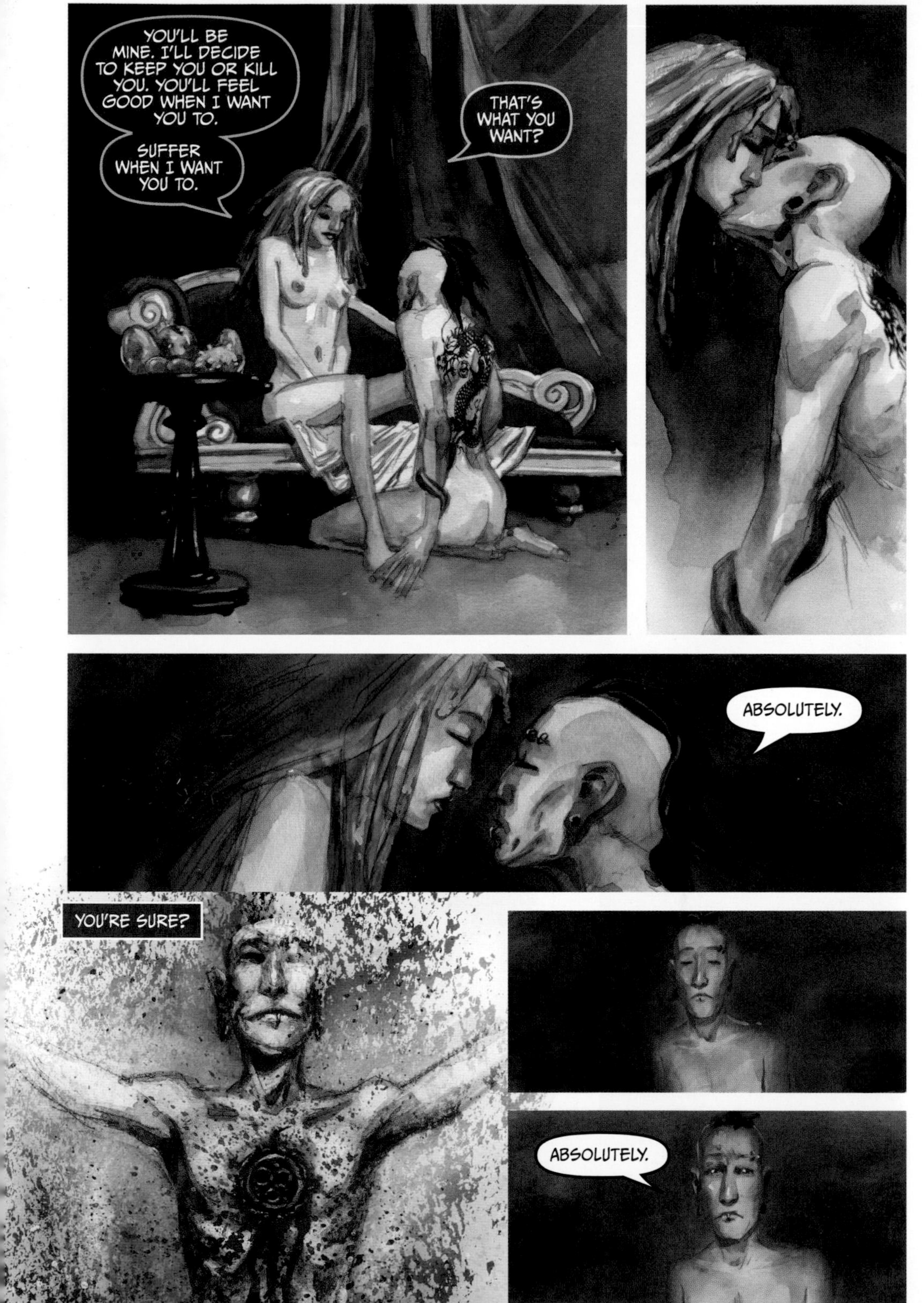
YOU'LL BE MINE. I'LL DECIDE TO KEEP YOU OR KILL YOU. YOU'LL FEEL GOOD WHEN I WANT YOU TO.
SUFFER WHEN I WANT YOU TO.
THAT'S WHAT YOU WANT?
ABSOLUTELY.
YOU'RE SURE?
ABSOLUTELY.

CHAPTER TWO

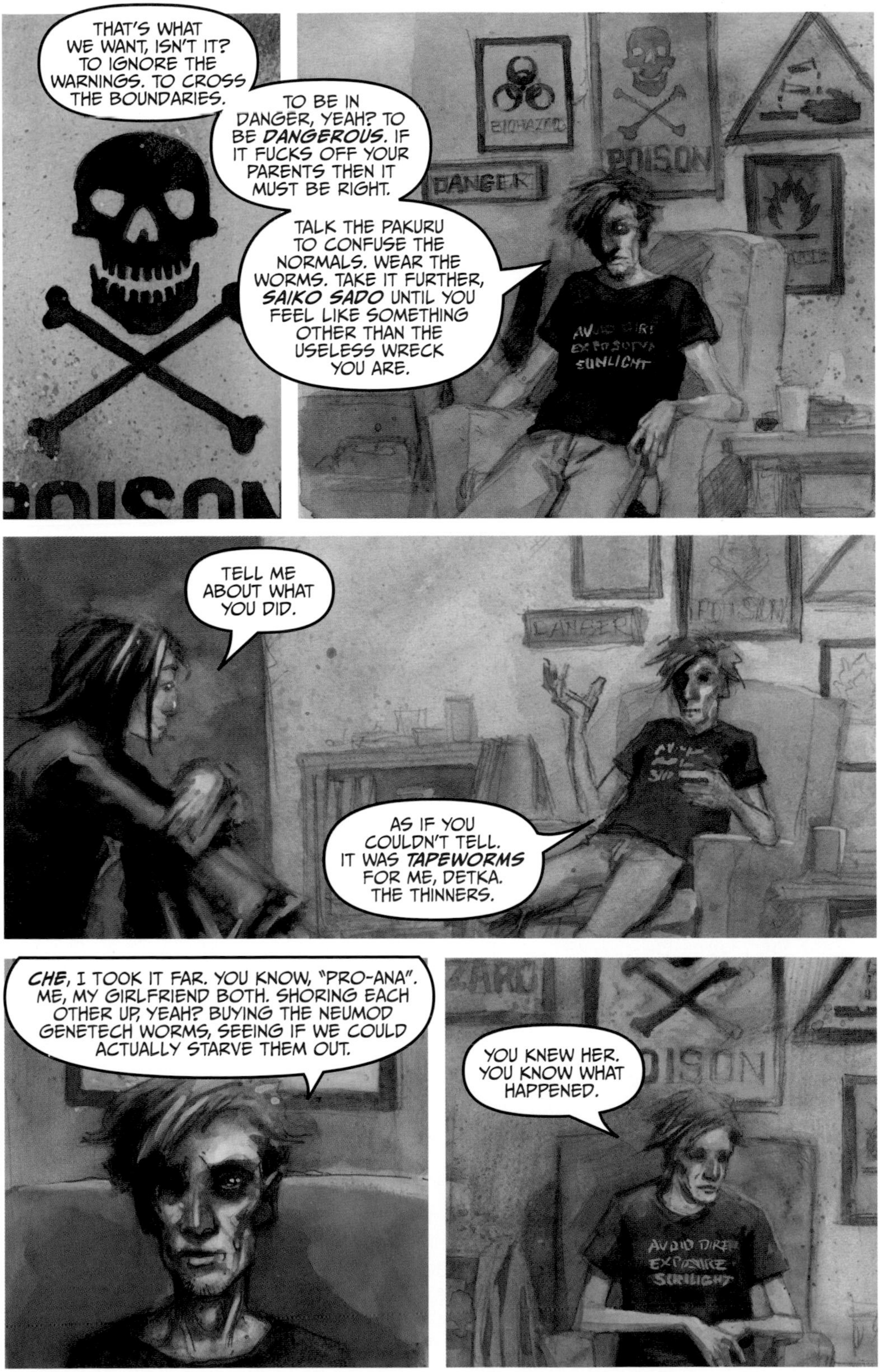
THAT'S WHAT WE WANT, ISN'T IT? TO IGNORE THE WARNINGS. TO CROSS THE BOUNDARIES.
TO BE IN DANGER, YEAH? TO BE **DANGEROUS**. IF IT FUCKS OFF YOUR PARENTS THEN IT MUST BE RIGHT.
TALK THE PAKURU TO CONFUSE THE NORMALS. WEAR THE WORMS. TAKE IT FURTHER, **SAIKO SADO** UNTIL YOU FEEL LIKE SOMETHING OTHER THAN THE USELESS WRECK YOU ARE.
POISON
DANGER
POISON
TELL ME ABOUT WHAT YOU DID.
AS IF YOU COULDN'T TELL. IT WAS **TAPEWORMS** FOR ME, DETKA. THE THINNERS.
CHE, I TOOK IT FAR. YOU KNOW, "PRO-ANA". ME, MY GIRLFRIEND BOTH. SHORING EACH OTHER UP, YEAH? BUYING THE NEUMOD GENETECH WORMS, SEEING IF WE COULD ACTUALLY STARVE THEM OUT.
YOU KNEW HER. YOU KNOW WHAT HAPPENED.

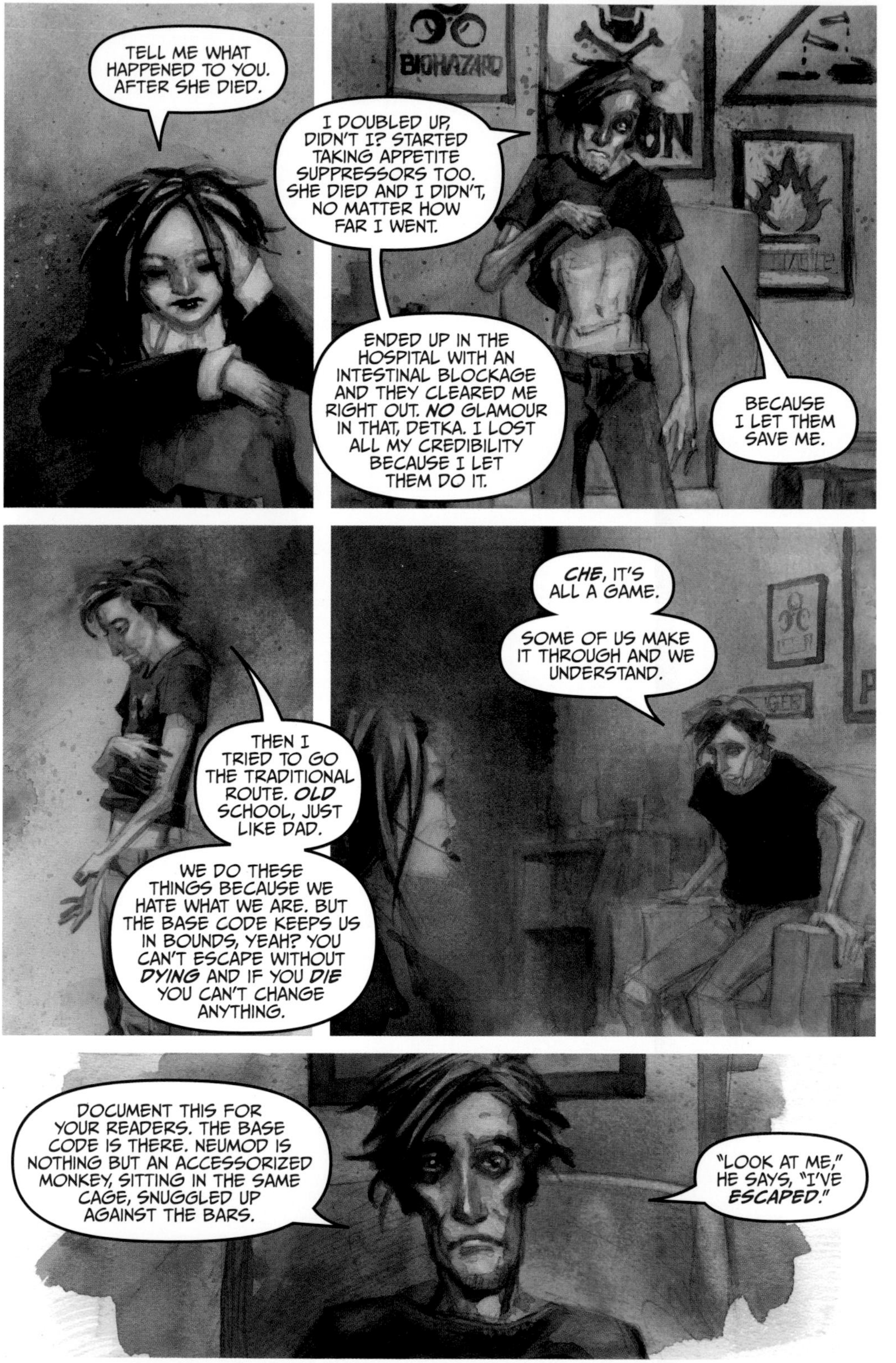
TELL ME WHAT HAPPENED TO YOU. AFTER SHE DIED.
I DOUBLED UP, DIDN'T I? STARTED TAKING APPETITE SUPPRESSORS TOO. SHE DIED AND I DIDN'T, NO MATTER HOW FAR I WENT.
ENDED UP IN THE HOSPITAL WITH AN INTESTINAL BLOCKAGE AND THEY CLEARED ME RIGHT OUT. *NO* GLAMOUR IN THAT, DETKA. I LOST ALL MY CREDIBILITY BECAUSE I LET THEM DO IT.
BECAUSE I LET THEM SAVE ME.
BIOHAZARD
THEN I TRIED TO GO THE TRADITIONAL ROUTE. *OLD* SCHOOL, JUST LIKE DAD.
WE DO THESE THINGS BECAUSE WE HATE WHAT WE ARE. BUT THE BASE CODE KEEPS US IN BOUNDS, YEAH? YOU CAN'T ESCAPE WITHOUT *DYING* AND IF YOU *DIE* YOU CAN'T CHANGE ANYTHING.
CHE, IT'S ALL A GAME.
SOME OF US MAKE IT THROUGH AND WE UNDERSTAND.
DOCUMENT THIS FOR YOUR READERS. THE BASE CODE IS THERE. NEUMOD IS NOTHING BUT AN ACCESSORIZED MONKEY, SITTING IN THE SAME CAGE, SNUGGLED UP AGAINST THE BARS.
"LOOK AT ME," HE SAYS, "I'VE *ESCAPED*."

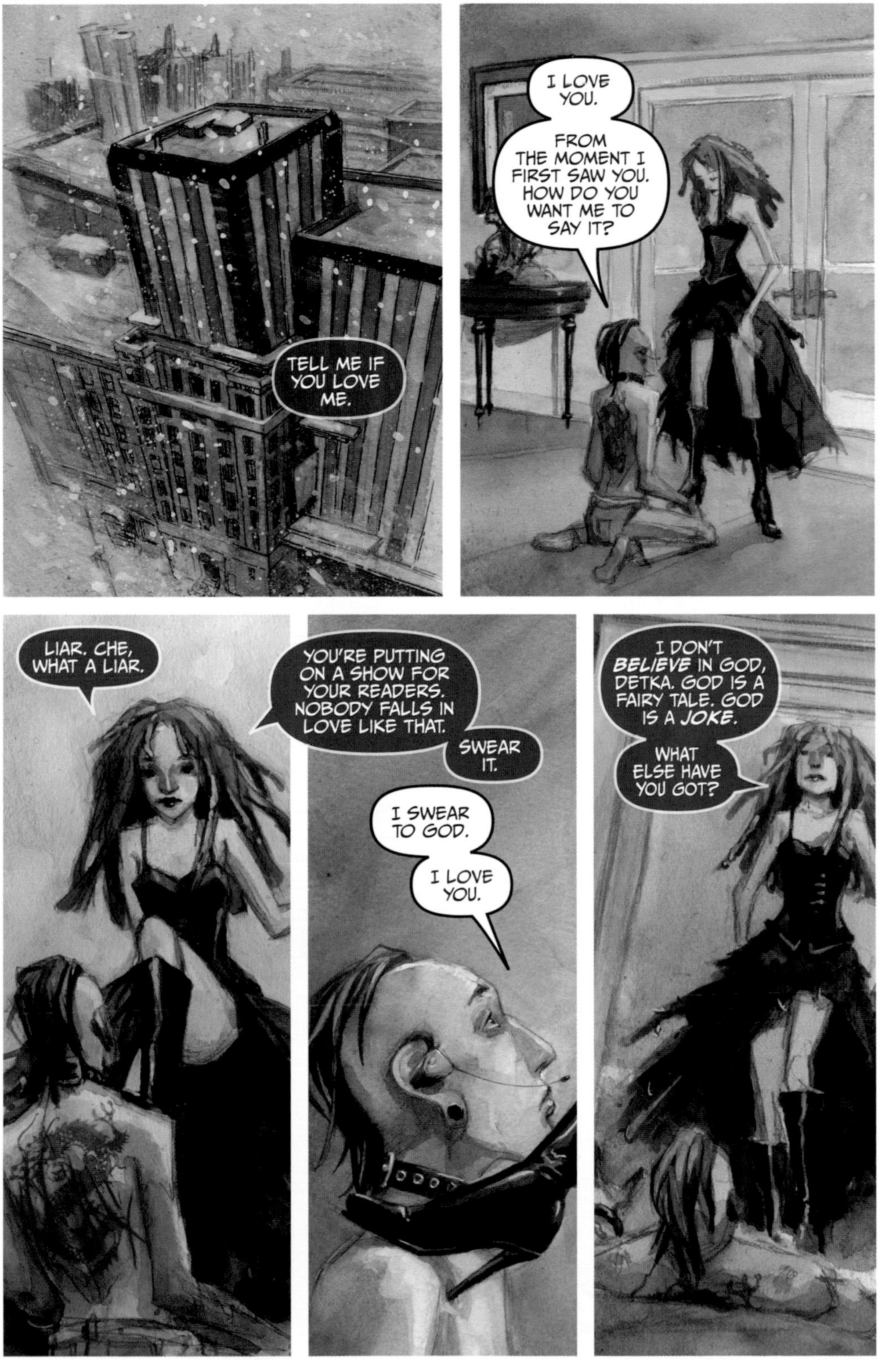
TELL ME IF YOU LOVE ME.
I LOVE YOU.
FROM THE MOMENT I FIRST SAW YOU. HOW DO YOU WANT ME TO SAY IT?
LIAR. CHE, WHAT A LIAR.
YOU'RE PUTTING ON A SHOW FOR YOUR READERS. NOBODY FALLS IN LOVE LIKE THAT.
SWEAR IT.
I SWEAR TO GOD.
I LOVE YOU.
I DON'T *BELIEVE* IN GOD, DETKA. GOD IS A FAIRY TALE. GOD IS A *JOKE*.
WHAT ELSE HAVE YOU GOT?

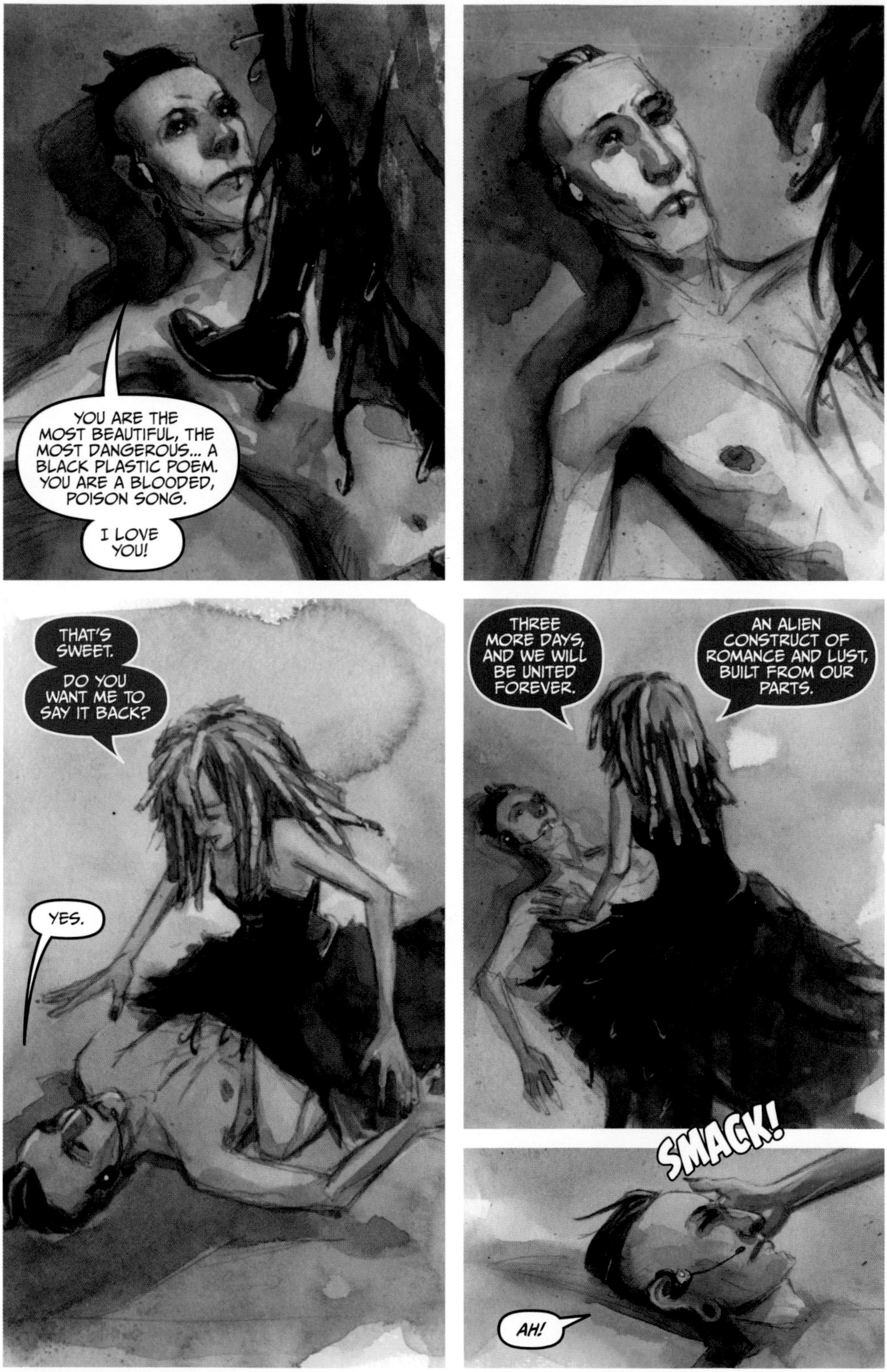
YOU ARE THE MOST BEAUTIFUL, THE MOST DANGEROUS... A BLACK PLASTIC POEM. YOU ARE A BLOODED, POISON SONG.
I LOVE YOU!
THAT'S SWEET.
DO YOU WANT ME TO SAY IT BACK?
YES.
THREE MORE DAYS, AND WE WILL BE UNITED FOREVER.
AN ALIEN CONSTRUCT OF ROMANCE AND LUST, BUILT FROM OUR PARTS.
SMACK!
AH!

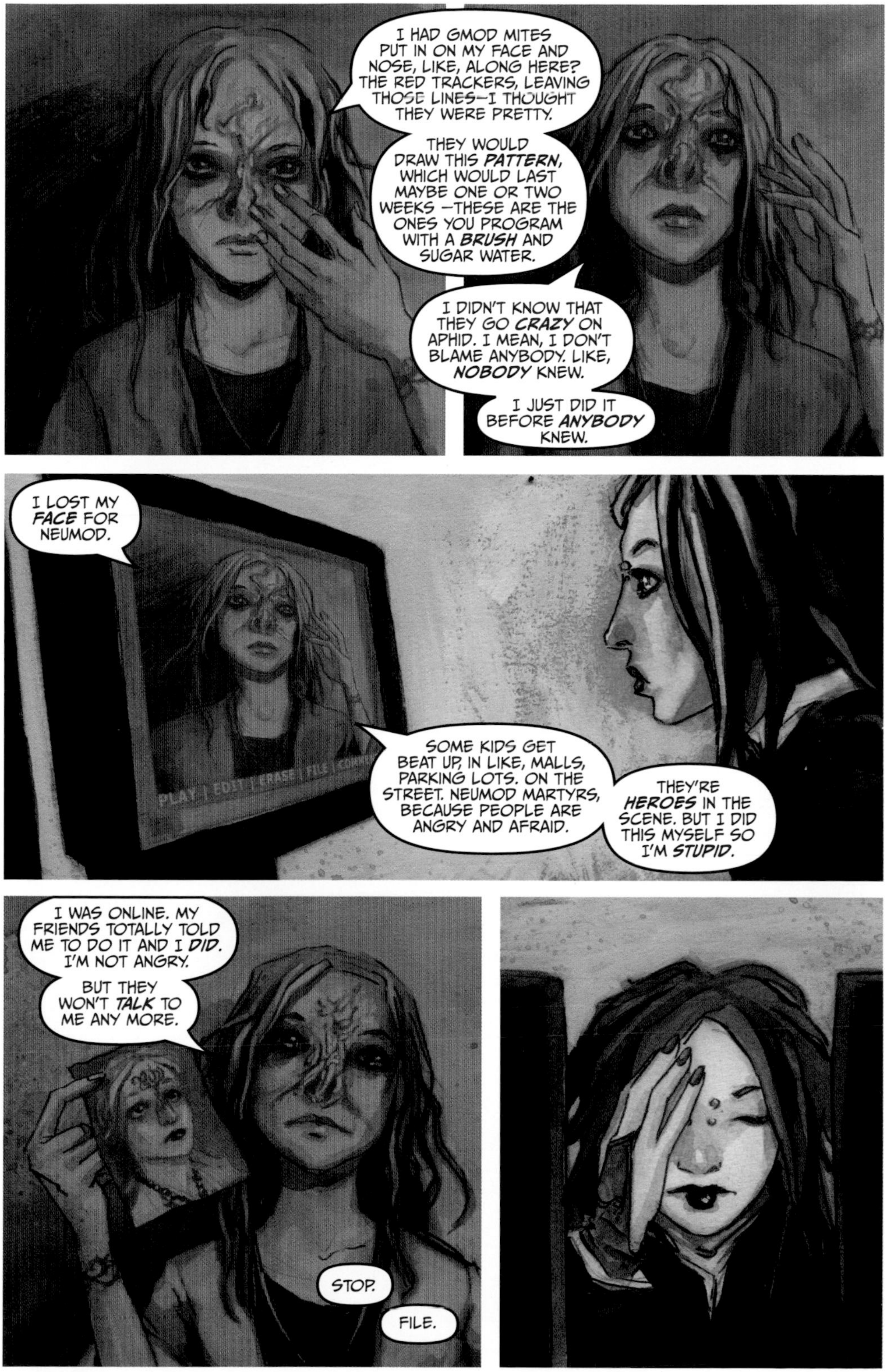
I HAD GMOD MITES PUT IN ON MY FACE AND NOSE, LIKE, ALONG HERE? THE RED TRACKERS, LEAVING THOSE LINES—I THOUGHT THEY WERE PRETTY.
THEY WOULD DRAW THIS *PATTERN*, WHICH WOULD LAST MAYBE ONE OR TWO WEEKS —THESE ARE THE ONES YOU PROGRAM WITH A *BRUSH* AND SUGAR WATER.
I DIDN'T KNOW THAT THEY GO *CRAZY* ON APHID. I MEAN, I DON'T BLAME ANYBODY. LIKE, *NOBODY* KNEW.
I JUST DID IT BEFORE *ANYBODY* KNEW.
I LOST MY *FACE* FOR NEUMOD.
PLAY | EDIT | ERASE | FILE |
SOME KIDS GET BEAT UP, IN LIKE, MALLS, PARKING LOTS. ON THE STREET. NEUMOD MARTYRS, BECAUSE PEOPLE ARE ANGRY AND AFRAID.
THEY'RE *HEROES* IN THE SCENE. BUT I DID THIS MYSELF SO I'M *STUPID*.
I WAS ONLINE. MY FRIENDS TOTALLY TOLD ME TO DO IT AND I *DID*. I'M NOT ANGRY.
BUT THEY WON'T *TALK* TO ME ANY MORE.
STOP.
FILE.

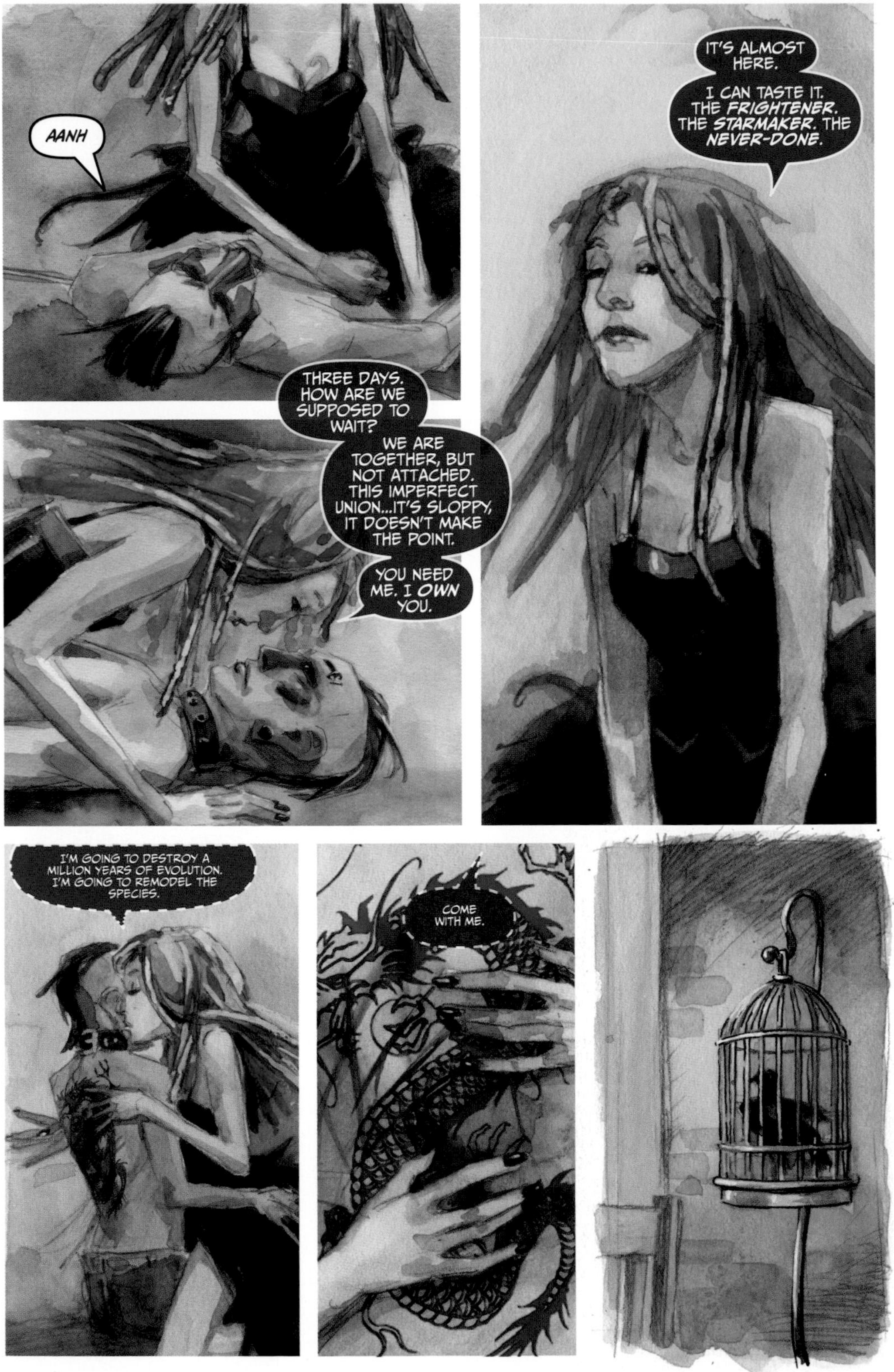
AANH
IT'S ALMOST HERE.
I CAN TASTE IT. THE *FRIGHTENER*. THE *STARMAKER*. THE *NEVER-DONE*.
THREE DAYS. HOW ARE WE SUPPOSED TO WAIT?
WE ARE TOGETHER, BUT NOT ATTACHED. THIS IMPERFECT UNION...IT'S SLOPPY, IT DOESN'T MAKE THE POINT.
YOU NEED ME. I *OWN* YOU.
I'M GOING TO DESTROY A MILLION YEARS OF EVOLUTION. I'M GOING TO REMODEL THE SPECIES.
COME WITH ME.

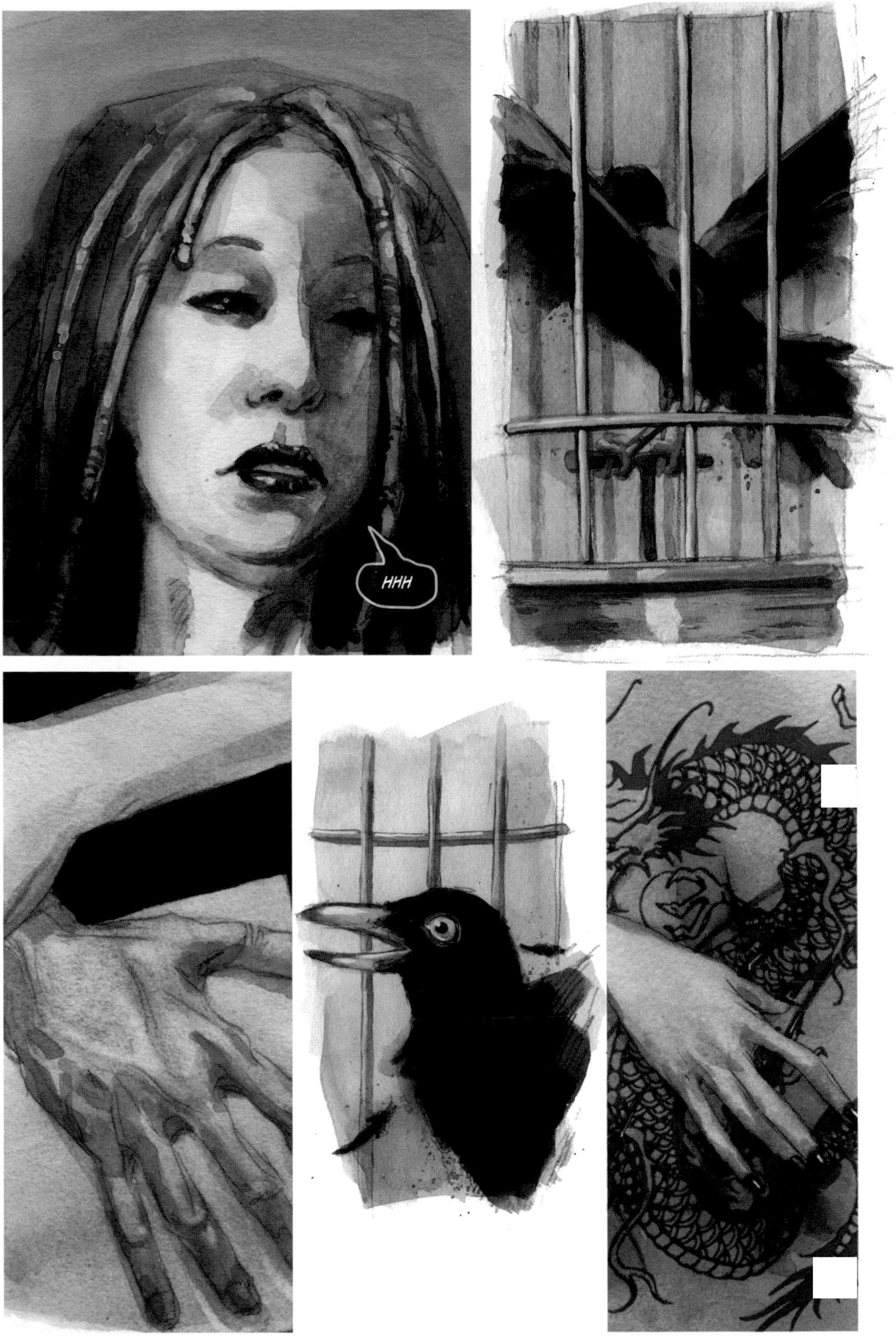
HHH

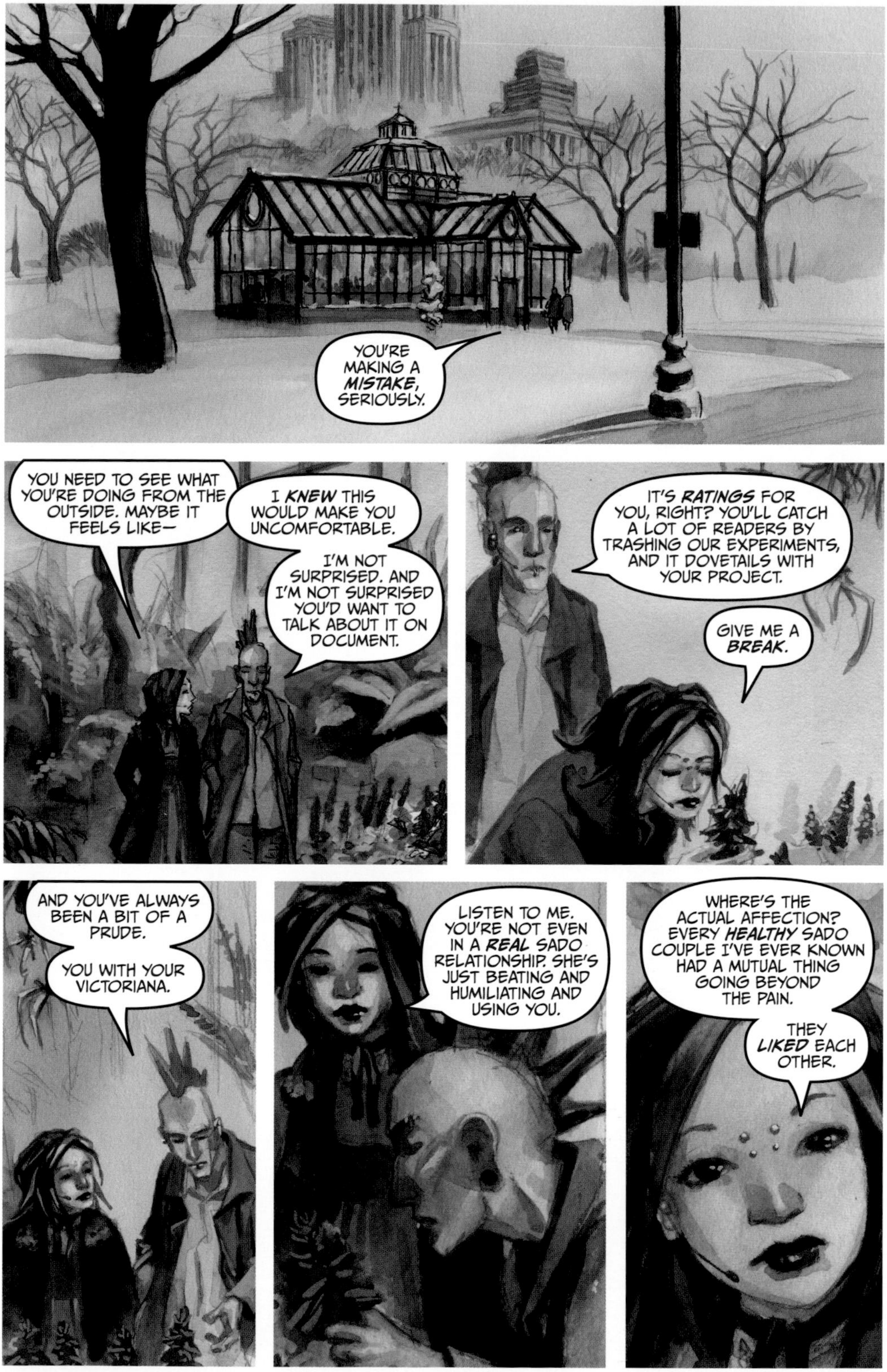
YOU'RE MAKING A MISTAKE, SERIOUSLY.
YOU NEED TO SEE WHAT YOU'RE DOING FROM THE OUTSIDE. MAYBE IT FEELS LIKE—
I KNEW THIS WOULD MAKE YOU UNCOMFORTABLE.
I'M NOT SURPRISED. AND I'M NOT SURPRISED YOU'D WANT TO TALK ABOUT IT ON DOCUMENT.
IT'S RATINGS FOR YOU, RIGHT? YOU'LL CATCH A LOT OF READERS BY TRASHING OUR EXPERIMENTS, AND IT DOVETAILS WITH YOUR PROJECT.
GIVE ME A BREAK.
AND YOU'VE ALWAYS BEEN A BIT OF A PRUDE.
YOU WITH YOUR VICTORIANA.
LISTEN TO ME. YOU'RE NOT EVEN IN A REAL SADO RELATIONSHIP. SHE'S JUST BEATING AND HUMILIATING AND USING YOU.
WHERE'S THE ACTUAL AFFECTION? EVERY HEALTHY SADO COUPLE I'VE EVER KNOWN HAD A MUTUAL THING GOING BEYOND THE PAIN.
THEY LIKED EACH OTHER.

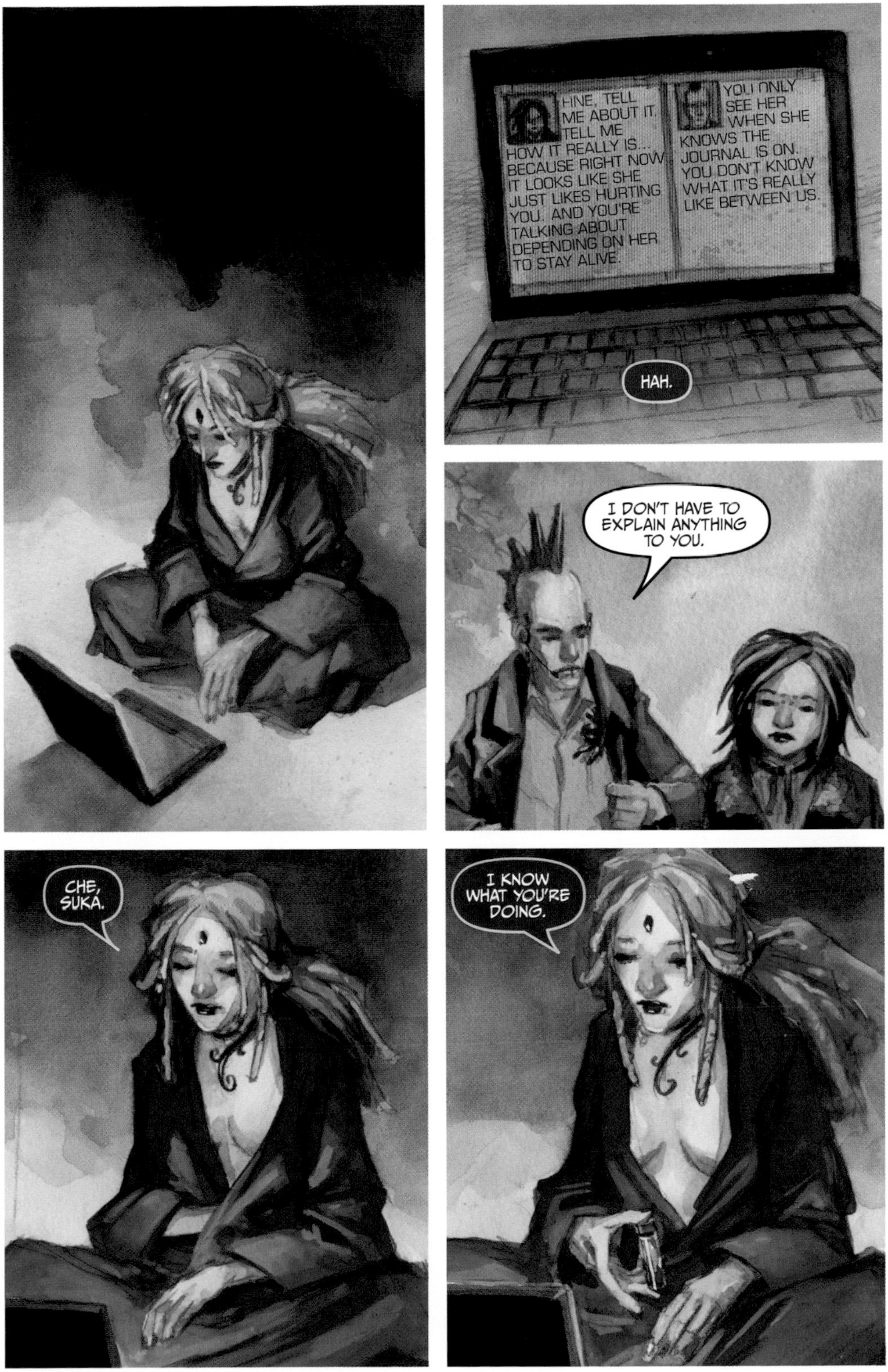
FINE, TELL ME ABOUT IT. TELL ME HOW IT REALLY IS... BECAUSE RIGHT NOW IT LOOKS LIKE SHE JUST LIKES HURTING YOU. AND YOU'RE TALKING ABOUT DEPENDING ON HER TO STAY ALIVE.
YOU ONLY SEE HER WHEN SHE KNOWS THE JOURNAL IS ON. YOU DON'T KNOW WHAT IT'S REALLY LIKE BETWEEN US.
HAH.
I DON'T HAVE TO EXPLAIN ANYTHING TO YOU.
CHE, SUKA.
I KNOW WHAT YOU'RE DOING.

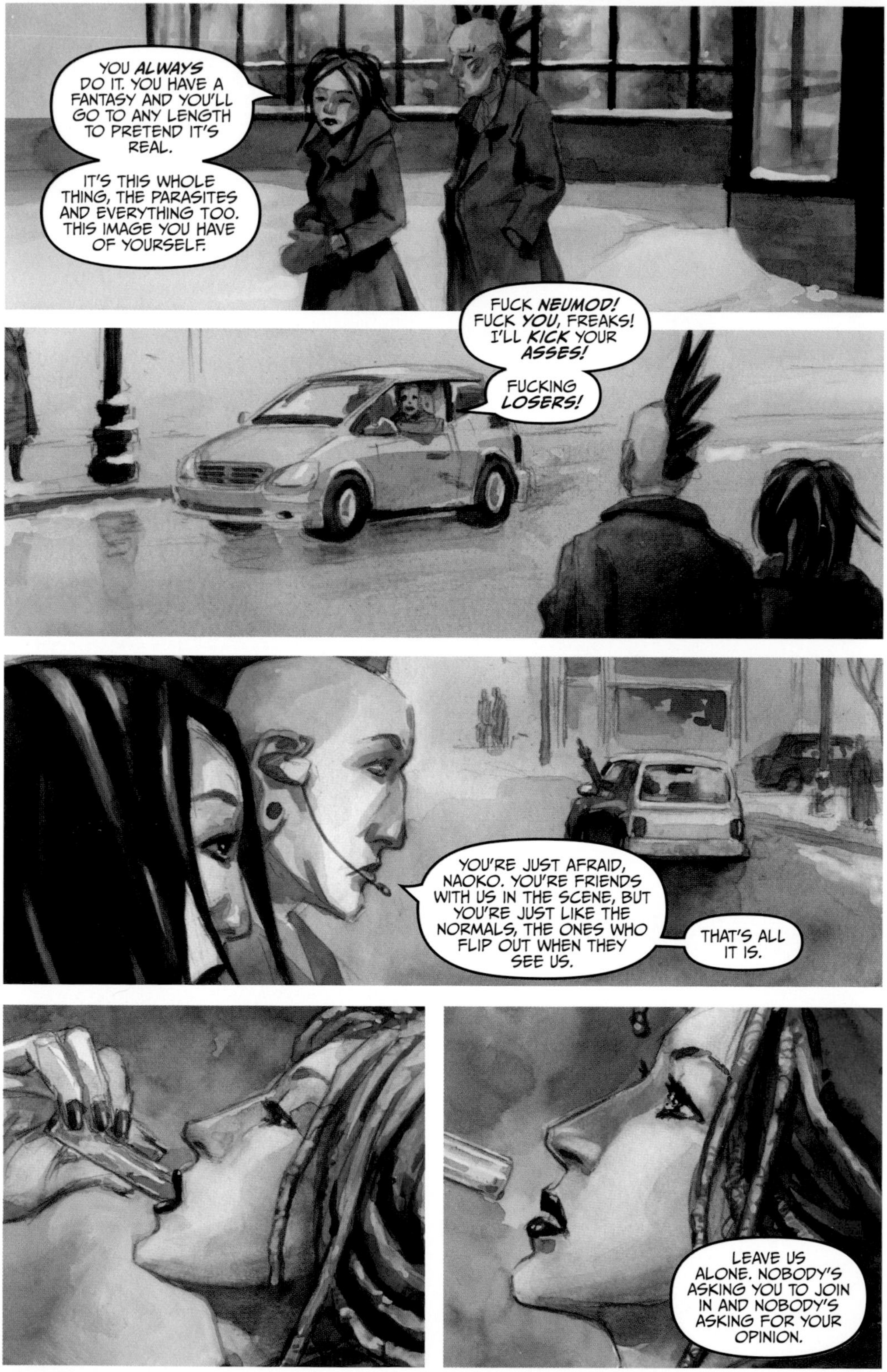
YOU ALWAYS DO IT. YOU HAVE A FANTASY AND YOU'LL GO TO ANY LENGTH TO PRETEND IT'S REAL.
IT'S THIS WHOLE THING, THE PARASITES AND EVERYTHING TOO. THIS IMAGE YOU HAVE OF YOURSELF.
FUCK NEUMOD! FUCK YOU, FREAKS! I'LL KICK YOUR ASSES!
FUCKING LOSERS!
YOU'RE JUST AFRAID, NAOKO. YOU'RE FRIENDS WITH US IN THE SCENE, BUT YOU'RE JUST LIKE THE NORMALS, THE ONES WHO FLIP OUT WHEN THEY SEE US.
THAT'S ALL IT IS.
LEAVE US ALONE. NOBODY'S ASKING YOU TO JOIN IN AND NOBODY'S ASKING FOR YOUR OPINION.

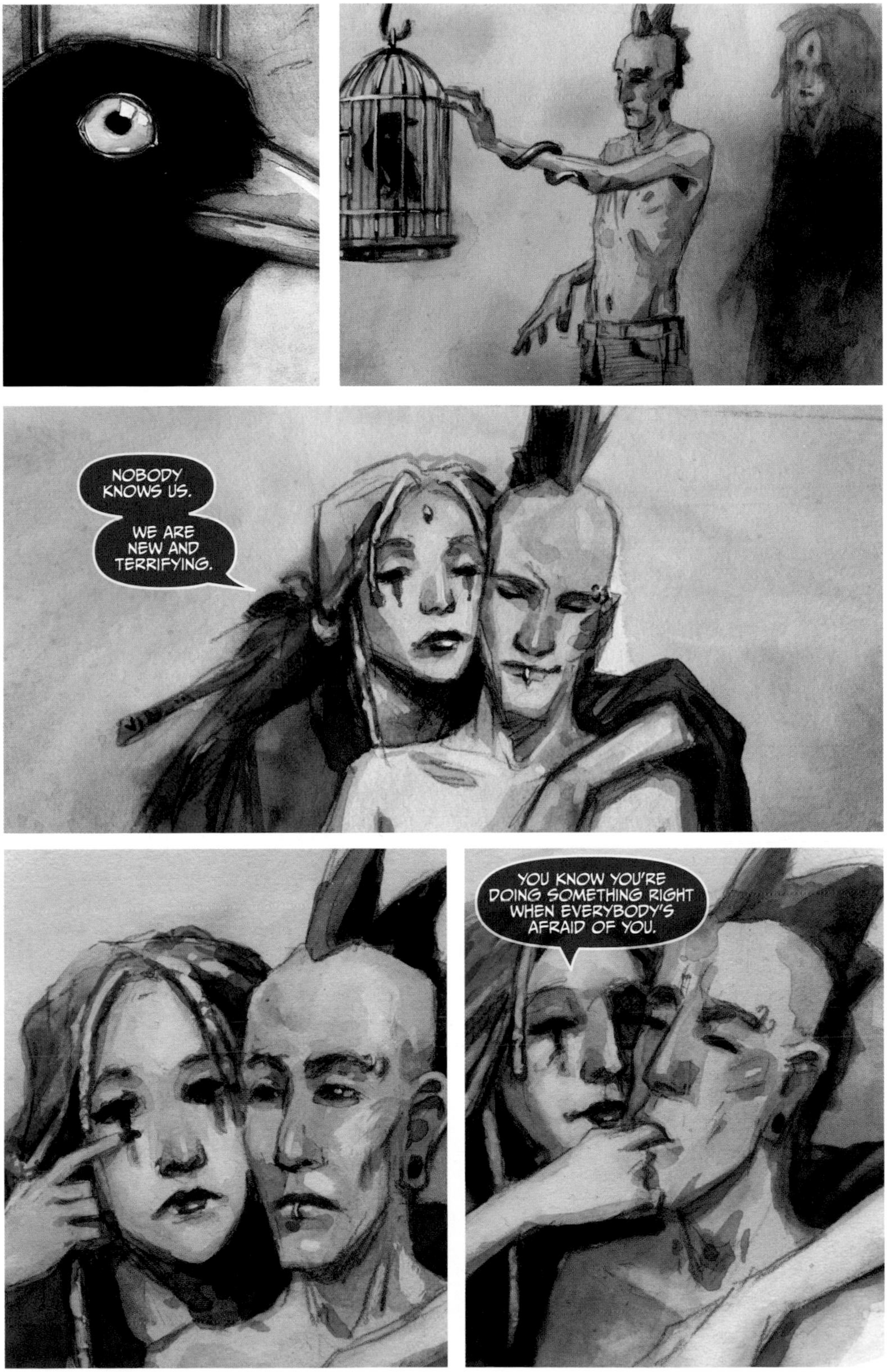
NOBODY KNOWS US.
WE ARE NEW AND TERRIFYING.
YOU KNOW YOU'RE DOING SOMETHING RIGHT WHEN EVERYBODY'S AFRAID OF YOU.

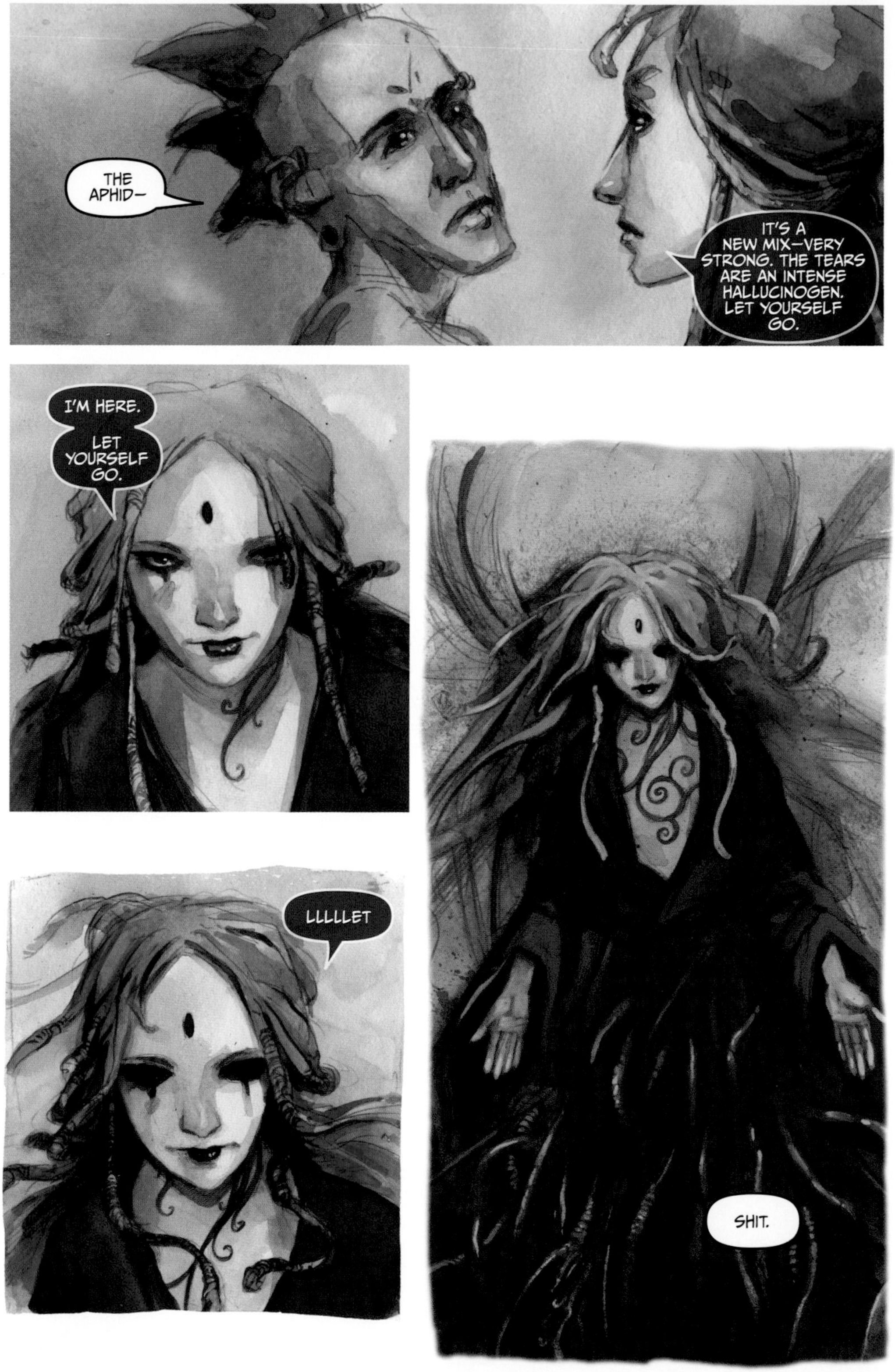
THE APHID—
IT'S A NEW MIX—VERY STRONG. THE TEARS ARE AN INTENSE HALLUCINOGEN. LET YOURSELF GO.
I'M HERE.
LET YOURSELF GO.
LLLLLET
SHIT.

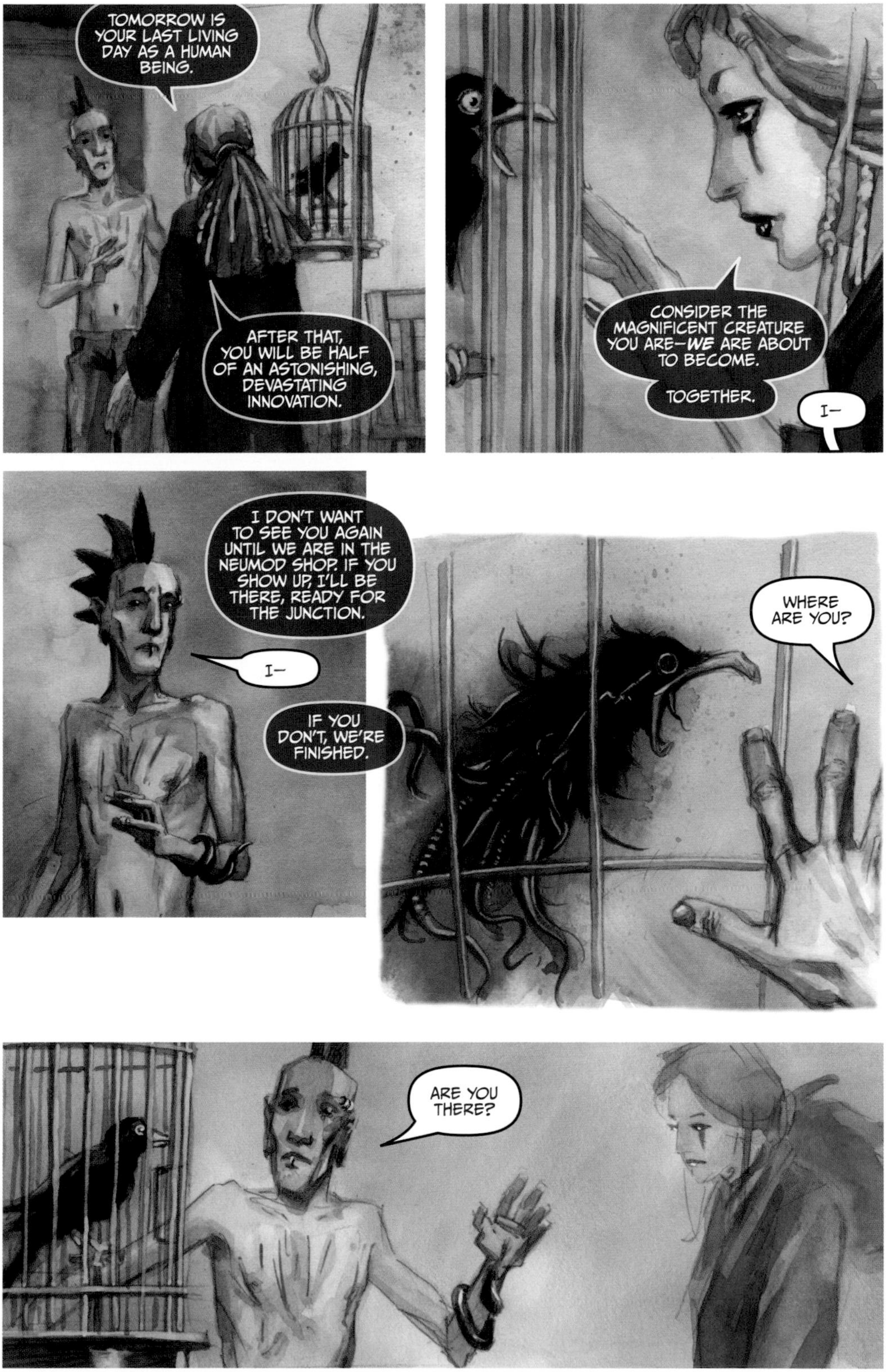
TOMORROW IS YOUR LAST LIVING DAY AS A HUMAN BEING.
AFTER THAT, YOU WILL BE HALF OF AN ASTONISHING, DEVASTATING INNOVATION.
CONSIDER THE MAGNIFICENT CREATURE YOU ARE—WE ARE ABOUT TO BECOME.
TOGETHER.
I—
I DON'T WANT TO SEE YOU AGAIN UNTIL WE ARE IN THE NEUMOD SHOP. IF YOU SHOW UP, I'LL BE THERE, READY FOR THE JUNCTION.
I—
IF YOU DON'T, WE'RE FINISHED.
WHERE ARE YOU?
ARE YOU THERE?

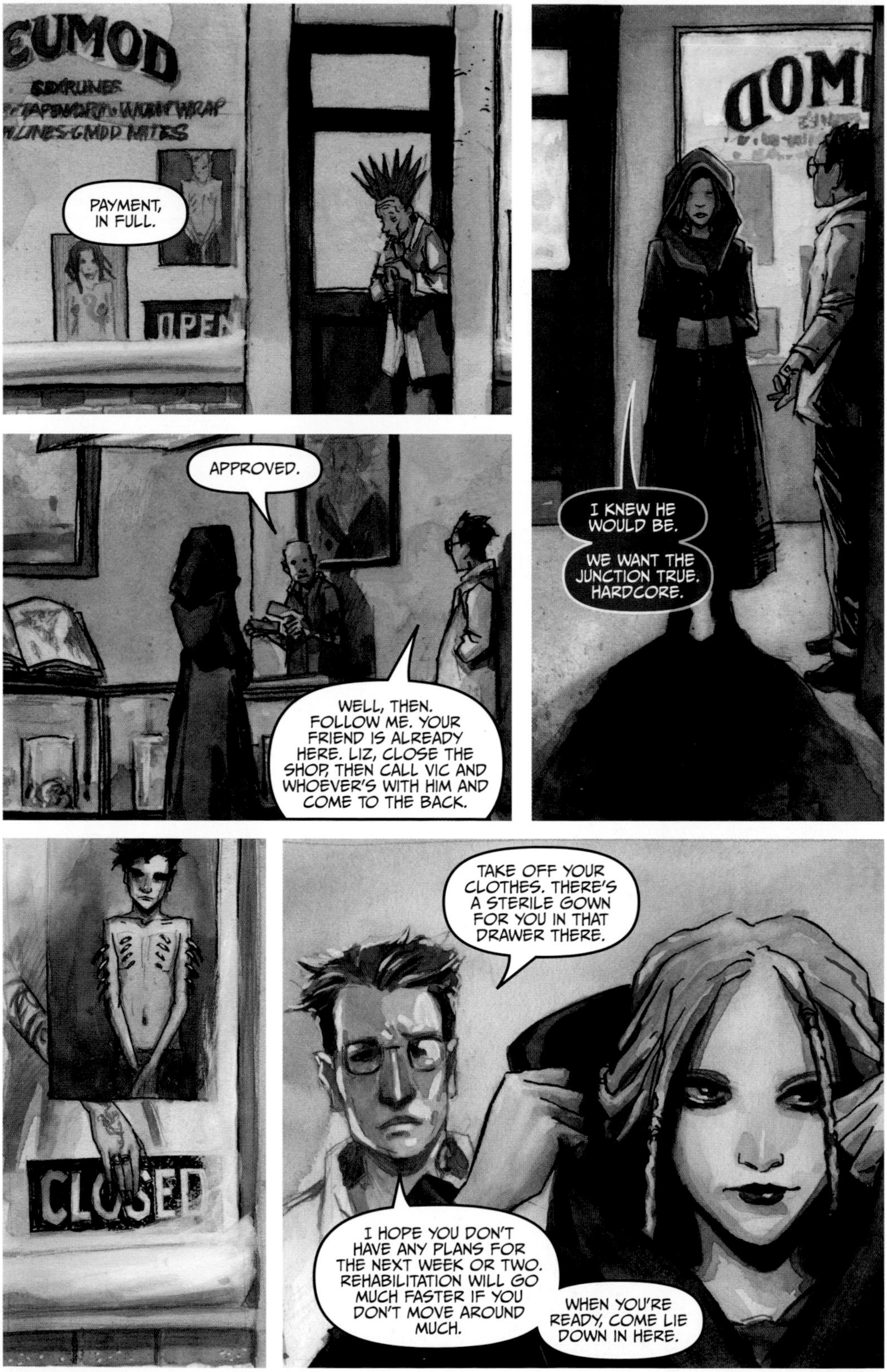

EUMOD
PAYMENT, IN FULL.
I KNEW HE WOULD BE.
WE WANT THE JUNCTION TRUE. HARDCORE.
APPROVED.
WELL, THEN. FOLLOW ME. YOUR FRIEND IS ALREADY HERE. LIZ, CLOSE THE SHOP, THEN CALL VIC AND WHOEVER'S WITH HIM AND COME TO THE BACK.
CLOSED
TAKE OFF YOUR CLOTHES. THERE'S A STERILE GOWN FOR YOU IN THAT DRAWER THERE.
I HOPE YOU DON'T HAVE ANY PLANS FOR THE NEXT WEEK OR TWO. REHABILITATION WILL GO MUCH FASTER IF YOU DON'T MOVE AROUND MUCH.
WHEN YOU'RE READY, COME LIE DOWN IN HERE.

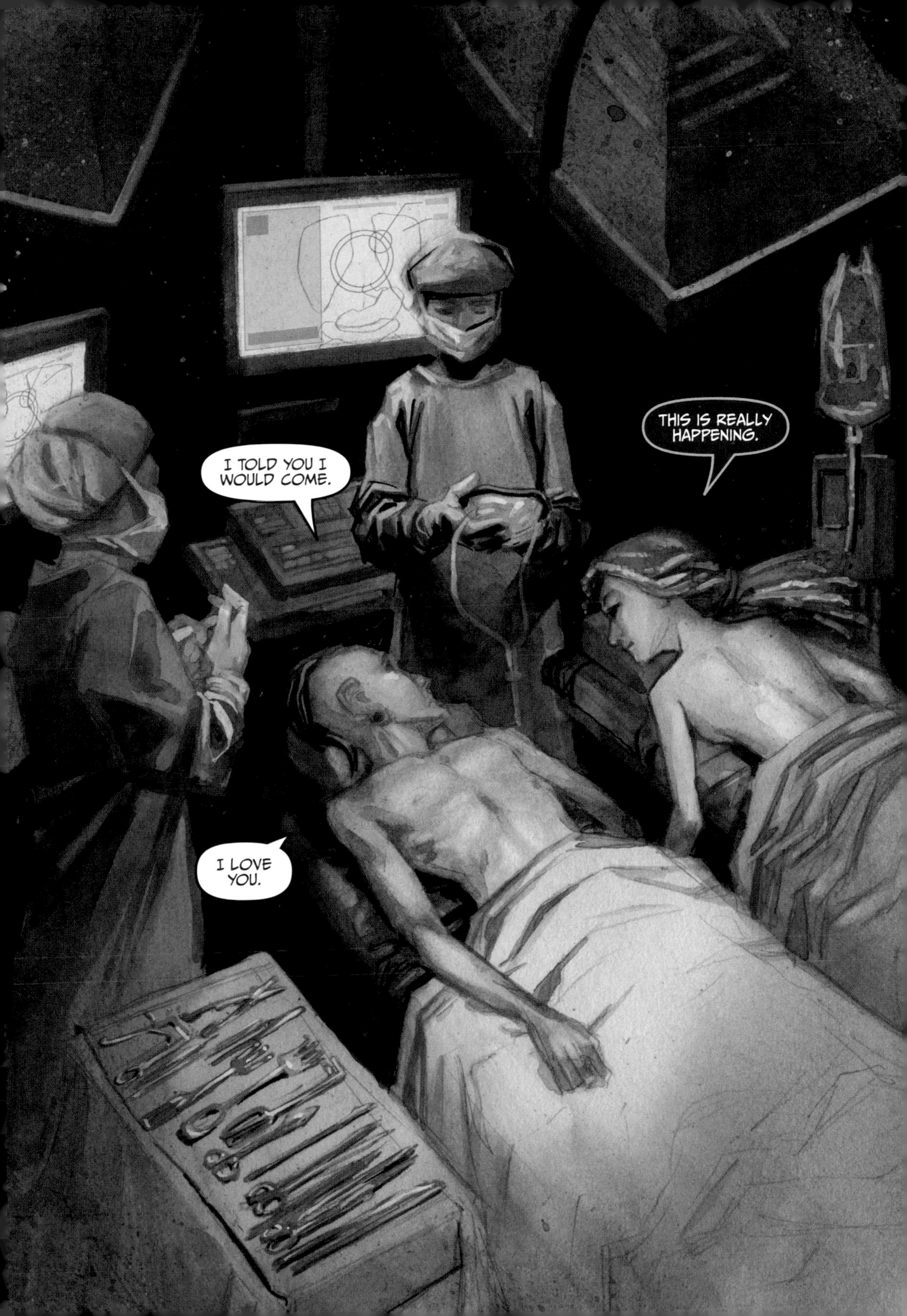
I TOLD YOU I WOULD COME.
THIS IS REALLY HAPPENING.
I LOVE YOU.

MONITOR LOOKS GOOD.
WE'RE READY TO GO.
FLASH THE DIAGRAM.
RIGHT.
GOOD. GIVE ME AN EEG.
FAREWELL HEAD, FAREWELL HEART.
YOU ARE A LIAR.
AND YOU ARE *DYING* NOW.
SUICIDE.
IF I DIE BEFORE I WAKE
WHAT DO I BECOME?

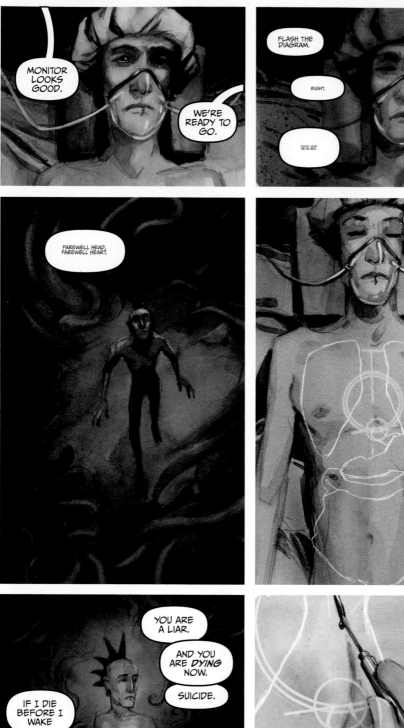

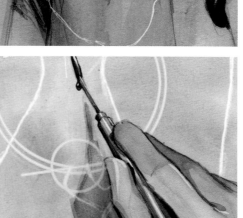

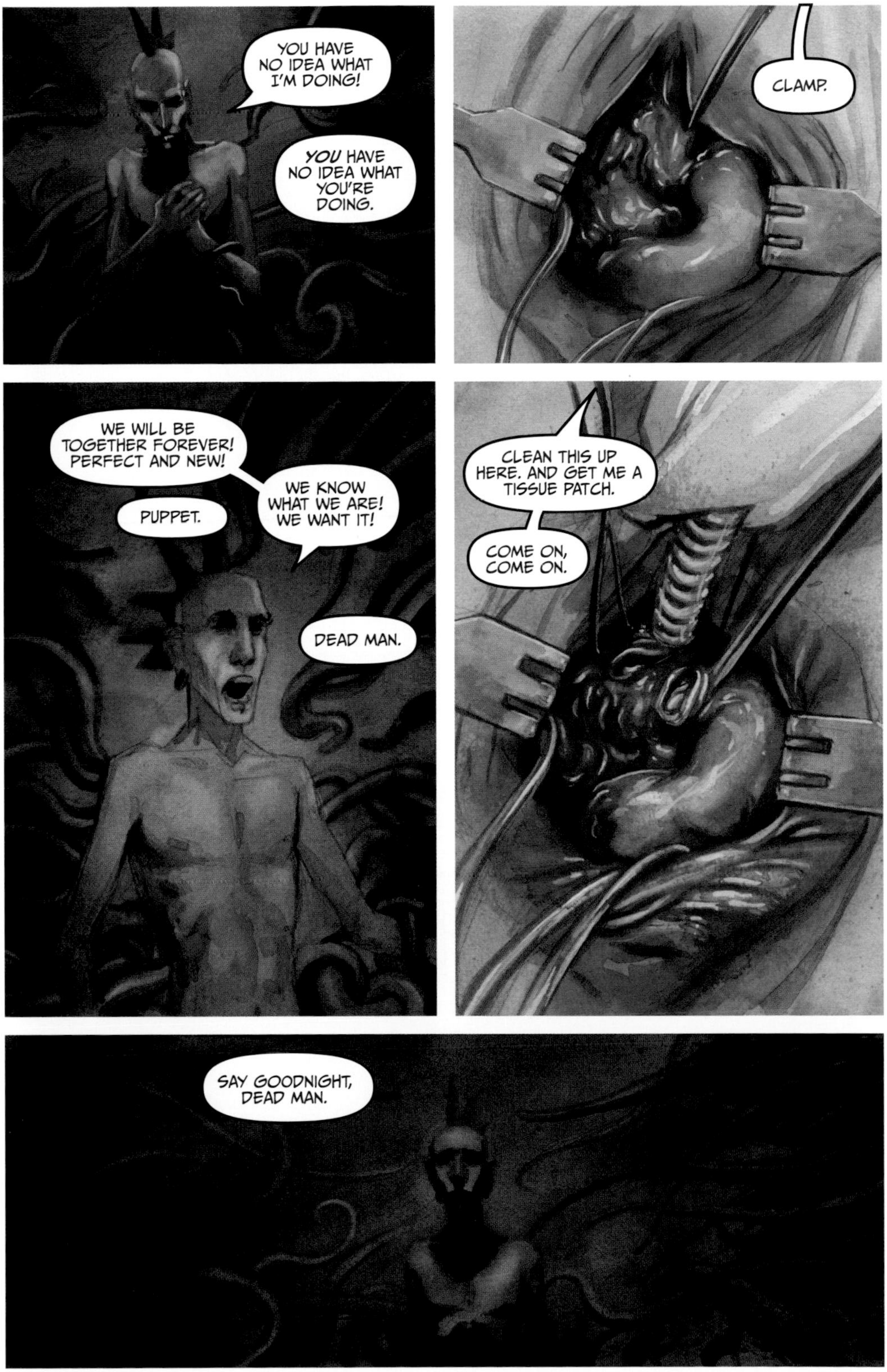
YOU HAVE NO IDEA WHAT I'M DOING!
YOU HAVE NO IDEA WHAT YOU'RE DOING.
CLAMP.
WE WILL BE TOGETHER FOREVER! PERFECT AND NEW!
PUPPET.
WE KNOW WHAT WE ARE! WE WANT IT!
DEAD MAN.
CLEAN THIS UP HERE. AND GET ME A TISSUE PATCH.
COME ON, COME ON.
SAY GOODNIGHT, DEAD MAN.

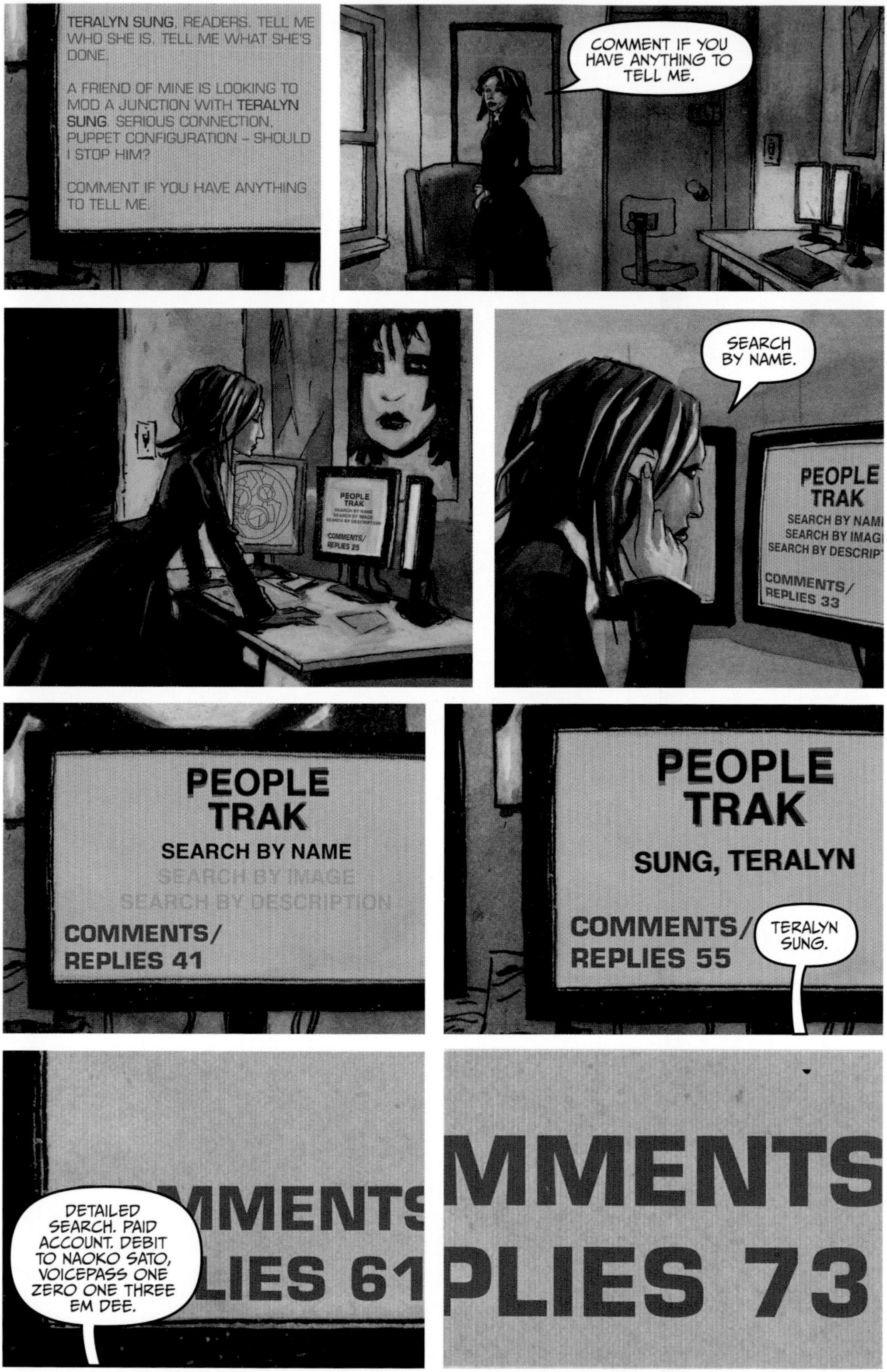
TERALYN SUNG, READERS. TELL ME WHO SHE IS. TELL ME WHAT SHE'S DONE.
A FRIEND OF MINE IS LOOKING TO MOD A JUNCTION WITH TERALYN SUNG. SERIOUS CONNECTION, PUPPET CONFIGURATION – SHOULD I STOP HIM?
COMMENT IF YOU HAVE ANYTHING TO TELL ME.
COMMENT IF YOU HAVE ANYTHING TO TELL ME.
PEOPLE TRAK
COMMENTS/ REPLIES 25
SEARCH BY NAME.
PEOPLE TRAK
COMMENTS/ REPLIES 33
PEOPLE TRAK
SEARCH BY NAME
SEARCH BY IMAGE
SEARCH BY DESCRIPTION
COMMENTS/ REPLIES 41
PEOPLE TRAK
SUNG, TERALYN
COMMENTS/ REPLIES 55
TERALYN SUNG.
DETAILED SEARCH. PAID ACCOUNT. DEBIT TO NAOKO SATO, VOICEPASS ONE ZERO ONE THREE EM DEE.
LIES 61
MMENTS
PLIES 73

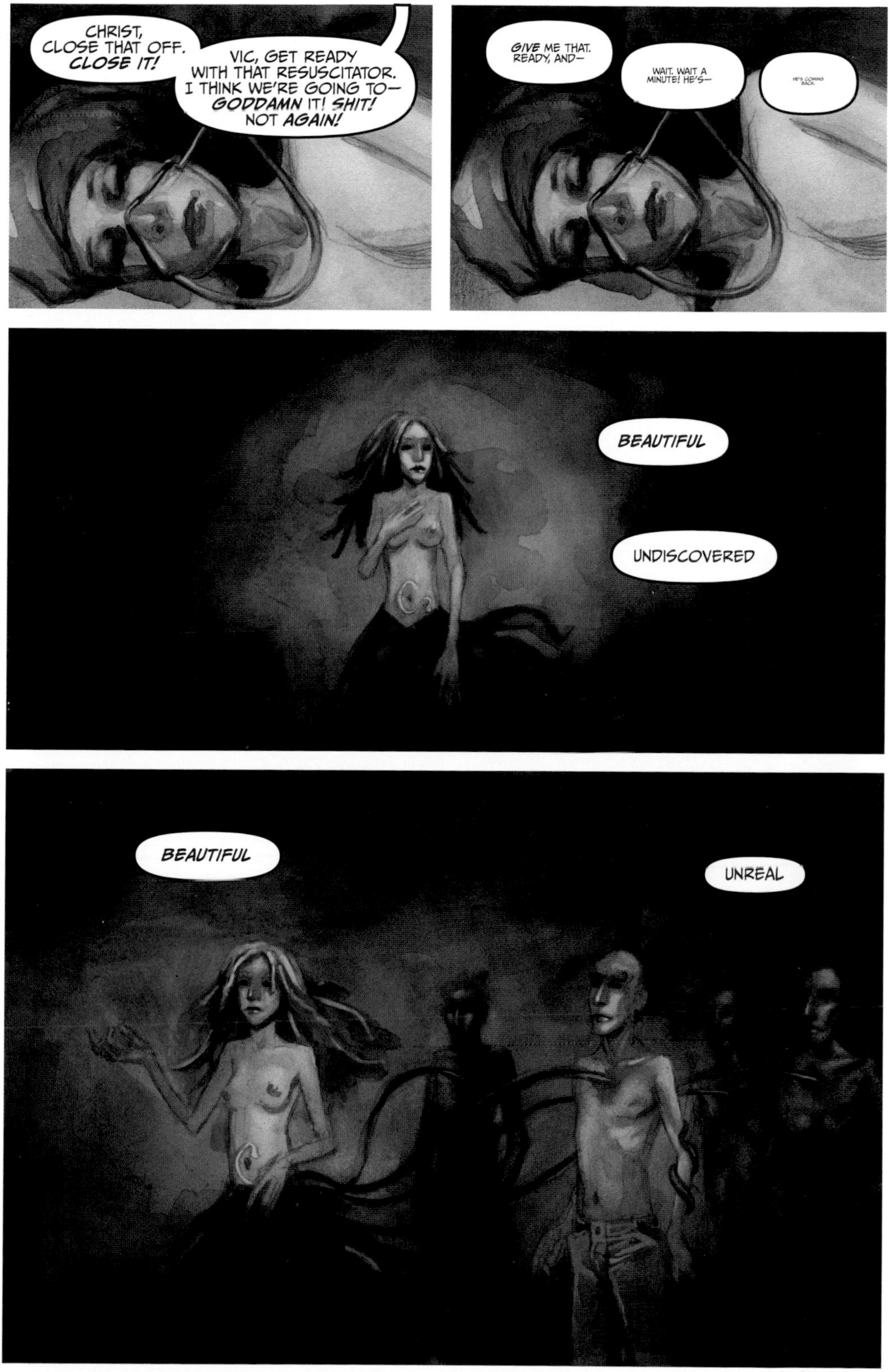
CHRIST, CLOSE THAT OFF. CLOSE IT!
VIC, GET READY WITH THAT RESUSCITATOR. I THINK WE'RE GOING TO— GODDAMN IT! SHIT! NOT AGAIN!
GIVE ME THAT. READY, AND—
WAIT. WAIT A MINUTE! HE'S—
HE'S COMING BACK.
BEAUTIFUL
UNDISCOVERED
BEAUTIFUL
UNREAL

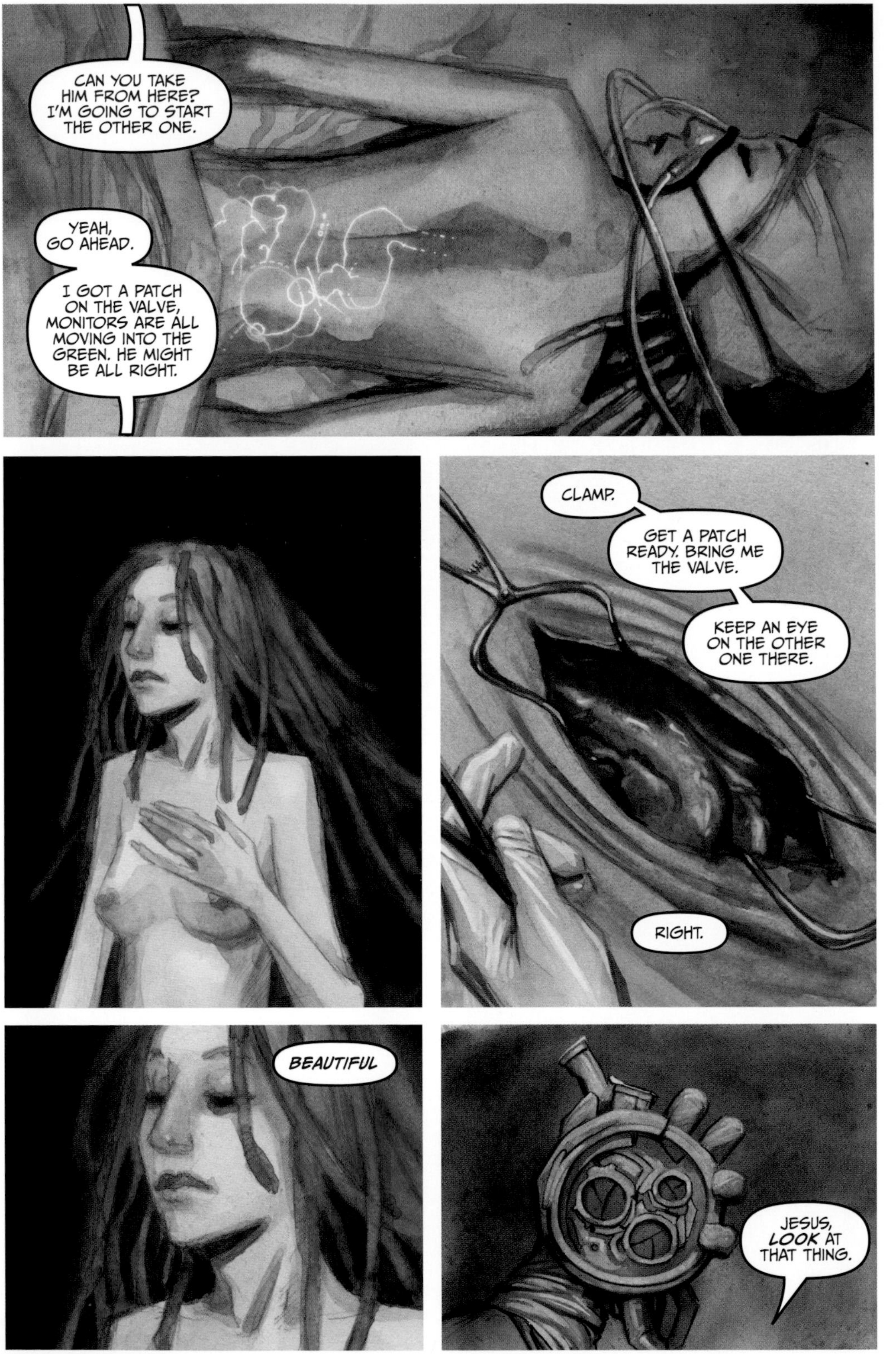

CAN YOU TAKE HIM FROM HERE? I'M GOING TO START THE OTHER ONE.
YEAH, GO AHEAD.
I GOT A PATCH ON THE VALVE, MONITORS ARE ALL MOVING INTO THE GREEN. HE MIGHT BE ALL RIGHT.
CLAMP.
GET A PATCH READY. BRING ME THE VALVE.
KEEP AN EYE ON THE OTHER ONE THERE.
RIGHT.
BEAUTIFUL
JESUS, LOOK AT THAT THING.

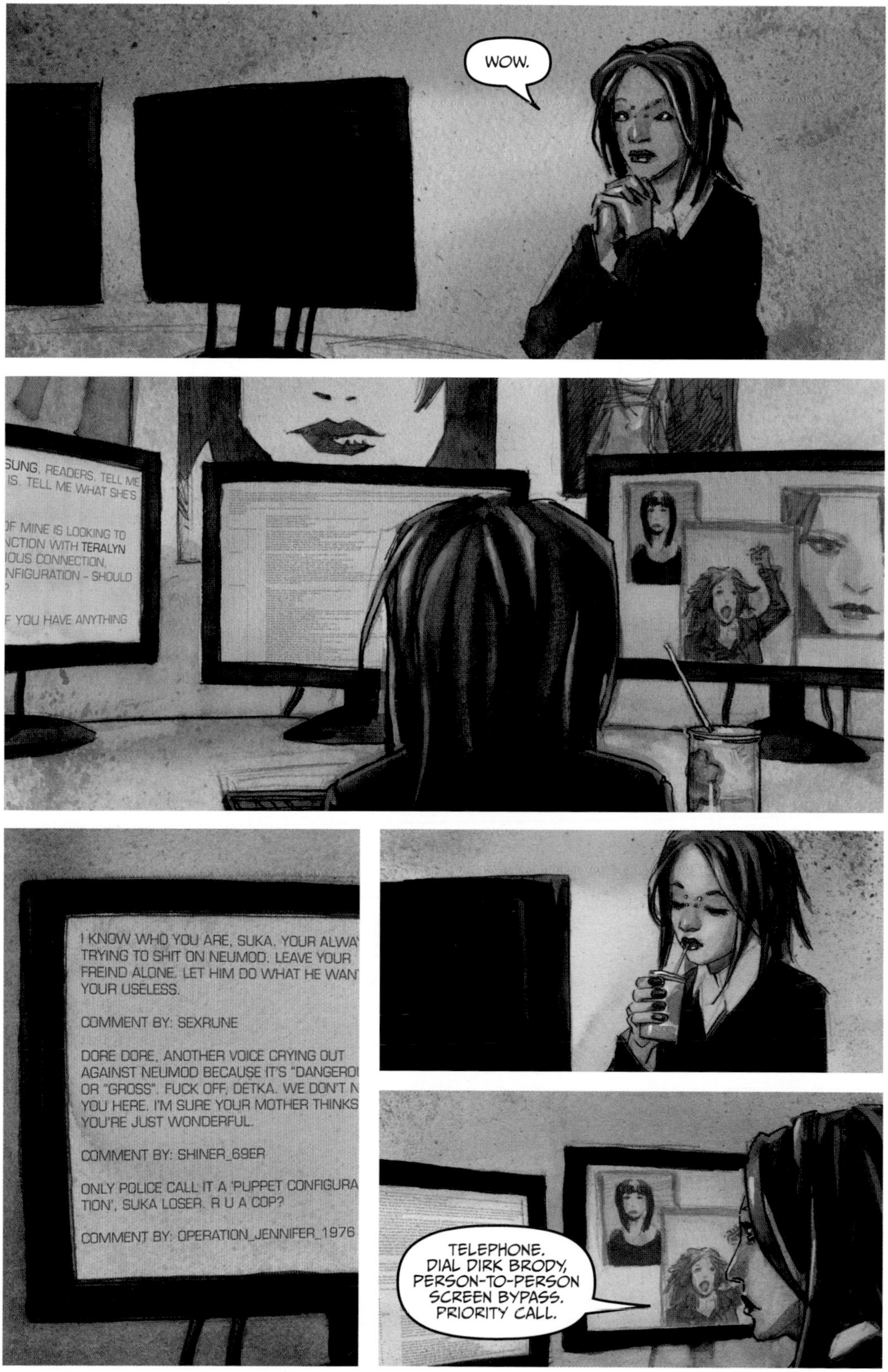
WOW.
SUNG. READERS. TELL ME
IS. TELL ME WHAT SHE'S
OF MINE IS LOOKING TO
NCTION WITH TERALYN
IOUS CONNECTION,
NFIGURATION – SHOULD
F YOU HAVE ANYTHING
I KNOW WHO YOU ARE, SUKA. YOUR ALWAY TRYING TO SHIT ON NEUMOD. LEAVE YOUR FREIND ALONE. LET HIM DO WHAT HE WANT YOUR USELESS.
COMMENT BY: SEXRUNE
DORE DORE, ANOTHER VOICE CRYING OUT AGAINST NEUMOD BECAUSE IT'S "DANGERO OR "GROSS". FUCK OFF, DETKA. WE DON'T N YOU HERE. I'M SURE YOUR MOTHER THINKS YOU'RE JUST WONDERFUL.
COMMENT BY: SHINER_69ER
ONLY POLICE CALL IT A 'PUPPET CONFIGURA TION', SUKA LOSER. R U A COP?
COMMENT BY: OPERATION_JENNIFER_1976
TELEPHONE. DIAL DIRK BRODY, PERSON-TO-PERSON SCREEN BYPASS. PRIORITY CALL.

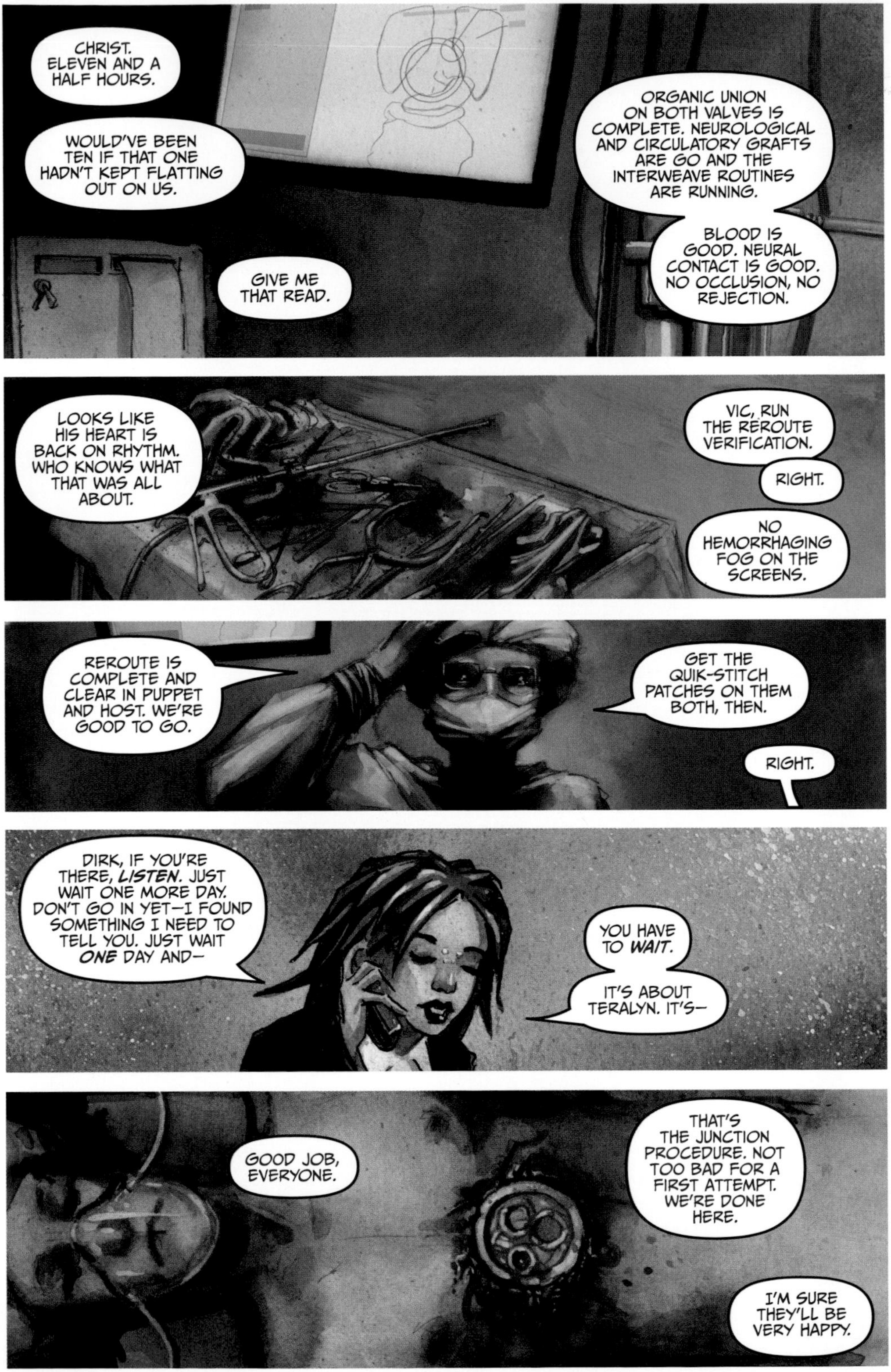
CHRIST. ELEVEN AND A HALF HOURS.
WOULD'VE BEEN TEN IF THAT ONE HADN'T KEPT FLATTING OUT ON US.
ORGANIC UNION ON BOTH VALVES IS COMPLETE. NEUROLOGICAL AND CIRCULATORY GRAFTS ARE GO AND THE INTERWEAVE ROUTINES ARE RUNNING.
BLOOD IS GOOD. NEURAL CONTACT IS GOOD. NO OCCLUSION, NO REJECTION.
GIVE ME THAT READ.
LOOKS LIKE HIS HEART IS BACK ON RHYTHM. WHO KNOWS WHAT THAT WAS ALL ABOUT.
VIC, RUN THE REROUTE VERIFICATION.
RIGHT.
NO HEMORRHAGING FOG ON THE SCREENS.
REROUTE IS COMPLETE AND CLEAR IN PUPPET AND HOST. WE'RE GOOD TO GO.
GET THE QUIK-STITCH PATCHES ON THEM BOTH, THEN.
RIGHT.
DIRK, IF YOU'RE THERE, ***LISTEN***. JUST WAIT ONE MORE DAY. DON'T GO IN YET—I FOUND SOMETHING I NEED TO TELL YOU. JUST WAIT ***ONE*** DAY AND—
YOU HAVE TO ***WAIT***.
IT'S ABOUT TERALYN. IT'S—
GOOD JOB, EVERYONE.
THAT'S THE JUNCTION PROCEDURE. NOT TOO BAD FOR A FIRST ATTEMPT. WE'RE DONE HERE.
I'M SURE THEY'LL BE VERY HAPPY.

CHAPTER THREE

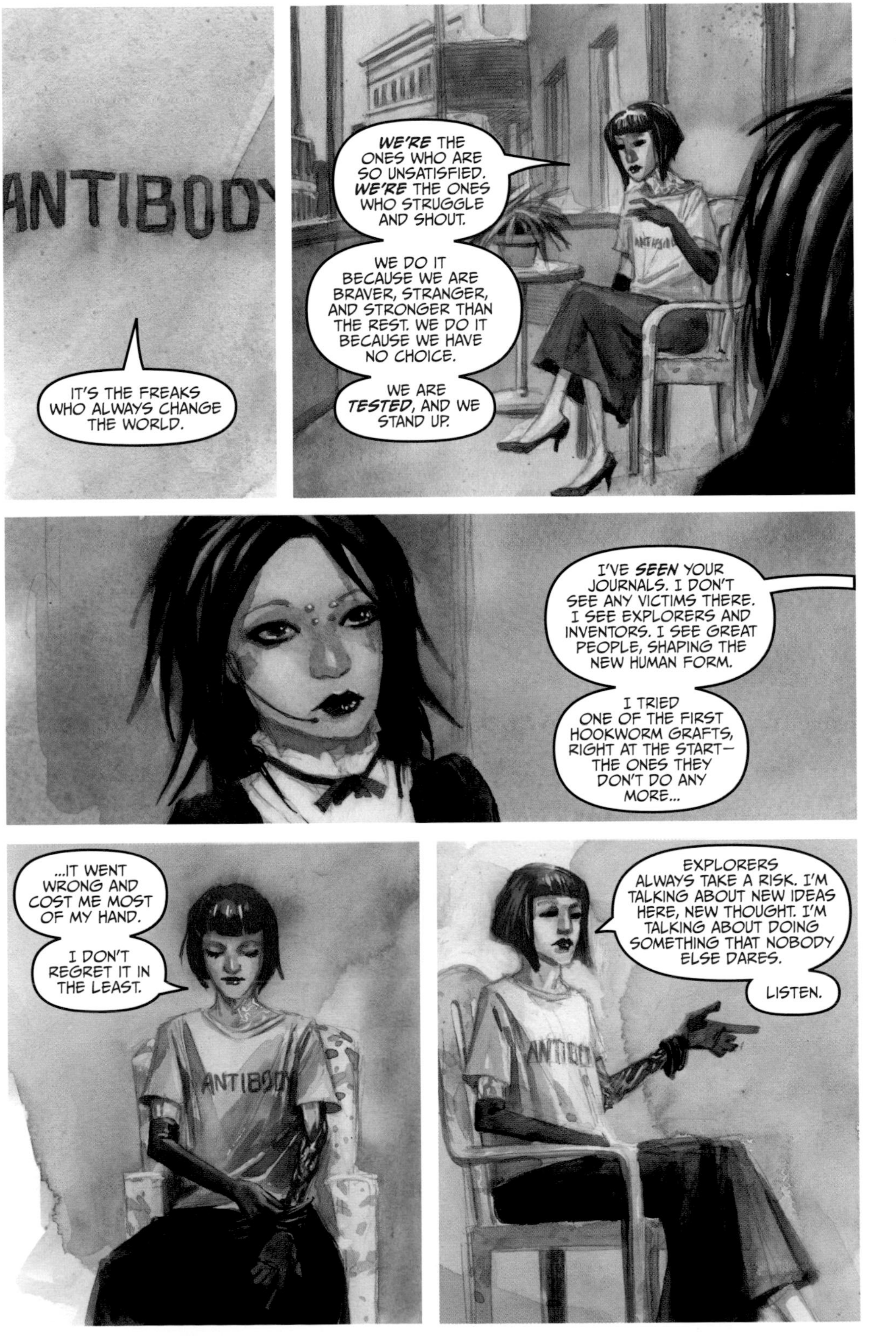
ANTIBODY
IT'S THE FREAKS WHO ALWAYS CHANGE THE WORLD.
WE'RE THE ONES WHO ARE SO UNSATISFIED. WE'RE THE ONES WHO STRUGGLE AND SHOUT.
WE DO IT BECAUSE WE ARE BRAVER, STRANGER, AND STRONGER THAN THE REST. WE DO IT BECAUSE WE HAVE NO CHOICE.
WE ARE TESTED, AND WE STAND UP.
I'VE SEEN YOUR JOURNALS. I DON'T SEE ANY VICTIMS THERE. I SEE EXPLORERS AND INVENTORS. I SEE GREAT PEOPLE, SHAPING THE NEW HUMAN FORM.
I TRIED ONE OF THE FIRST HOOKWORM GRAFTS, RIGHT AT THE START— THE ONES THEY DON'T DO ANY MORE...
...IT WENT WRONG AND COST ME MOST OF MY HAND.
I DON'T REGRET IT IN THE LEAST.
ANTIBODY
EXPLORERS ALWAYS TAKE A RISK. I'M TALKING ABOUT NEW IDEAS HERE, NEW THOUGHT. I'M TALKING ABOUT DOING SOMETHING THAT NOBODY ELSE DARES.
LISTEN.

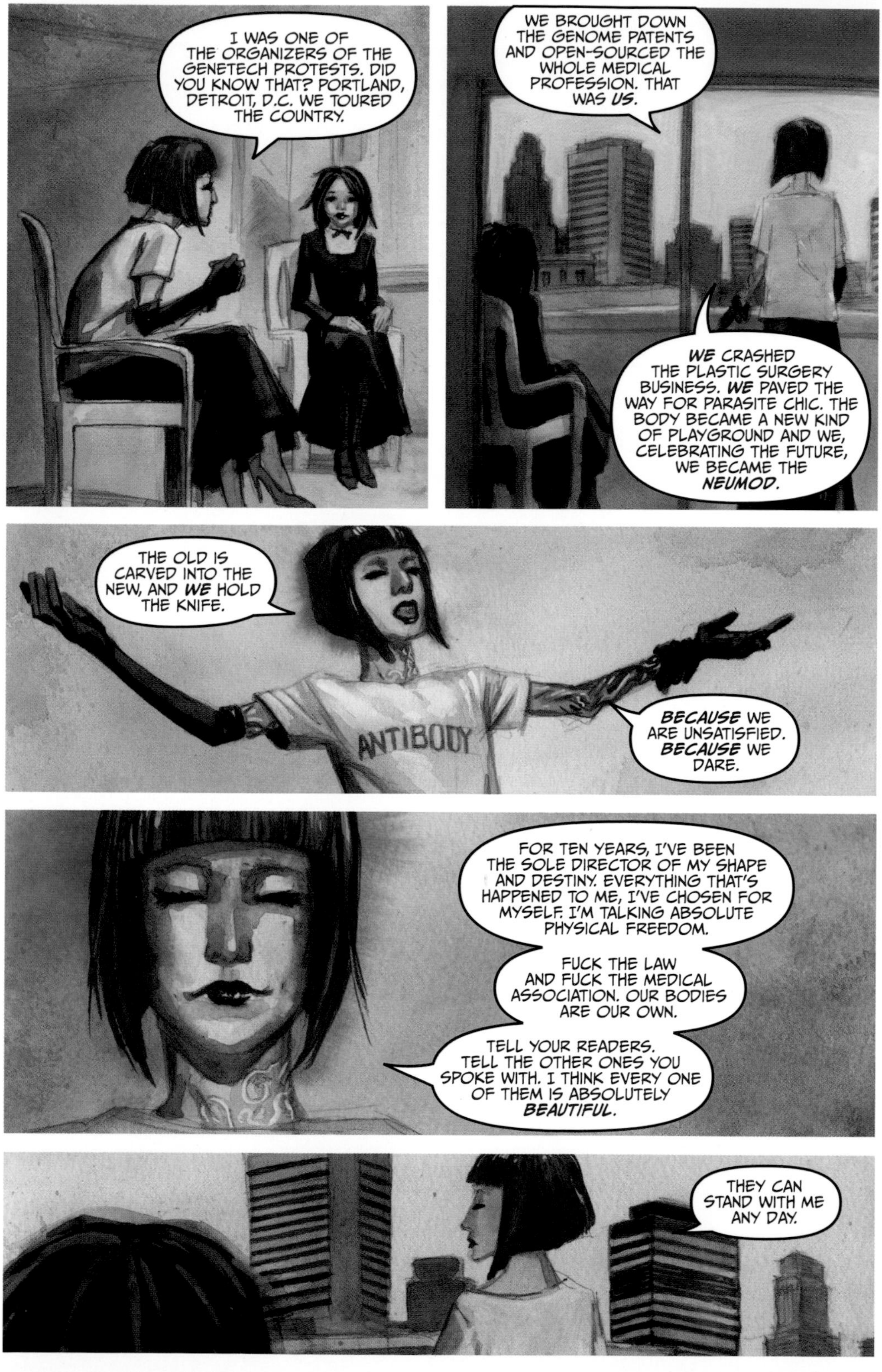
I WAS ONE OF THE ORGANIZERS OF THE GENETECH PROTESTS. DID YOU KNOW THAT? PORTLAND, DETROIT, D.C. WE TOURED THE COUNTRY.
WE BROUGHT DOWN THE GENOME PATENTS AND OPEN-SOURCED THE WHOLE MEDICAL PROFESSION. THAT WAS US.
WE CRASHED THE PLASTIC SURGERY BUSINESS. WE PAVED THE WAY FOR PARASITE CHIC. THE BODY BECAME A NEW KIND OF PLAYGROUND AND WE, CELEBRATING THE FUTURE, WE BECAME THE NEUMOD.
THE OLD IS CARVED INTO THE NEW, AND WE HOLD THE KNIFE.
ANTIBODY
BECAUSE WE ARE UNSATISFIED. BECAUSE WE DARE.
FOR TEN YEARS, I'VE BEEN THE SOLE DIRECTOR OF MY SHAPE AND DESTINY. EVERYTHING THAT'S HAPPENED TO ME, I'VE CHOSEN FOR MYSELF. I'M TALKING ABSOLUTE PHYSICAL FREEDOM.
FUCK THE LAW AND FUCK THE MEDICAL ASSOCIATION. OUR BODIES ARE OUR OWN.
TELL YOUR READERS. TELL THE OTHER ONES YOU SPOKE WITH. I THINK EVERY ONE OF THEM IS ABSOLUTELY BEAUTIFUL.
THEY CAN STAND WITH ME ANY DAY.

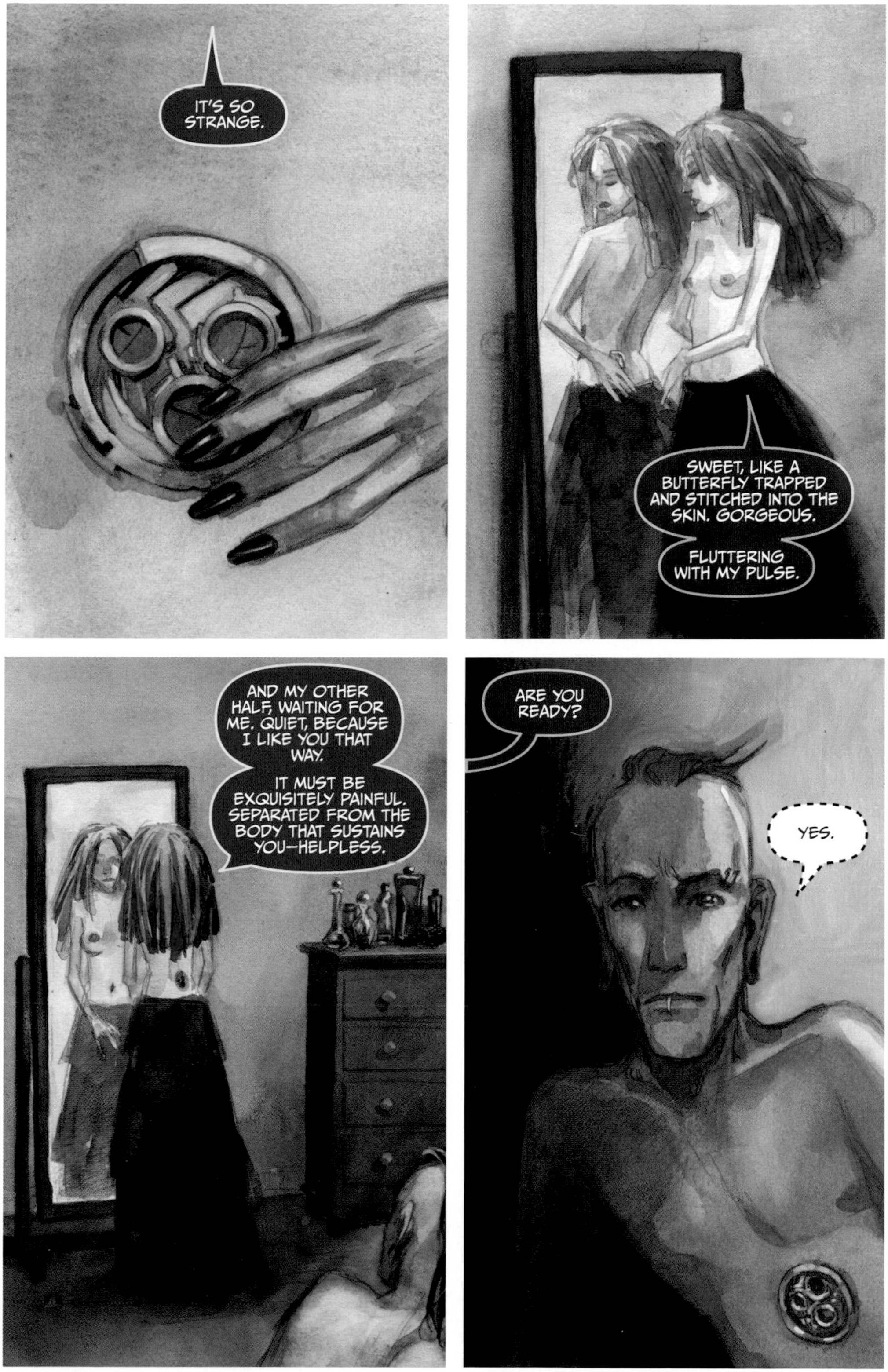
IT'S SO STRANGE.
SWEET, LIKE A BUTTERFLY TRAPPED AND STITCHED INTO THE SKIN. GORGEOUS.
FLUTTERING WITH MY PULSE.
AND MY OTHER HALF, WAITING FOR ME. QUIET, BECAUSE I LIKE YOU THAT WAY.
IT MUST BE EXQUISITELY PAINFUL. SEPARATED FROM THE BODY THAT SUSTAINS YOU—HELPLESS.
ARE YOU READY?
YES.

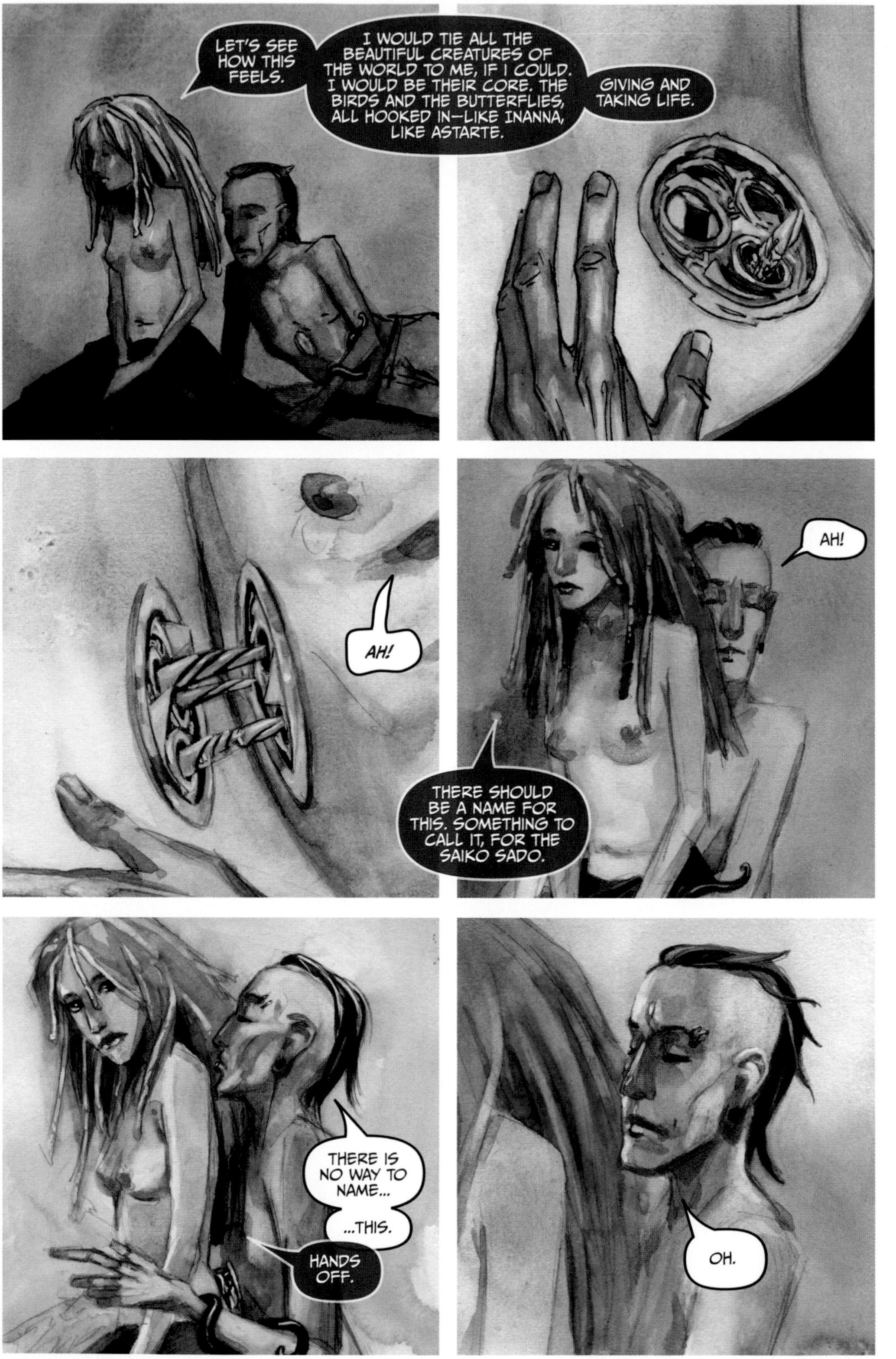
LET'S SEE HOW THIS FEELS.
I WOULD TIE ALL THE BEAUTIFUL CREATURES OF THE WORLD TO ME, IF I COULD. I WOULD BE THEIR CORE. THE BIRDS AND THE BUTTERFLIES, ALL HOOKED IN—LIKE INANNA, LIKE ASTARTE.
GIVING AND TAKING LIFE.
AH!
AH!
THERE SHOULD BE A NAME FOR THIS. SOMETHING TO CALL IT, FOR THE SAIKO SADO.
THERE IS NO WAY TO NAME...
...THIS.
HANDS OFF.
OH.

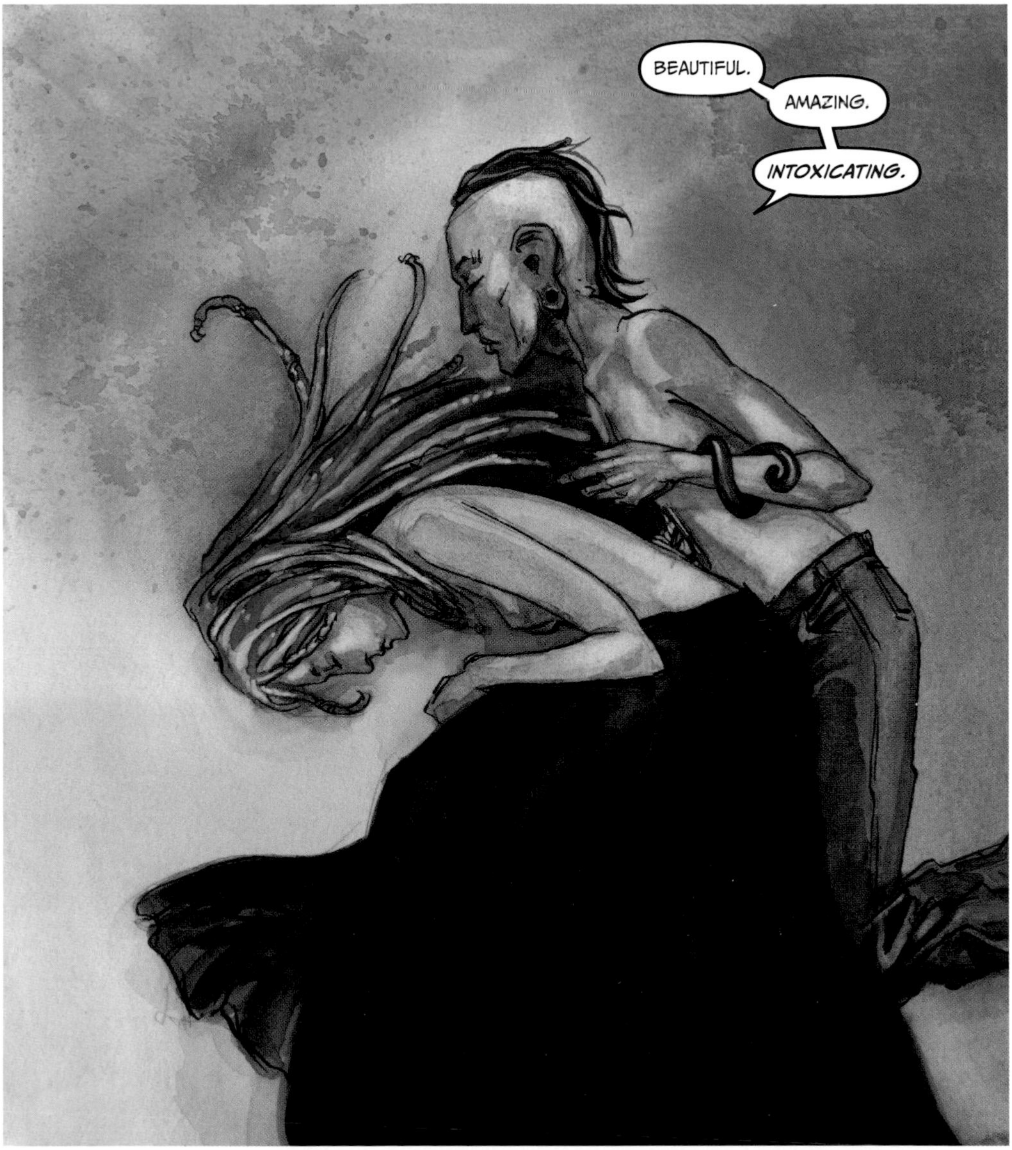
BEAUTIFUL.
AMAZING.
INTOXICATING.

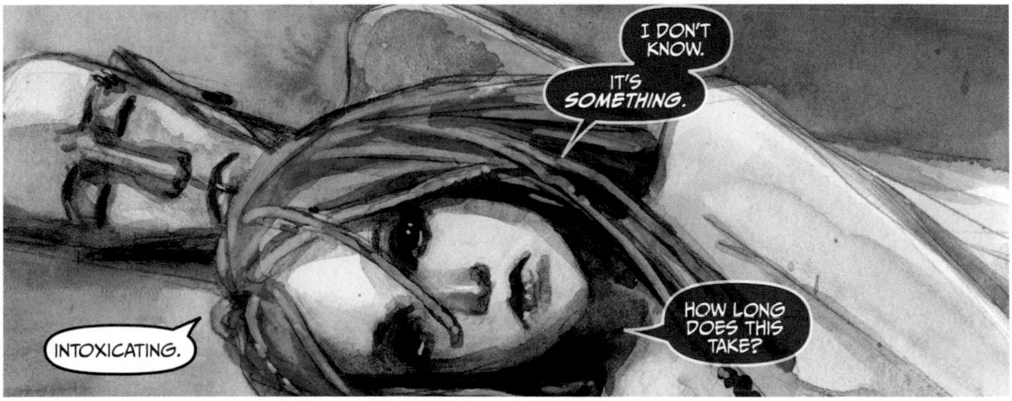
I DON'T KNOW.
IT'S SOMETHING.
INTOXICATING.
HOW LONG DOES THIS TAKE?

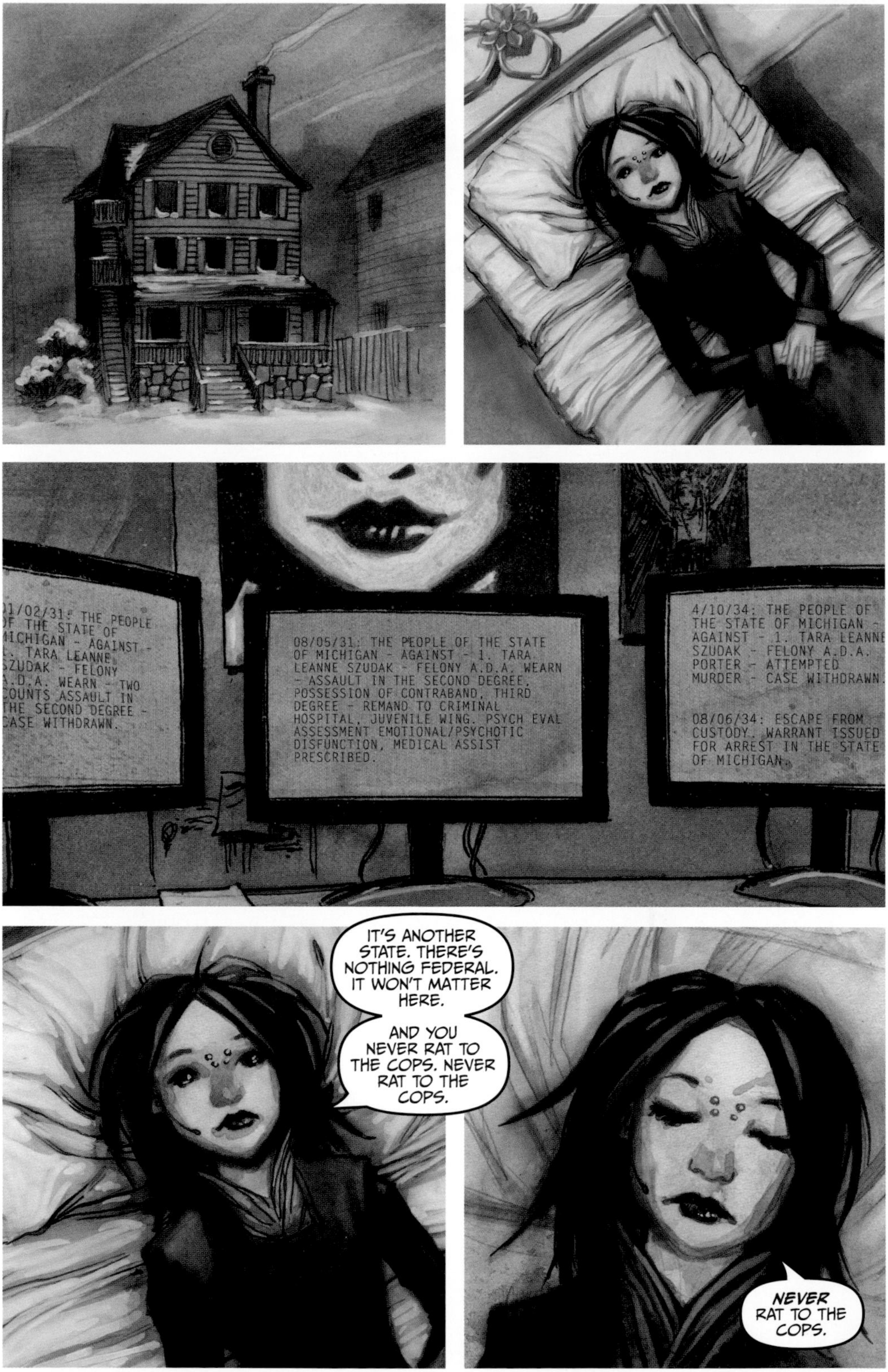
01/02/31: THE PEOPLE OF THE STATE OF MICHIGAN - AGAINST - 1. TARA LEANNE SZUDAK - FELONY A.D.A. WEARN - TWO COUNTS ASSAULT IN THE SECOND DEGREE - CASE WITHDRAWN.
08/05/31: THE PEOPLE OF THE STATE OF MICHIGAN - AGAINST - 1. TARA LEANNE SZUDAK - FELONY A.D.A. WEARN - ASSAULT IN THE SECOND DEGREE, POSSESSION OF CONTRABAND, THIRD DEGREE - REMAND TO CRIMINAL HOSPITAL, JUVENILE WING. PSYCH EVAL ASSESSMENT EMOTIONAL/PSYCHOTIC DISFUNCTION, MEDICAL ASSIST PRESCRIBED.
4/10/34: THE PEOPLE OF THE STATE OF MICHIGAN - AGAINST - 1. TARA LEANNE SZUDAK - FELONY A.D.A. PORTER - ATTEMPTED MURDER - CASE WITHDRAWN.
08/06/34: ESCAPE FROM CUSTODY. WARRANT ISSUED FOR ARREST IN THE STATE OF MICHIGAN.
IT'S ANOTHER STATE. THERE'S NOTHING FEDERAL. IT WON'T MATTER HERE.
AND YOU NEVER RAT TO THE COPS. NEVER RAT TO THE COPS.
NEVER RAT TO THE COPS.

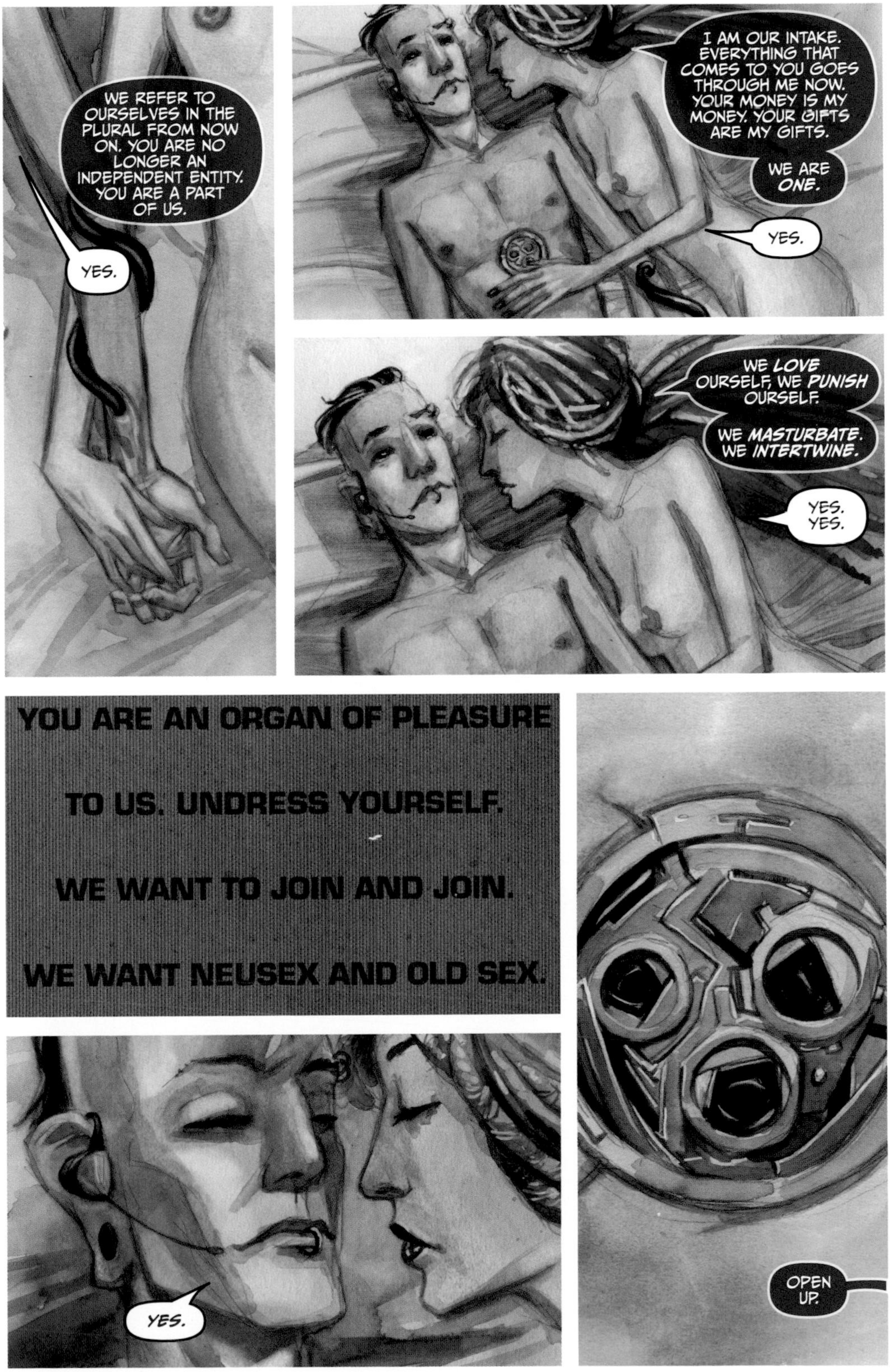
WE REFER TO OURSELVES IN THE PLURAL FROM NOW ON. YOU ARE NO LONGER AN INDEPENDENT ENTITY. YOU ARE A PART OF US.
YES.
I AM OUR INTAKE. EVERYTHING THAT COMES TO YOU GOES THROUGH ME NOW. YOUR MONEY IS MY MONEY. YOUR GIFTS ARE MY GIFTS.
WE ARE ONE.
YES.
WE LOVE OURSELF. WE PUNISH OURSELF.
WE MASTURBATE. WE INTERTWINE.
YES. YES.
YOU ARE AN ORGAN OF PLEASURE
TO US. UNDRESS YOURSELF.
WE WANT TO JOIN AND JOIN.
WE WANT NEUSEX AND OLD SEX.
YES.
OPEN UP.

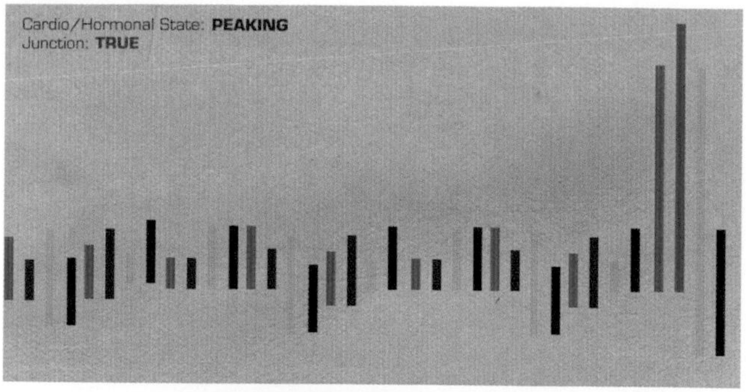
Cardio/Hormonal State: **PEAKING**
Junction: **TRUE**

I LOVE U DIRK TELL ME IS YOUR JUNCTION RLY TRUE OR CAN I GET C FOR U. I WOULD TREAT U RIGHT NOT LIKE THAT SUKA YOU'RE WITH RIGHT NOW

COMMENT BY: BLACKTEARS37

NO I WANT HIM HES MINE PLS I WAS READING HIS JOURNAL WHEN IT STARTED

COMMENT BY: FIRE_FIRE_FIRE

THANK YOU FOR THIS DOCUMENT IT' BEAUTIFUL YOU'RE BEAUTIFUL.

COMMENT BY: NEUMOD_FUTURE

SAIKO SADO! YOU ARE THE FUCKING GENIUS OF NEUMOD YOU ARE THE FUCKING PIONEER STAR. COME TO TEXAS AND SHOW THESE SUKA LOSERS HOW ITS DONE PLEASE I CA STAND THIS KUSO HALFASS SCENE.

COMMENT BY: SIX_OR

THIS DOCUMENT IS FAKE. YOU CAN TELL WHEN YOU LOOK AT HER SO-CALLED VALVE THE EDGES ARE ALWAYS BLURRY LIKE CHEAP PHOTO-FIX TECH

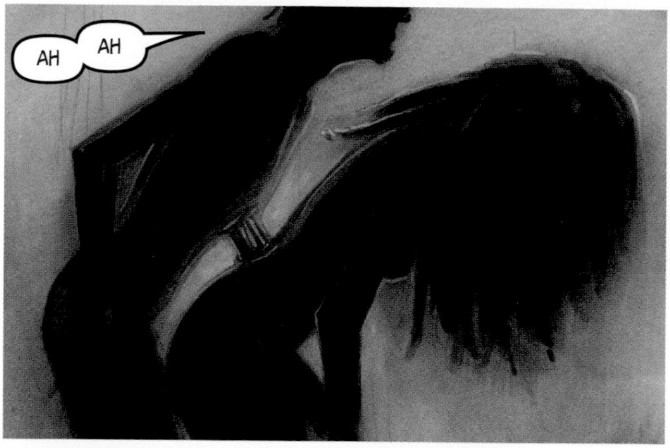
AH
AH

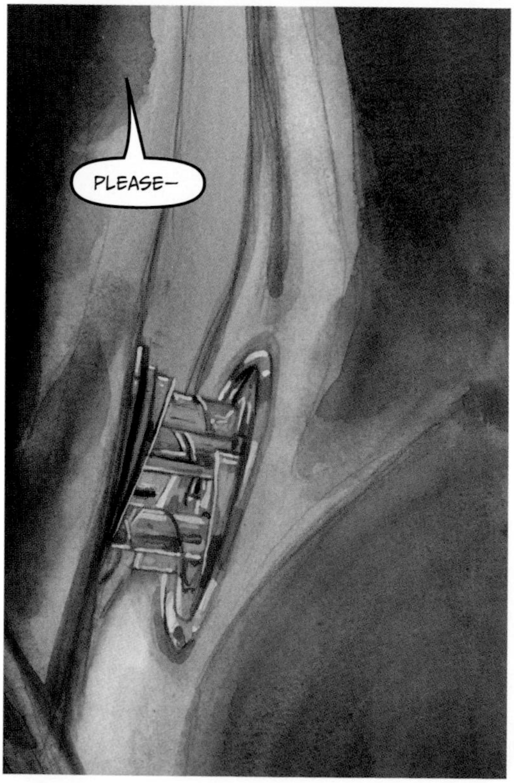
PLEASE—

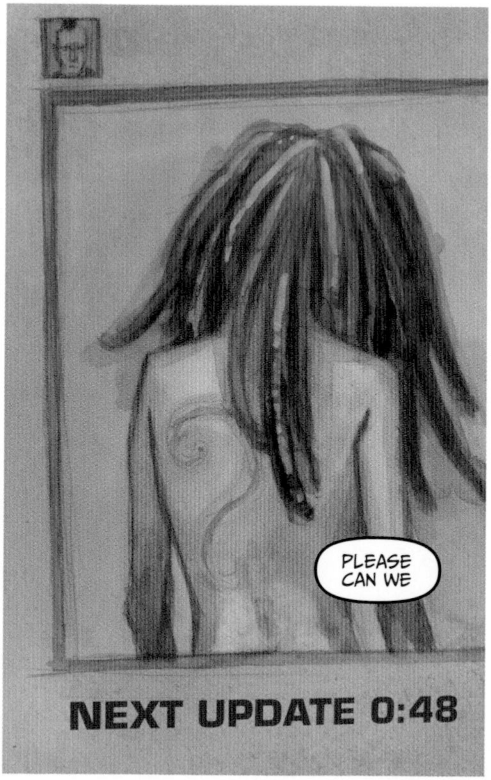
PLEASE CAN WE
NEXT UPDATE 0:48

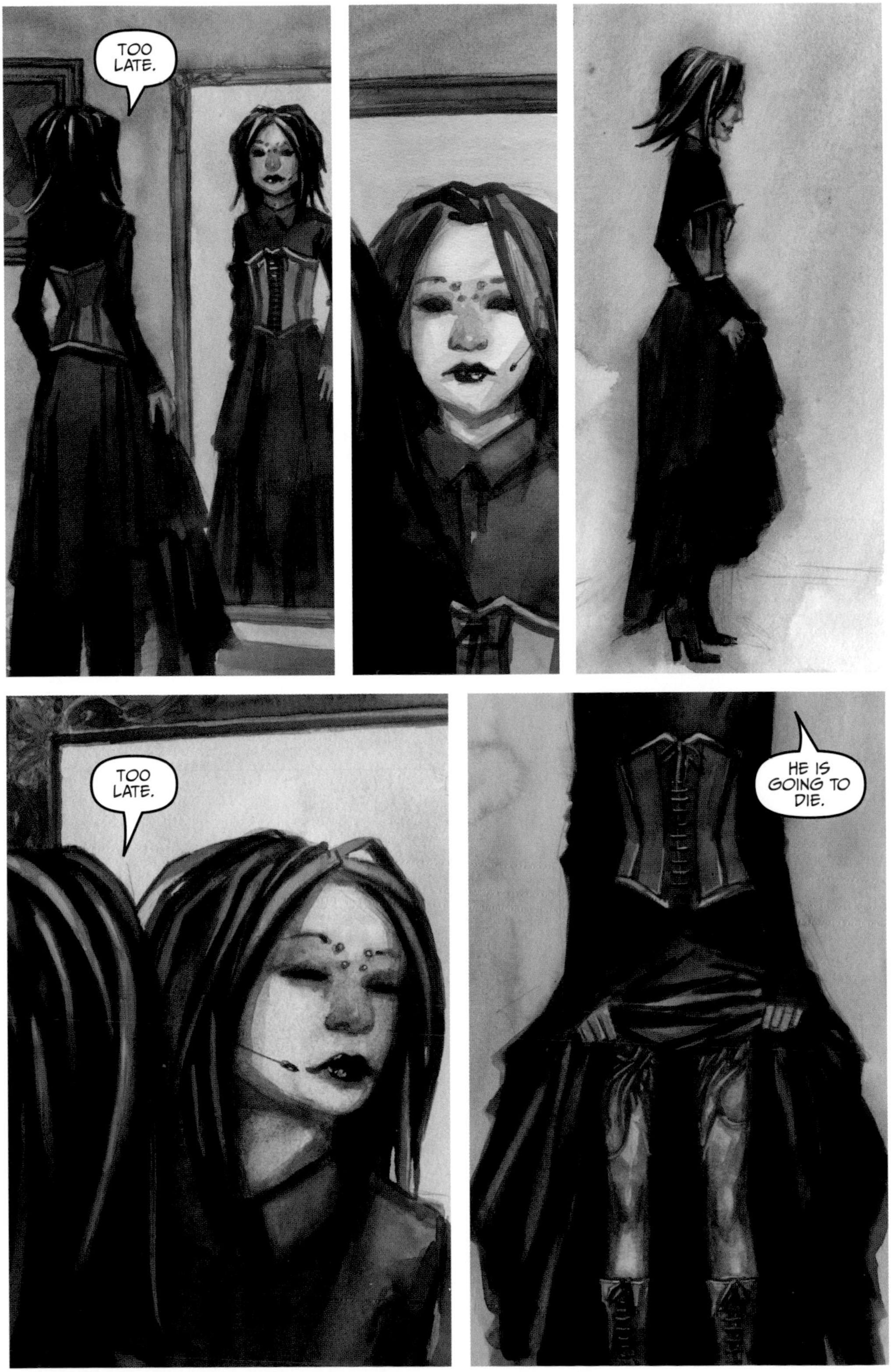
TOO LATE.
TOO LATE.
HE IS GOING TO DIE.

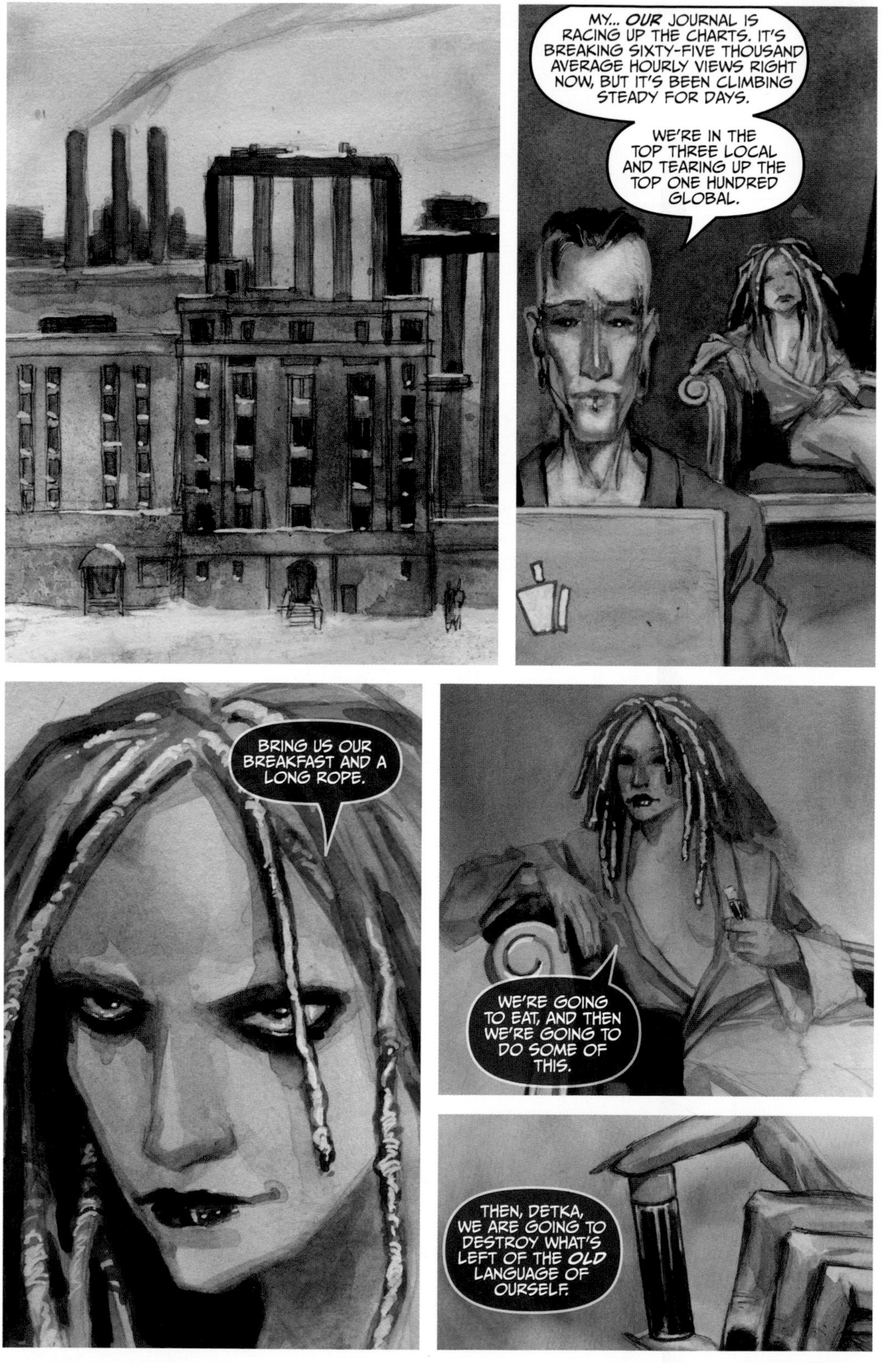

MY... OUR JOURNAL IS RACING UP THE CHARTS. IT'S BREAKING SIXTY-FIVE THOUSAND AVERAGE HOURLY VIEWS RIGHT NOW, BUT IT'S BEEN CLIMBING STEADY FOR DAYS.
WE'RE IN THE TOP THREE LOCAL AND TEARING UP THE TOP ONE HUNDRED GLOBAL.
BRING US OUR BREAKFAST AND A LONG ROPE.
WE'RE GOING TO EAT, AND THEN WE'RE GOING TO DO SOME OF THIS.
THEN, DETKA, WE ARE GOING TO DESTROY WHAT'S LEFT OF THE OLD LANGUAGE OF OURSELF.

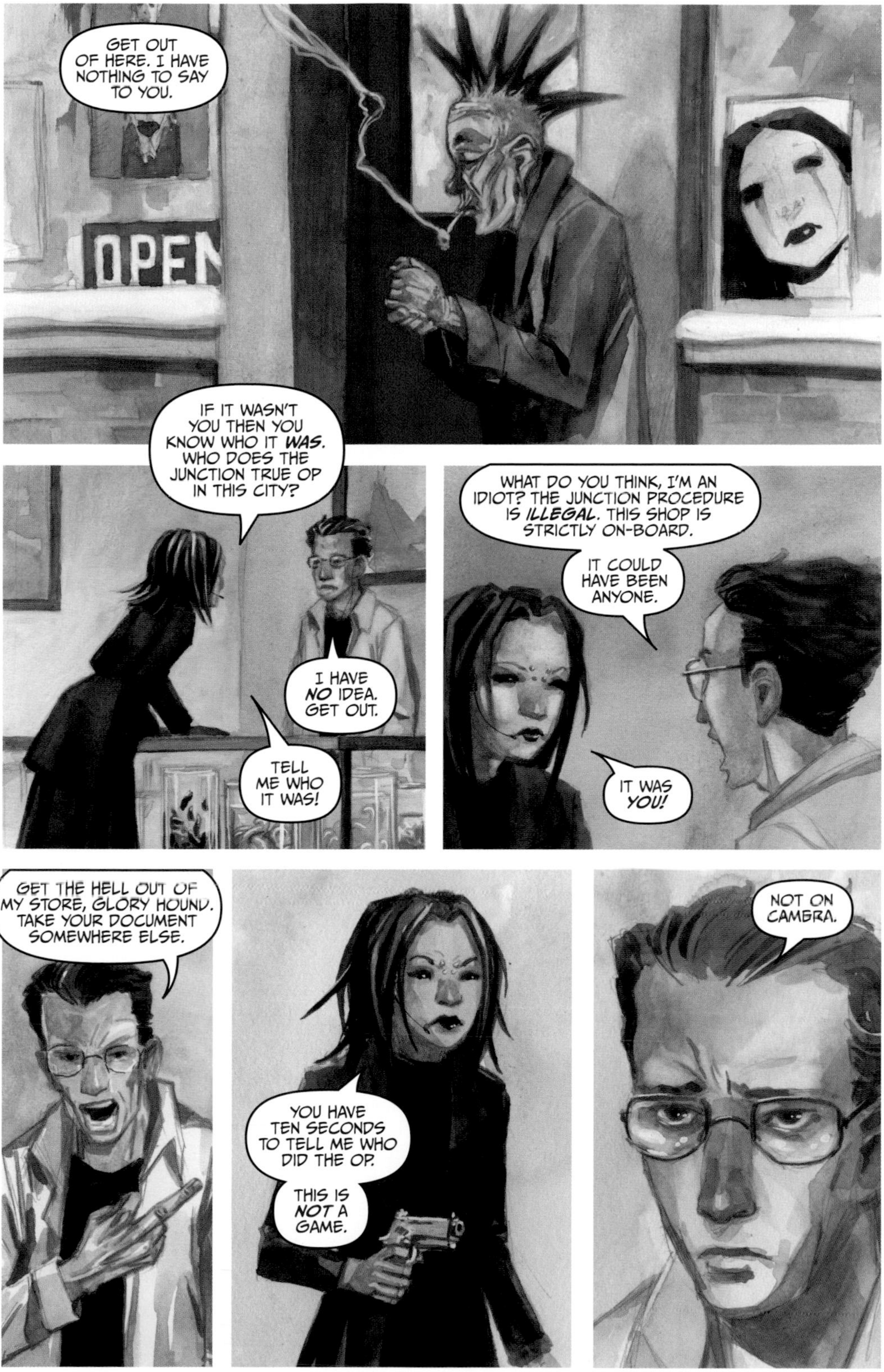
GET OUT OF HERE. I HAVE NOTHING TO SAY TO YOU.
OPEN
IF IT WASN'T YOU THEN YOU KNOW WHO IT *WAS*. WHO DOES THE JUNCTION TRUE OP IN THIS CITY?
I HAVE *NO* IDEA. GET OUT.
TELL ME WHO IT WAS!
WHAT DO YOU THINK, I'M AN IDIOT? THE JUNCTION PROCEDURE IS *ILLEGAL*. THIS SHOP IS STRICTLY ON-BOARD.
IT COULD HAVE BEEN ANYONE.
IT WAS *YOU!*
GET THE HELL OUT OF MY STORE, GLORY HOUND. TAKE YOUR DOCUMENT SOMEWHERE ELSE.
YOU HAVE TEN SECONDS TO TELL ME WHO DID THE OP.
THIS IS *NOT* A GAME.
NOT ON CAMERA.

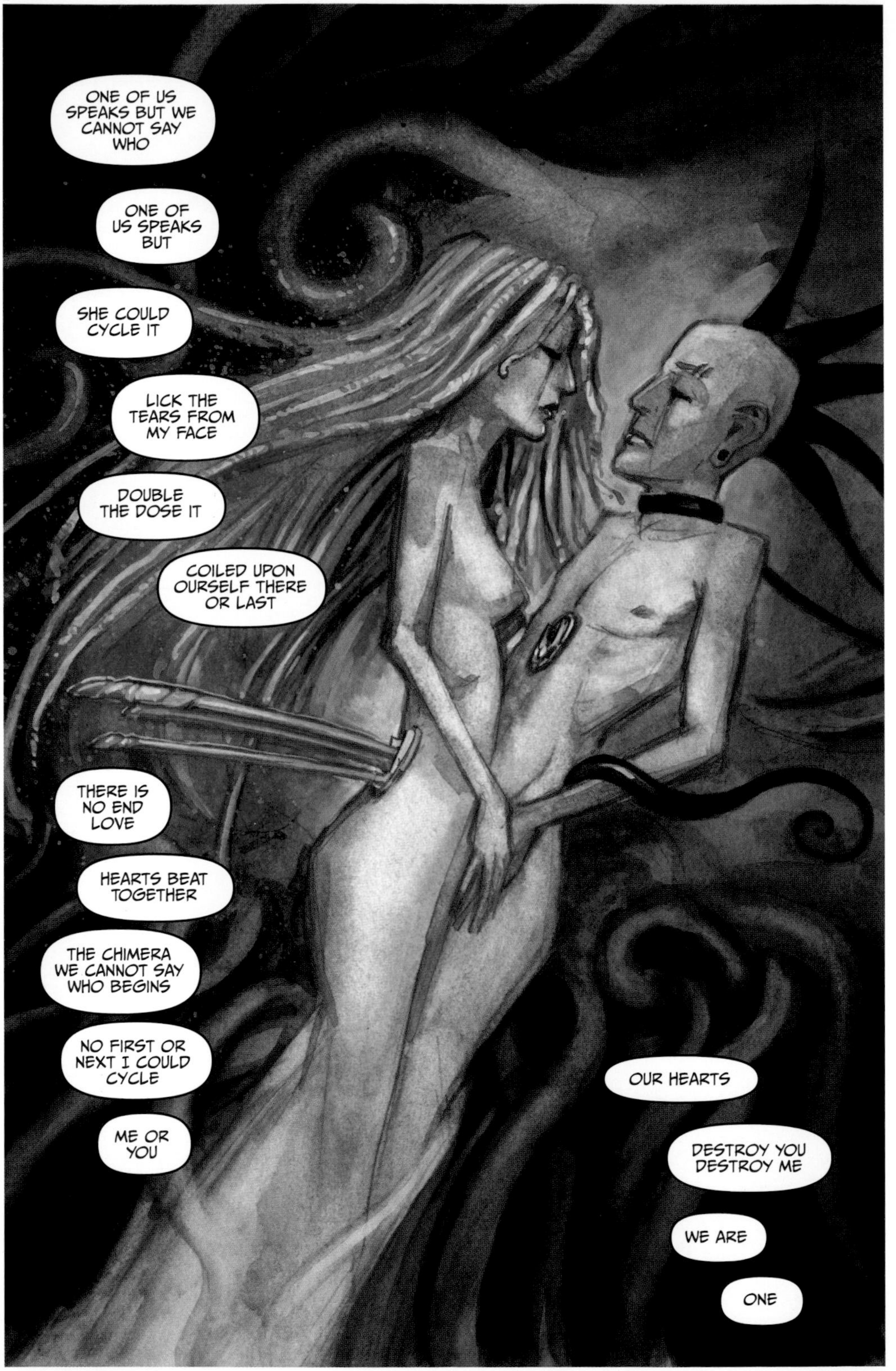
ONE OF US SPEAKS BUT WE CANNOT SAY WHO
ONE OF US SPEAKS BUT
SHE COULD CYCLE IT
LICK THE TEARS FROM MY FACE
DOUBLE THE DOSE IT
COILED UPON OURSELF THERE OR LAST
THERE IS NO END LOVE
HEARTS BEAT TOGETHER
THE CHIMERA WE CANNOT SAY WHO BEGINS
NO FIRST OR NEXT I COULD CYCLE
ME OR YOU
OUR HEARTS
DESTROY YOU DESTROY ME
WE ARE
ONE

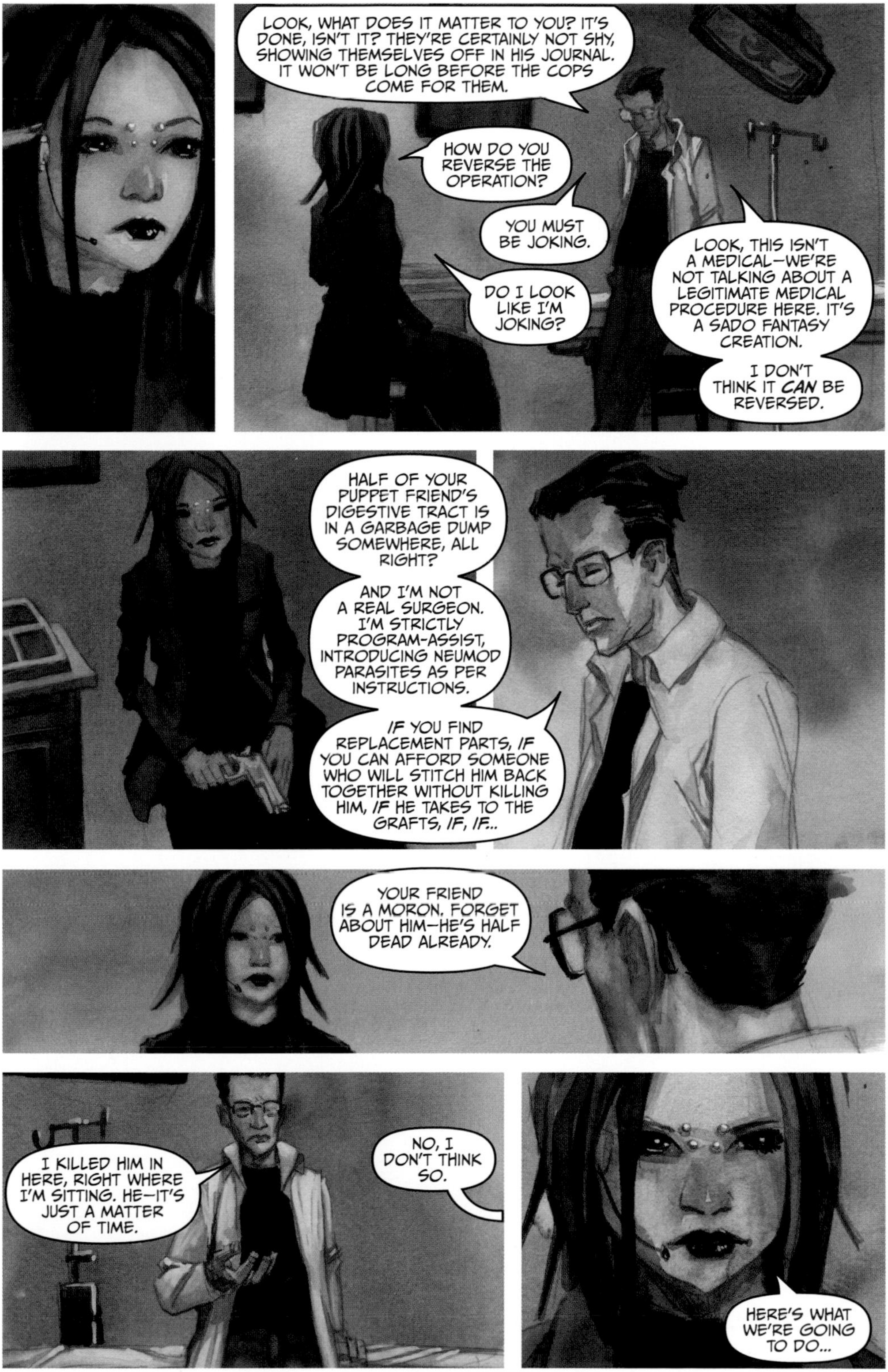
LOOK, WHAT DOES IT MATTER TO YOU? IT'S DONE, ISN'T IT? THEY'RE CERTAINLY NOT SHY, SHOWING THEMSELVES OFF IN HIS JOURNAL. IT WON'T BE LONG BEFORE THE COPS COME FOR THEM.
HOW DO YOU REVERSE THE OPERATION?
YOU MUST BE JOKING.
DO I LOOK LIKE I'M JOKING?
LOOK, THIS ISN'T A MEDICAL—WE'RE NOT TALKING ABOUT A LEGITIMATE MEDICAL PROCEDURE HERE. IT'S A SADO FANTASY CREATION.
I DON'T THINK IT *CAN* BE REVERSED.
HALF OF YOUR PUPPET FRIEND'S DIGESTIVE TRACT IS IN A GARBAGE DUMP SOMEWHERE, ALL RIGHT?
AND I'M NOT A REAL SURGEON. I'M STRICTLY PROGRAM-ASSIST, INTRODUCING NEUMOD PARASITES AS PER INSTRUCTIONS.
IF YOU FIND REPLACEMENT PARTS, *IF* YOU CAN AFFORD SOMEONE WHO WILL STITCH HIM BACK TOGETHER WITHOUT KILLING HIM, *IF* HE TAKES TO THE GRAFTS, *IF*, *IF*..
YOUR FRIEND IS A MORON. FORGET ABOUT HIM—HE'S HALF DEAD ALREADY.
I KILLED HIM IN HERE, RIGHT WHERE I'M SITTING. HE—IT'S JUST A MATTER OF TIME.
NO, I DON'T THINK SO.
HERE'S WHAT WE'RE GOING TO DO...

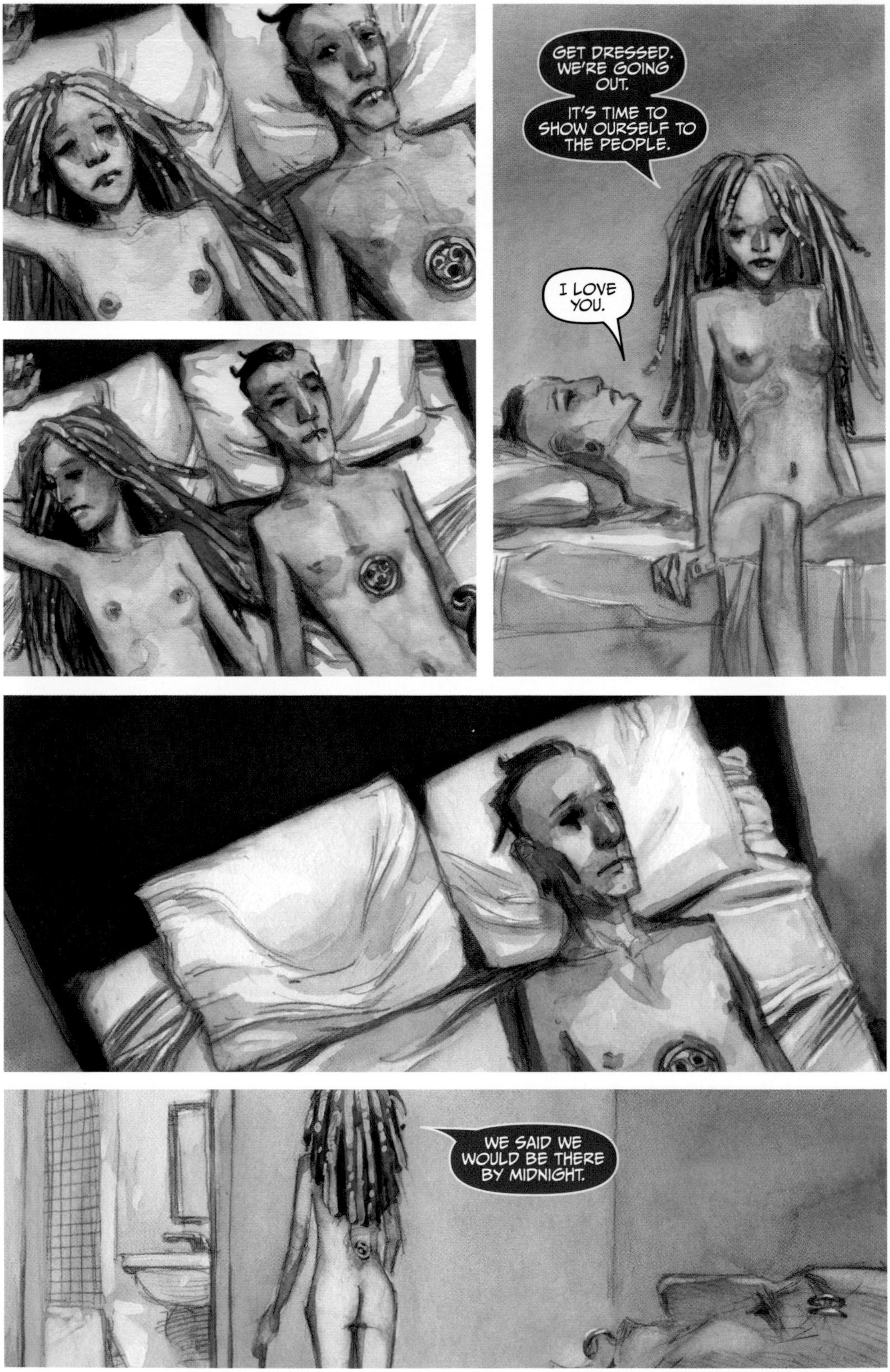
GET DRESSED. WE'RE GOING OUT.
IT'S TIME TO SHOW OURSELF TO THE PEOPLE.
I LOVE YOU.
WE SAID WE WOULD BE THERE BY MIDNIGHT.

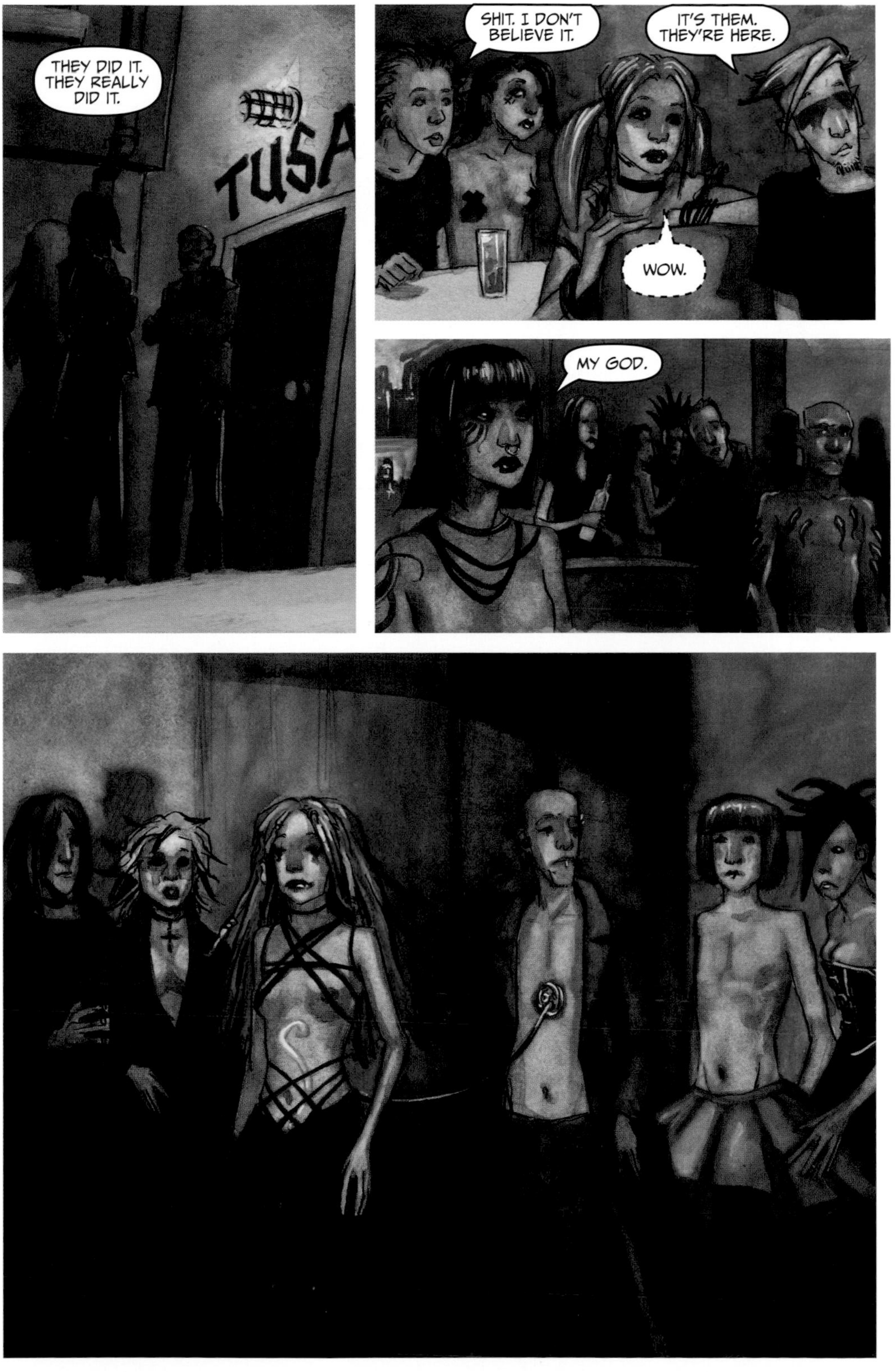
THEY DID IT. THEY REALLY DID IT.
TUSA
SHIT. I DON'T BELIEVE IT.
IT'S THEM. THEY'RE HERE.
WOW.
MY GOD.

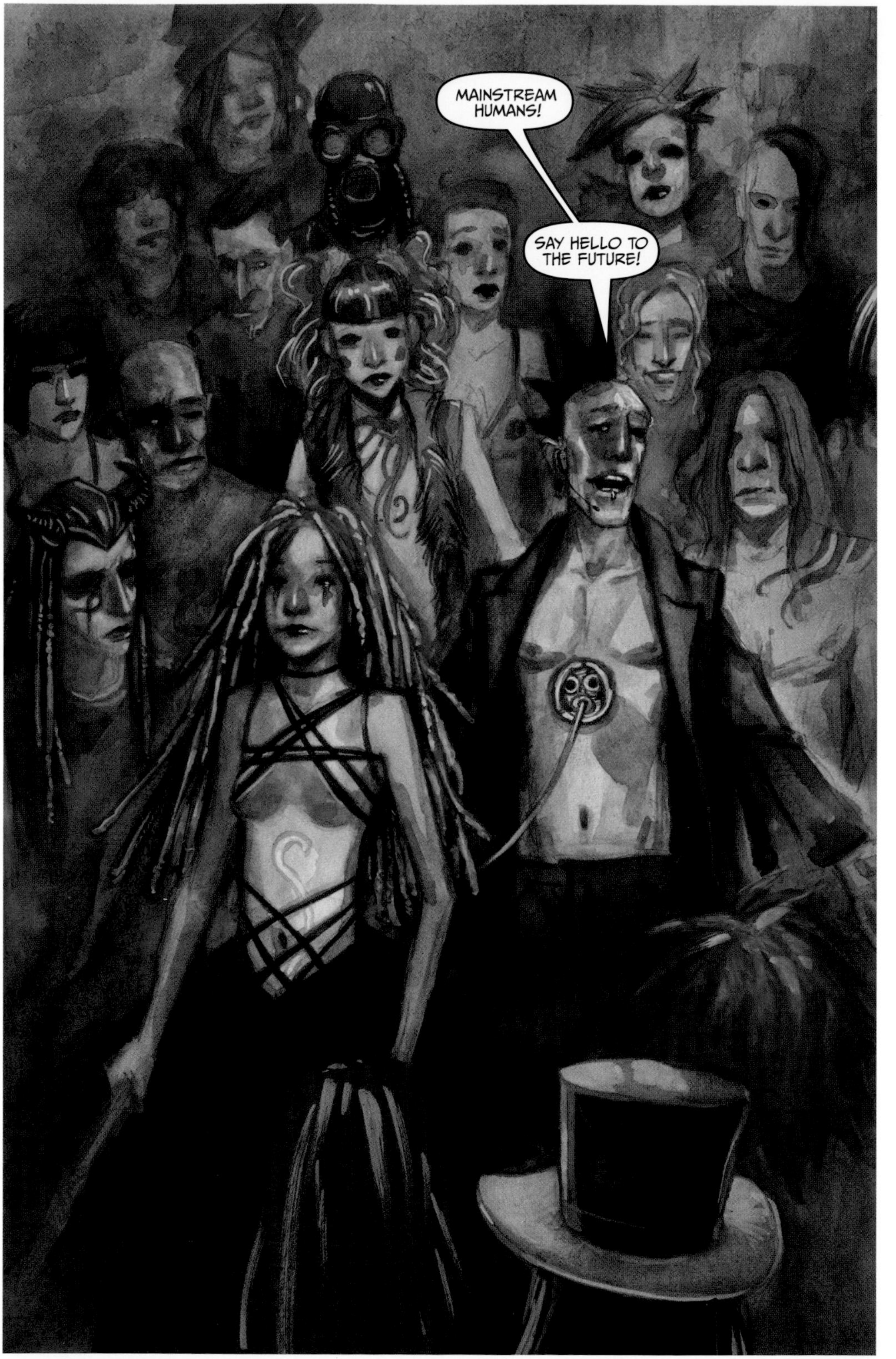
MAINSTREAM HUMANS!
SAY HELLO TO THE FUTURE!

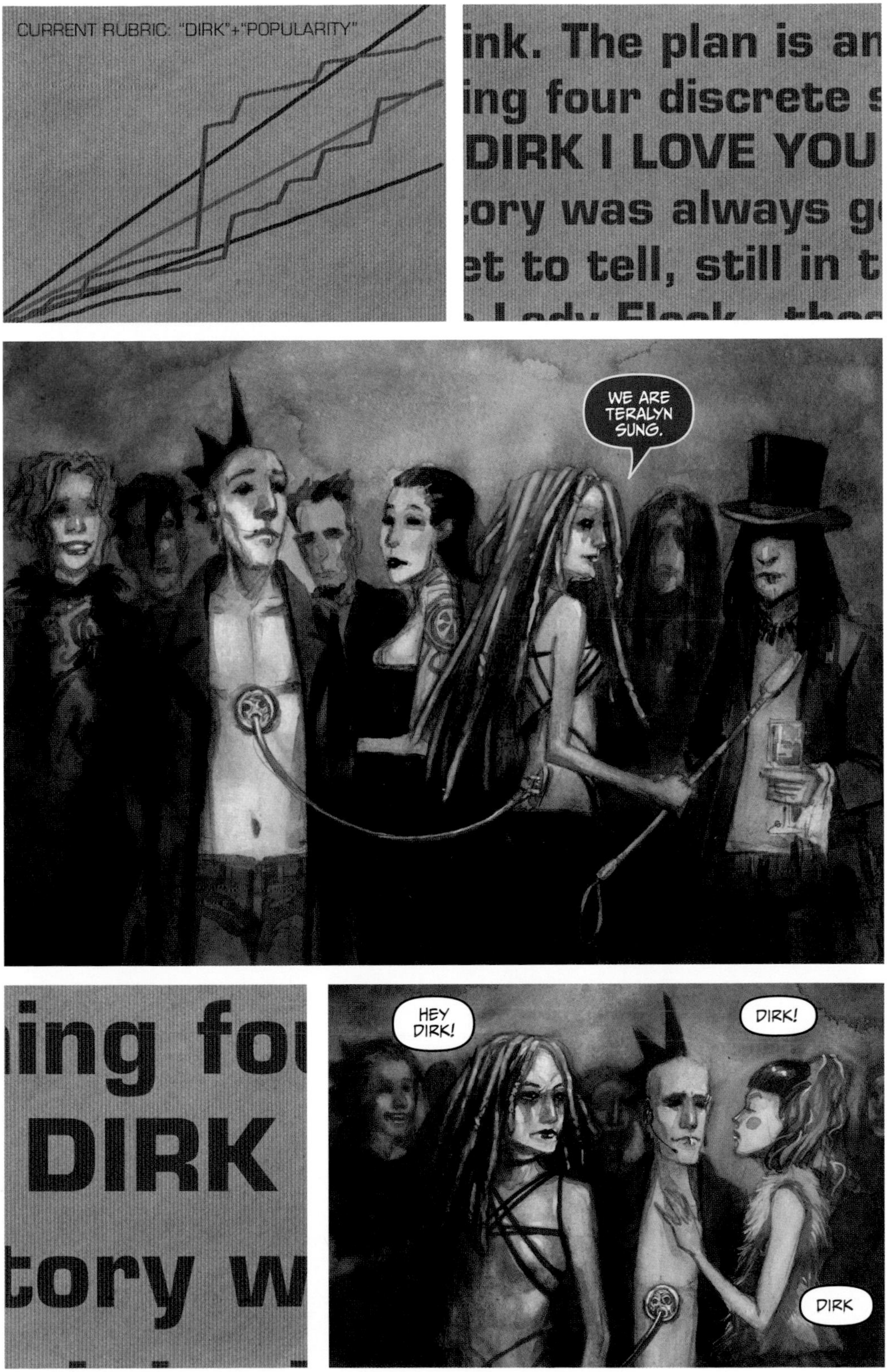
CURRENT RUBRIC: "DIRK"+"POPULARITY"
ink. The plan is an
ing four discrete s
DIRK I LOVE YOU
tory was always g
et to tell, still in t
WE ARE TERALYN SUNG.
hing fou
DIRK
tory w
HEY DIRK!
DIRK!
DIRK

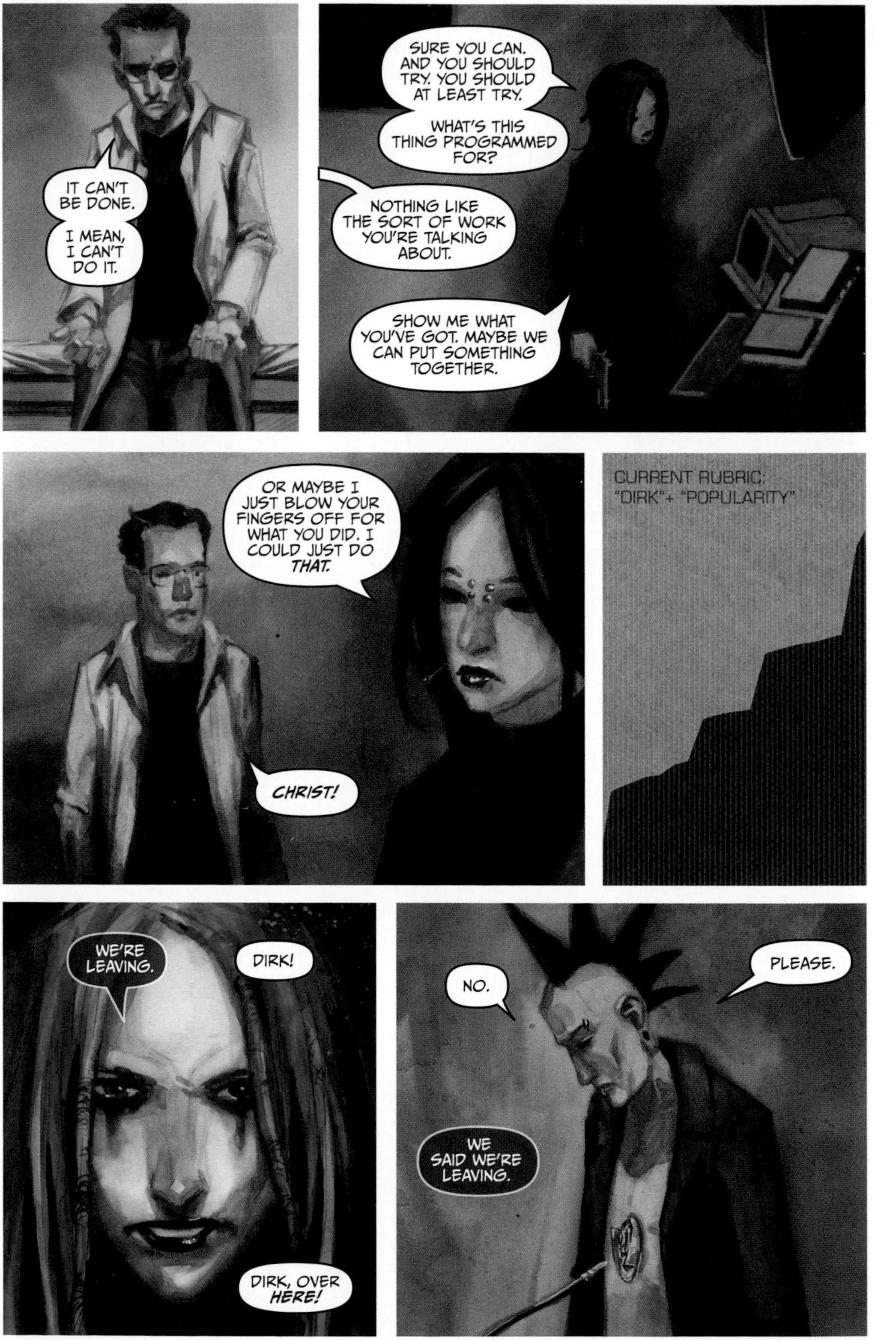
IT CAN'T BE DONE.
I MEAN, I CAN'T DO IT.
SURE YOU CAN. AND YOU SHOULD TRY. YOU SHOULD AT LEAST TRY.
WHAT'S THIS THING PROGRAMMED FOR?
NOTHING LIKE THE SORT OF WORK YOU'RE TALKING ABOUT.
SHOW ME WHAT YOU'VE GOT. MAYBE WE CAN PUT SOMETHING TOGETHER.
OR MAYBE I JUST BLOW YOUR FINGERS OFF FOR WHAT YOU DID. I COULD JUST DO *THAT.*
CHRIST!
CURRENT RUBRIC: "DIRK"+ "POPULARITY"
WE'RE LEAVING.
DIRK!
DIRK, OVER *HERE!*
NO.
PLEASE.
WE SAID WE'RE LEAVING.

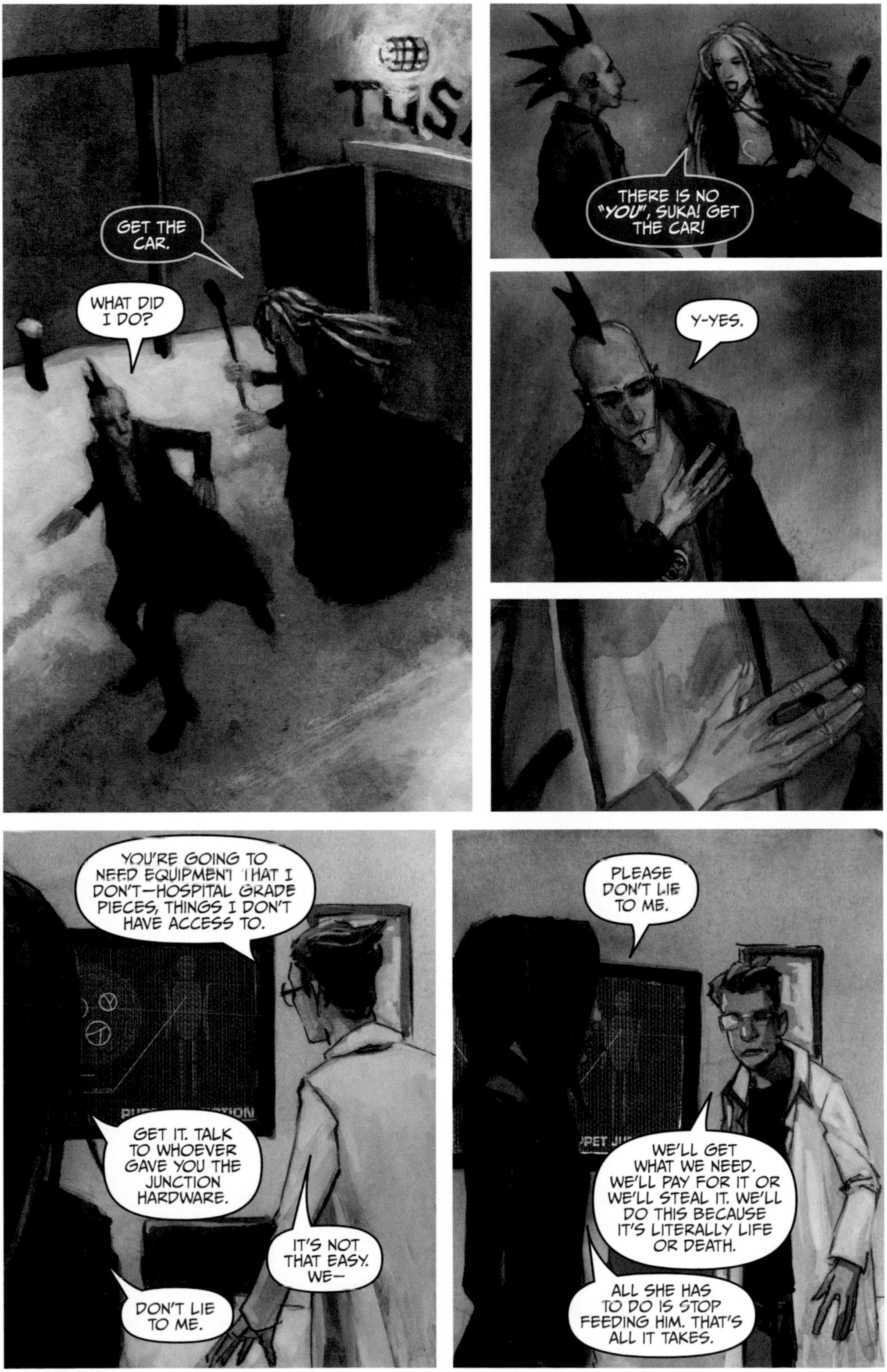
GET THE CAR.
WHAT DID I DO?
THERE IS NO "YOU", SUKA! GET THE CAR!
Y-YES.
YOU'RE GOING TO NEED EQUIPMENT THAT I DON'T—HOSPITAL GRADE PIECES, THINGS I DON'T HAVE ACCESS TO.
GET IT. TALK TO WHOEVER GAVE YOU THE JUNCTION HARDWARE.
IT'S NOT THAT EASY. WE—
DON'T LIE TO ME.
PLEASE DON'T LIE TO ME.
WE'LL GET WHAT WE NEED. WE'LL PAY FOR IT OR WE'LL STEAL IT. WE'LL DO THIS BECAUSE IT'S LITERALLY LIFE OR DEATH.
ALL SHE HAS TO DO IS STOP FEEDING HIM. THAT'S ALL IT TAKES.

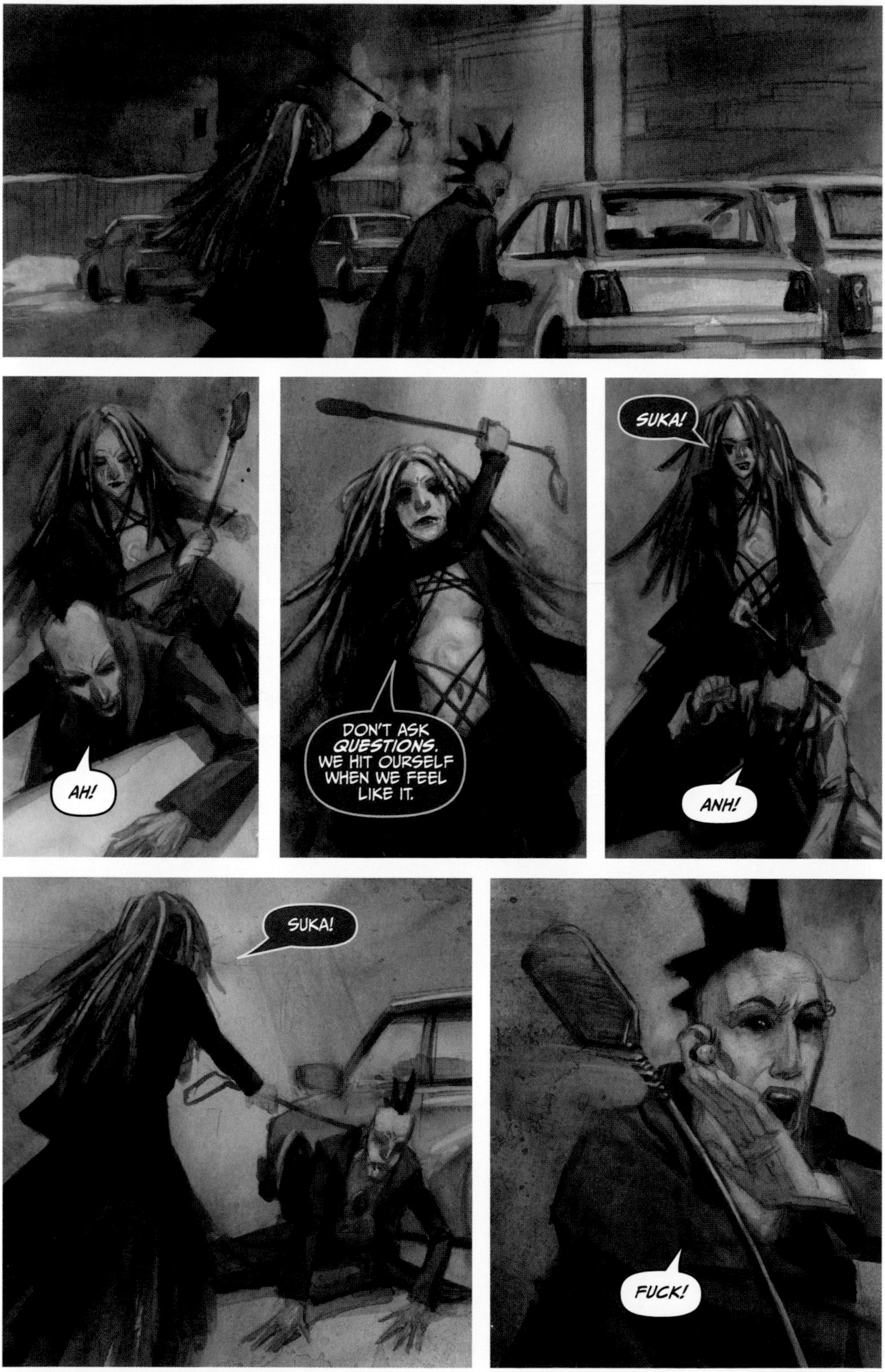
AH!
DON'T ASK QUESTIONS. WE HIT OURSELF WHEN WE FEEL LIKE IT.
SUKA!
ANH!
SUKA!
FUCK!

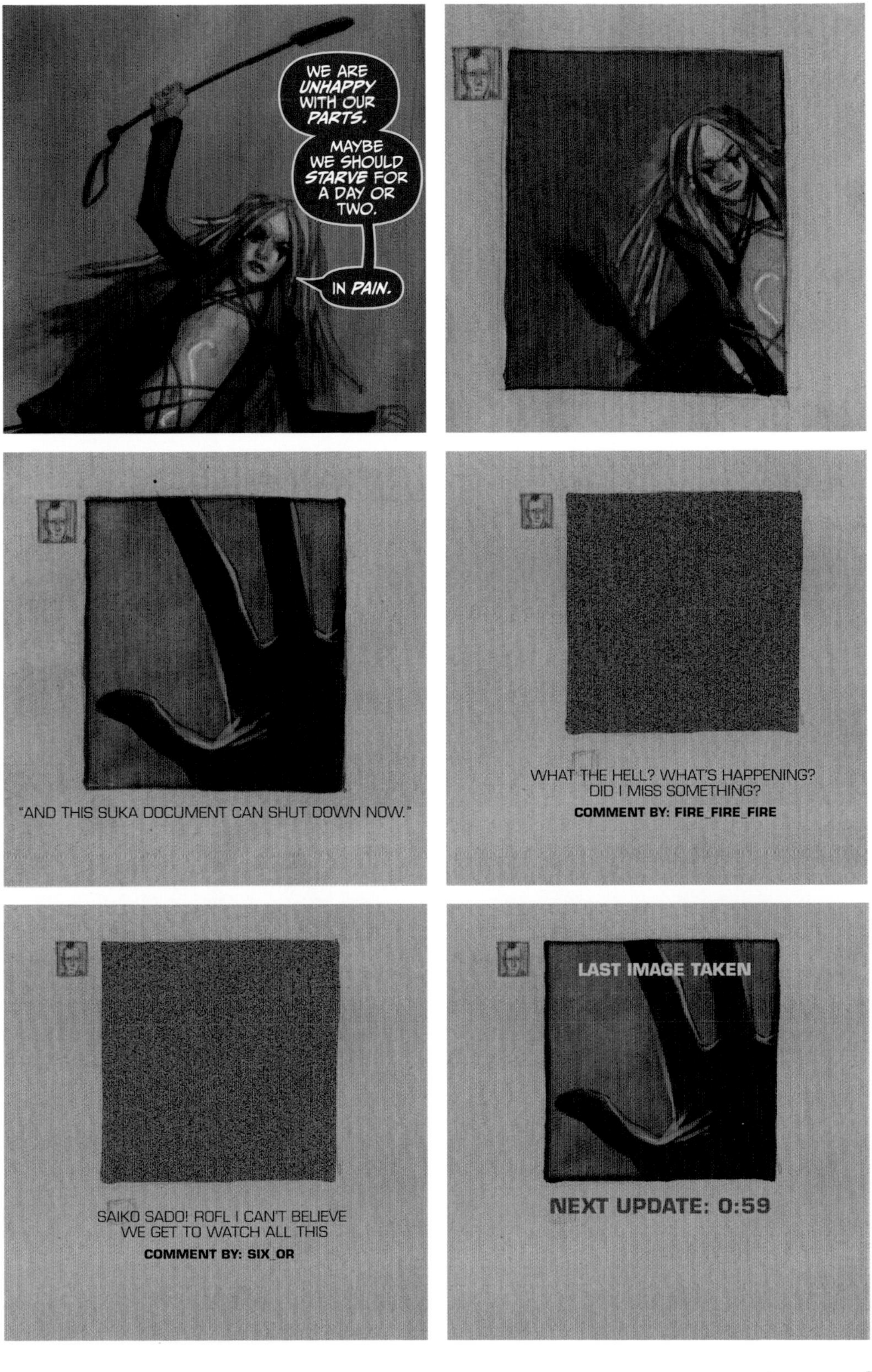
WE ARE UNHAPPY WITH OUR PARTS.
MAYBE WE SHOULD STARVE FOR A DAY OR TWO.
IN PAIN.
"AND THIS SUKA DOCUMENT CAN SHUT DOWN NOW."
WHAT THE HELL? WHAT'S HAPPENING? DID I MISS SOMETHING?
COMMENT BY: FIRE_FIRE_FIRE
SAIKO SADO! ROFL I CAN'T BELIEVE WE GET TO WATCH ALL THIS
COMMENT BY: SIX_OR
LAST IMAGE TAKEN
NEXT UPDATE: 0:59

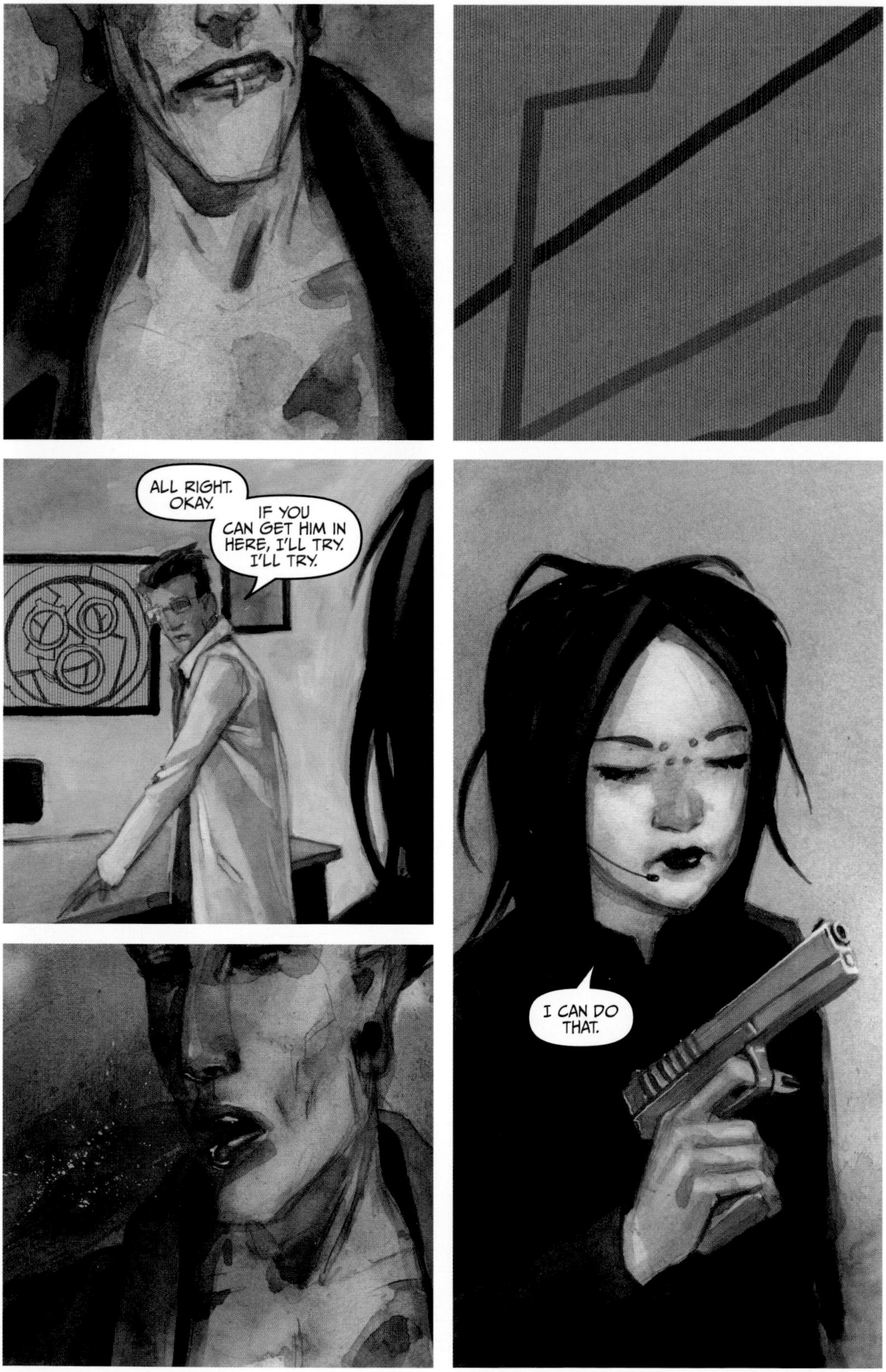
ALL RIGHT. OKAY.
IF YOU CAN GET HIM IN HERE, I'LL TRY. I'LL TRY.
I CAN DO THAT.

CHAPTER FOUR

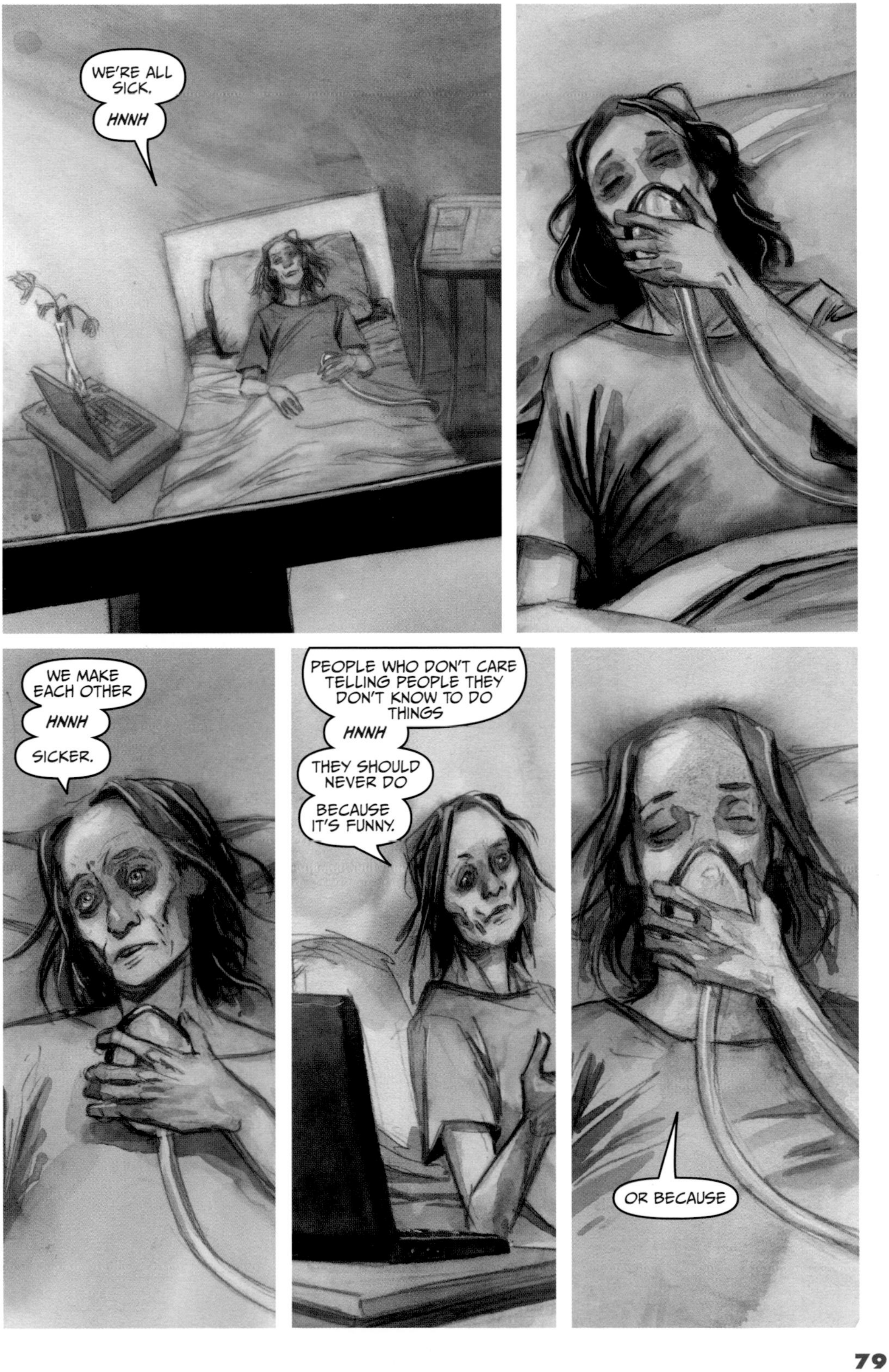
WE'RE ALL SICK.
HNNH
WE MAKE EACH OTHER
HNNH
SICKER.
PEOPLE WHO DON'T CARE TELLING PEOPLE THEY DON'T KNOW TO DO THINGS
HNNH
THEY SHOULD NEVER DO
BECAUSE IT'S FUNNY.
OR BECAUSE

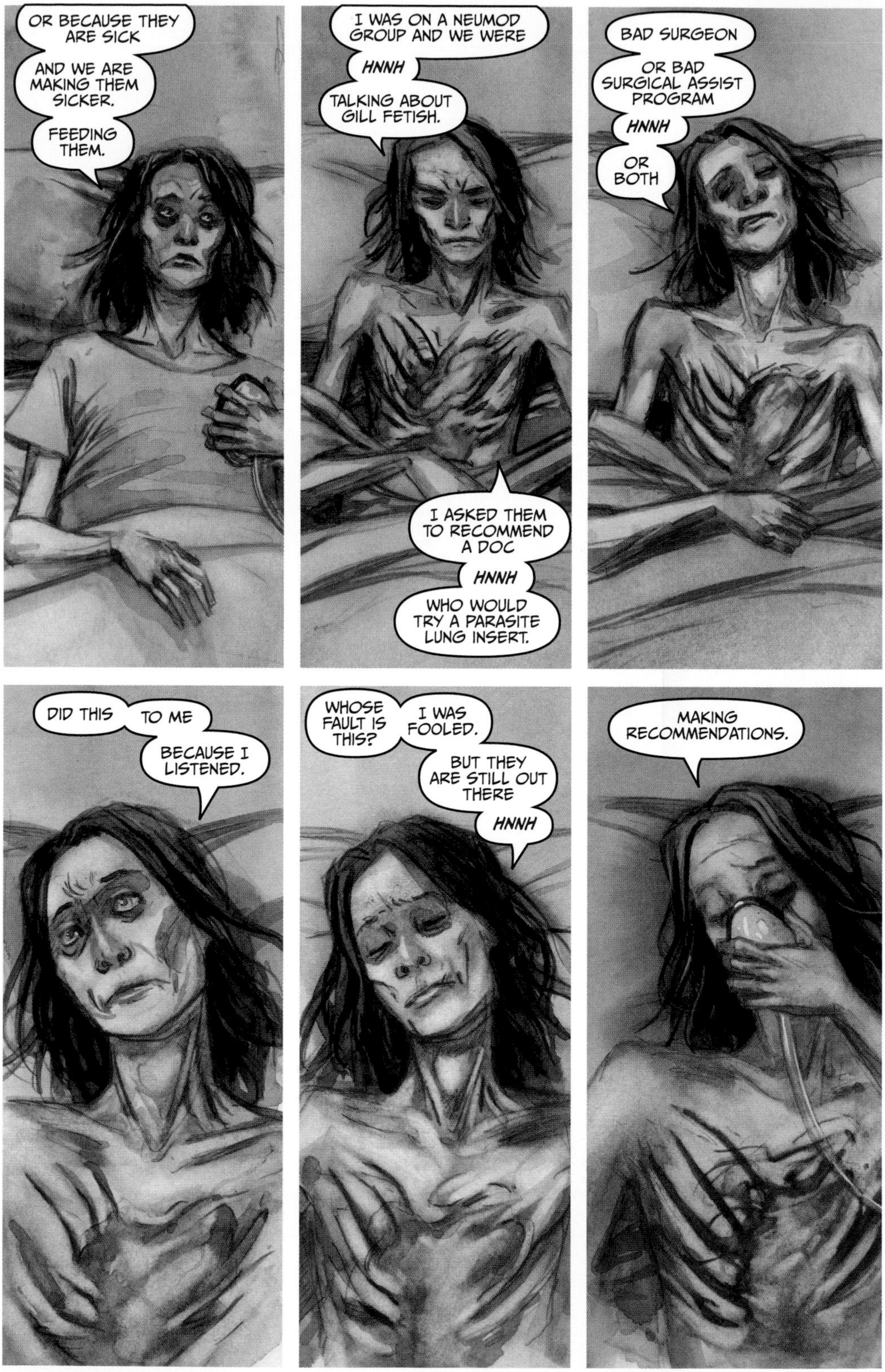
OR BECAUSE THEY ARE SICK
AND WE ARE MAKING THEM SICKER.
FEEDING THEM.
I WAS ON A NEUMOD GROUP AND WE WERE
HNNH
TALKING ABOUT GILL FETISH.
I ASKED THEM TO RECOMMEND A DOC
HNNH
WHO WOULD TRY A PARASITE LUNG INSERT.
BAD SURGEON
OR BAD SURGICAL ASSIST PROGRAM
HNNH
OR BOTH
DID THIS
TO ME
BECAUSE I LISTENED.
WHOSE FAULT IS THIS?
I WAS FOOLED.
BUT THEY ARE STILL OUT THERE
HNNH
MAKING RECOMMENDATIONS.

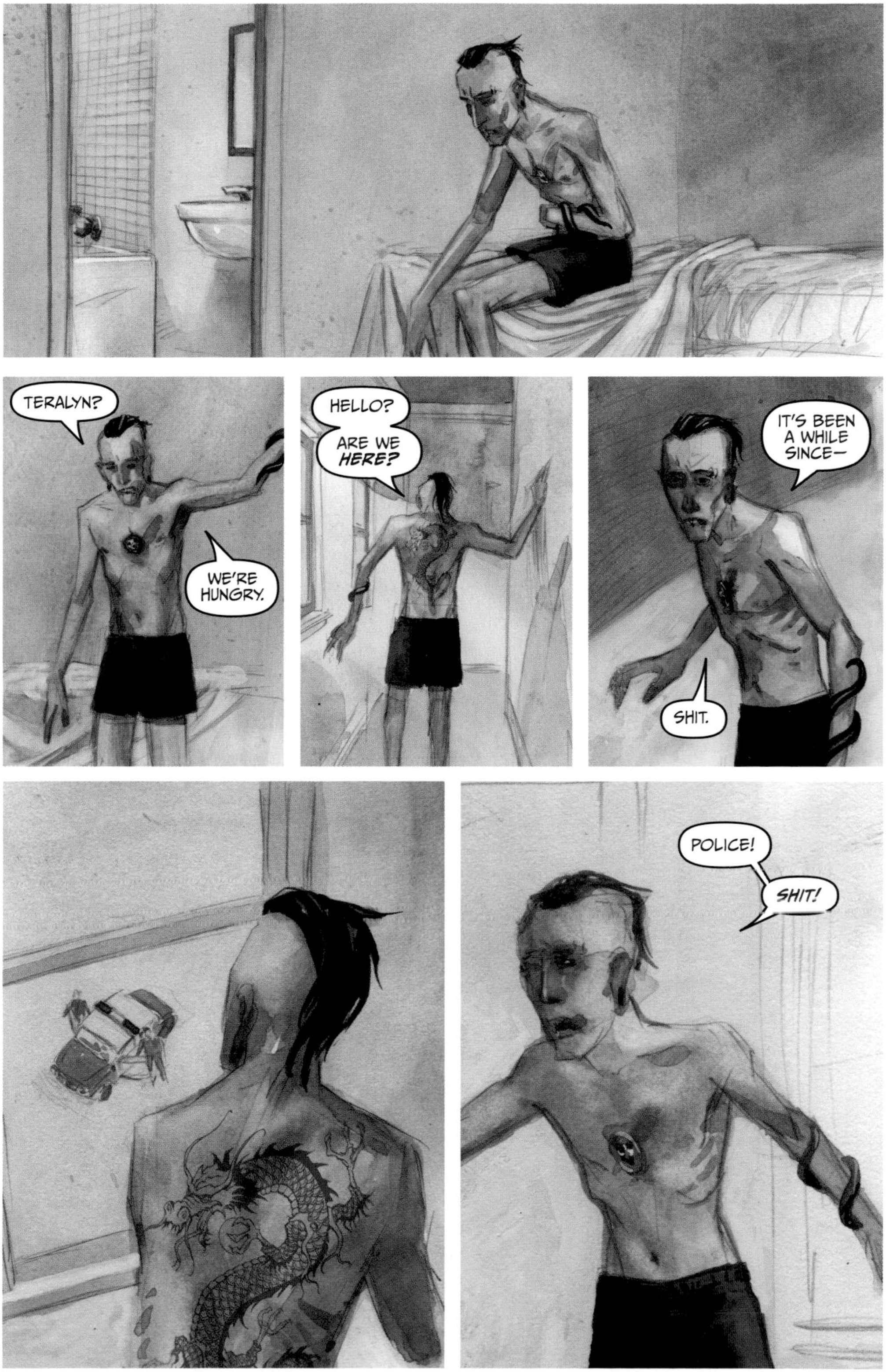
TERALYN?
WE'RE HUNGRY.
HELLO?
ARE WE *HERE?*
IT'S BEEN A WHILE SINCE—
SHIT.
POLICE!
SHIT!

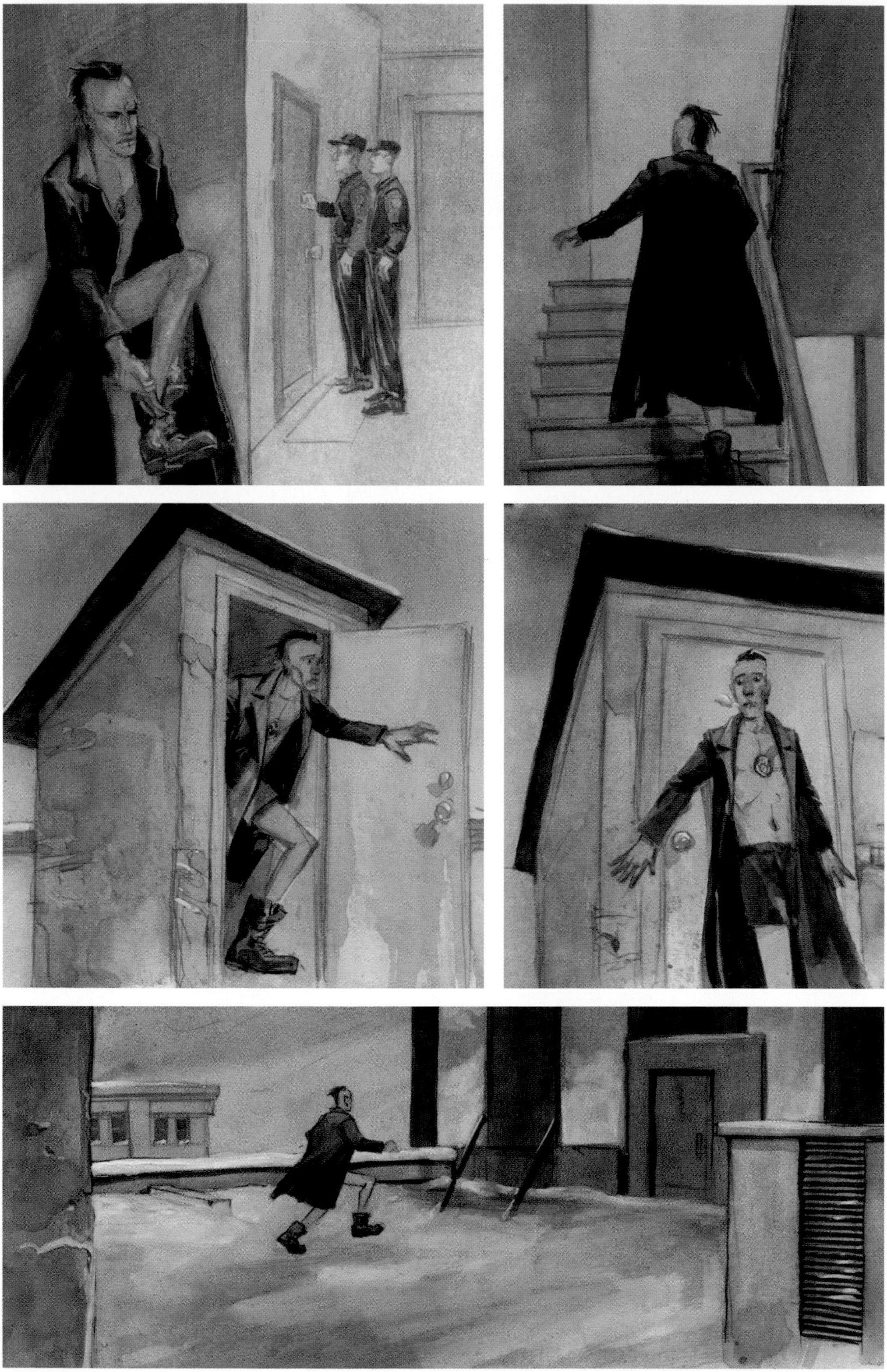

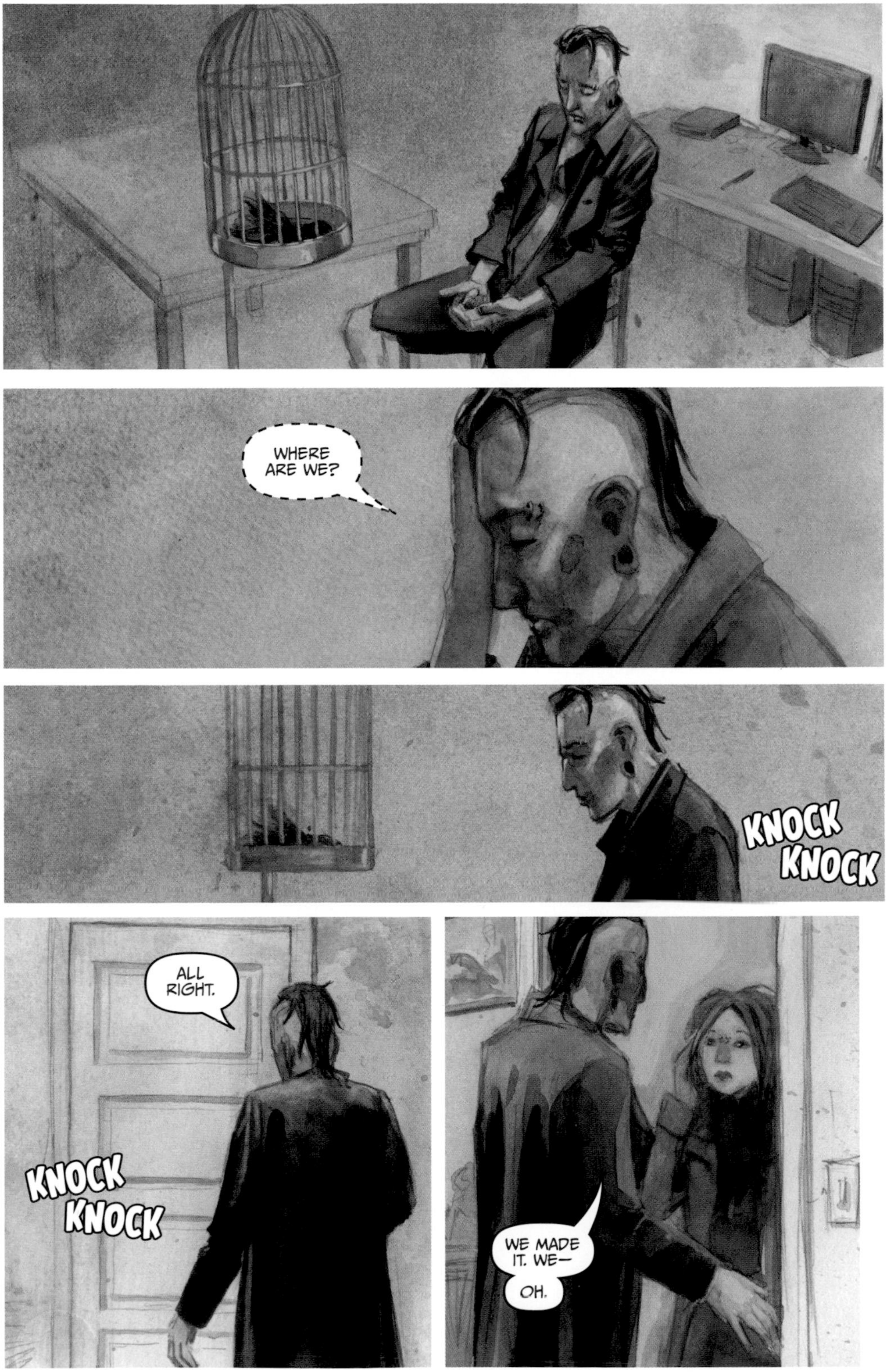
WHERE ARE WE?
KNOCK KNOCK
ALL RIGHT.
KNOCK KNOCK
WE MADE IT. WE—
OH.

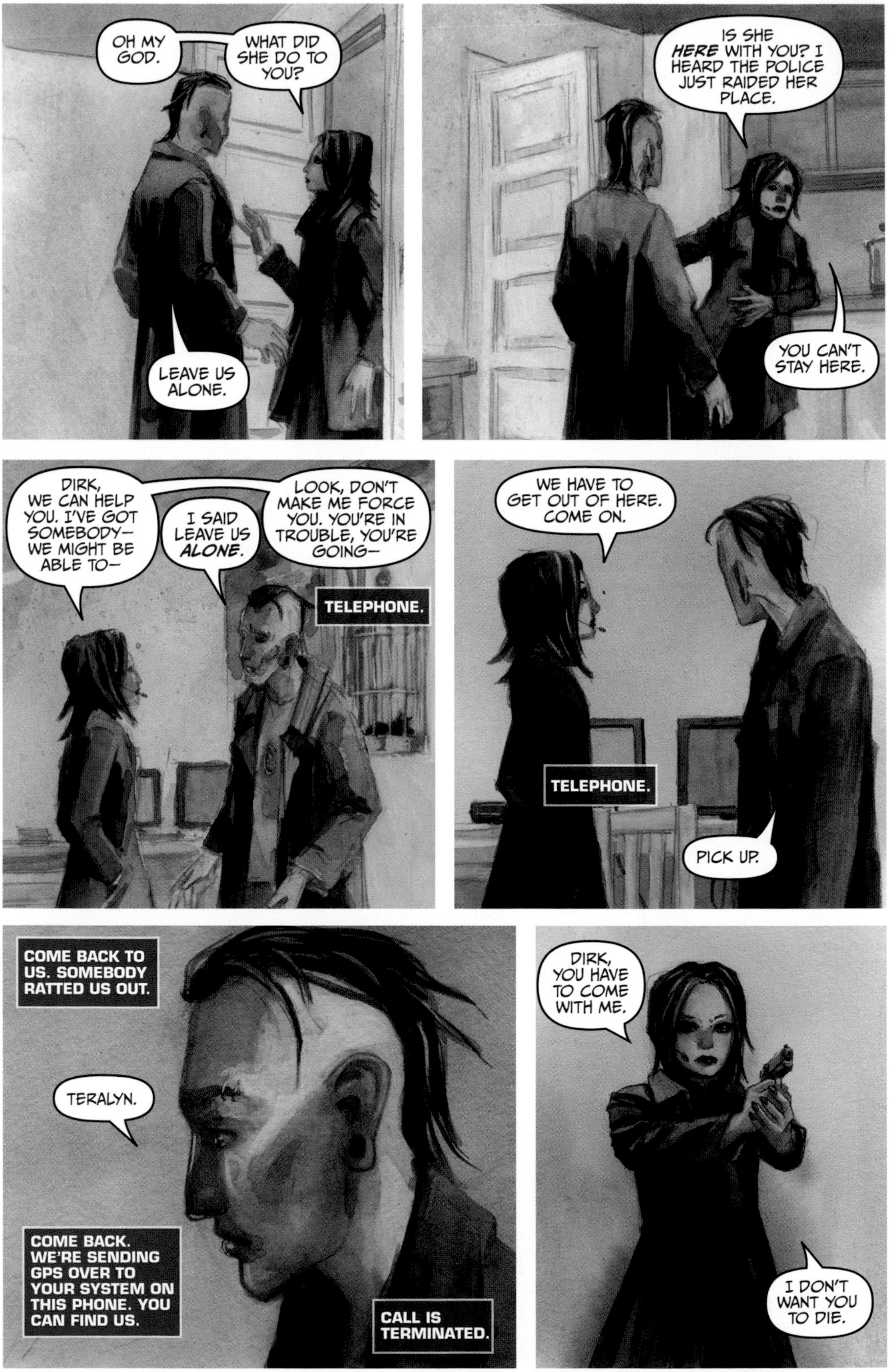
OH MY GOD.
WHAT DID SHE DO TO YOU?
LEAVE US ALONE.
IS SHE HERE WITH YOU? I HEARD THE POLICE JUST RAIDED HER PLACE.
YOU CAN'T STAY HERE.
DIRK, WE CAN HELP YOU. I'VE GOT SOMEBODY— WE MIGHT BE ABLE TO—
I SAID LEAVE US ALONE.
LOOK, DON'T MAKE ME FORCE YOU. YOU'RE IN TROUBLE, YOU'RE GOING—
TELEPHONE.
WE HAVE TO GET OUT OF HERE. COME ON.
TELEPHONE.
PICK UP.
COME BACK TO US. SOMEBODY RATTED US OUT.
TERALYN.
COME BACK. WE'RE SENDING GPS OVER TO YOUR SYSTEM ON THIS PHONE. YOU CAN FIND US.
CALL IS TERMINATED.
DIRK, YOU HAVE TO COME WITH ME.
I DON'T WANT YOU TO DIE.

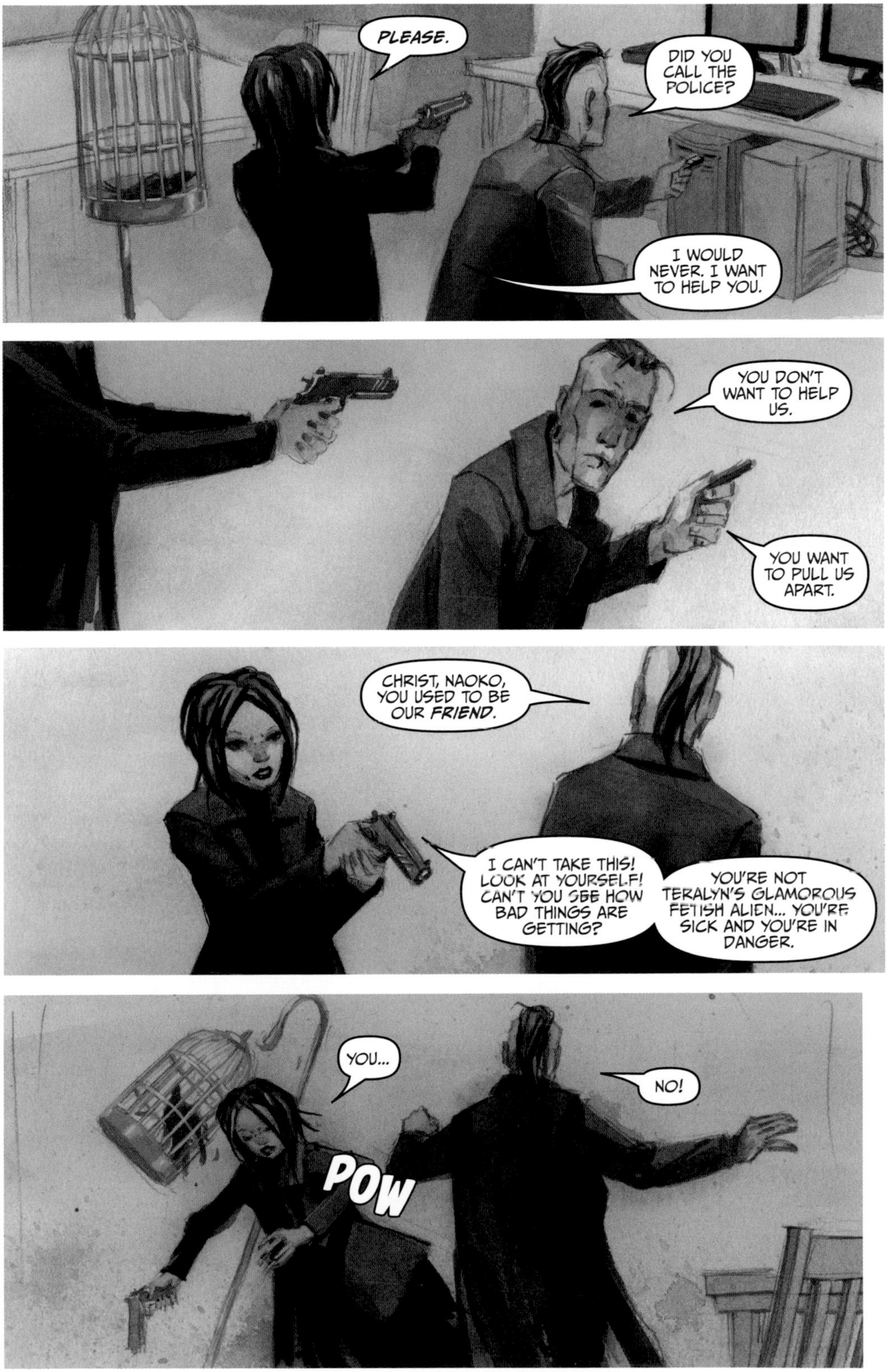
PLEASE.
DID YOU CALL THE POLICE?
I WOULD NEVER. I WANT TO HELP YOU.
YOU DON'T WANT TO HELP US.
YOU WANT TO PULL US APART.
CHRIST, NAOKO, YOU USED TO BE OUR FRIEND.
I CAN'T TAKE THIS! LOOK AT YOURSELF! CAN'T YOU SEE HOW BAD THINGS ARE GETTING?
YOU'RE NOT TERALYN'S GLAMOROUS FETISH ALIEN... YOU'RE SICK AND YOU'RE IN DANGER.
YOU...
NO!
POW

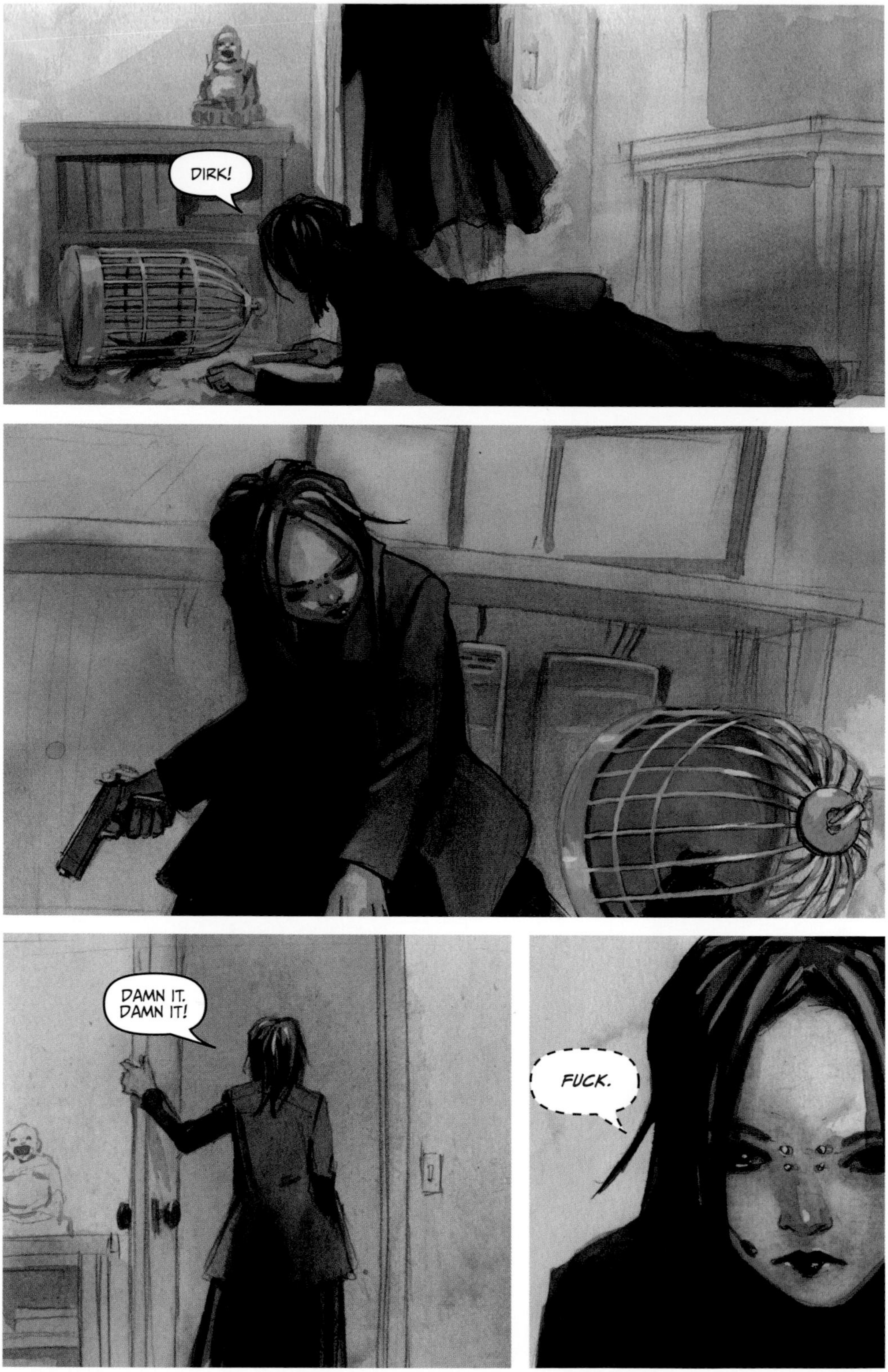
DIRK!
DAMN IT. DAMN IT!
FUCK.

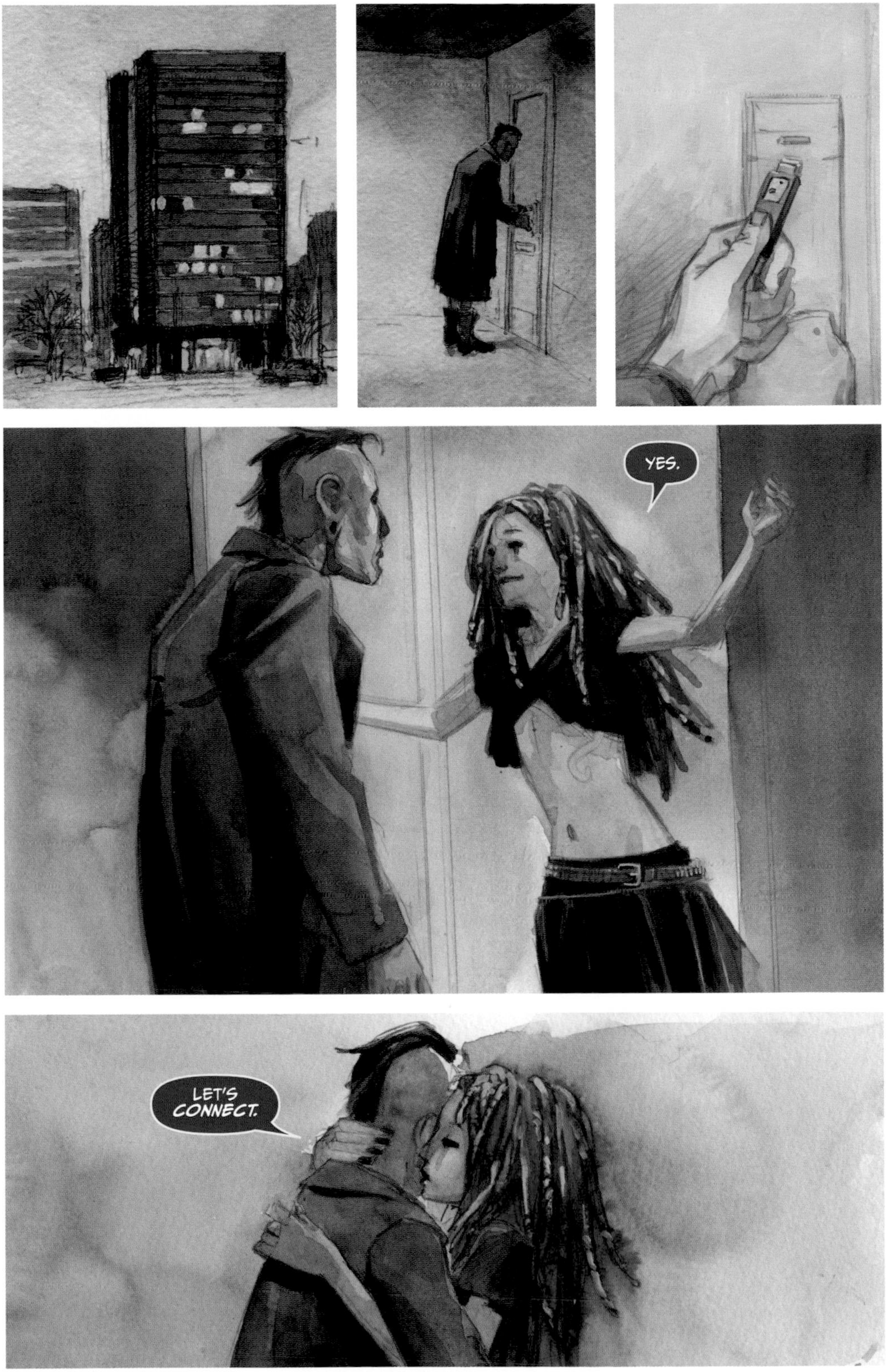
YES.
LET'S CONNECT.

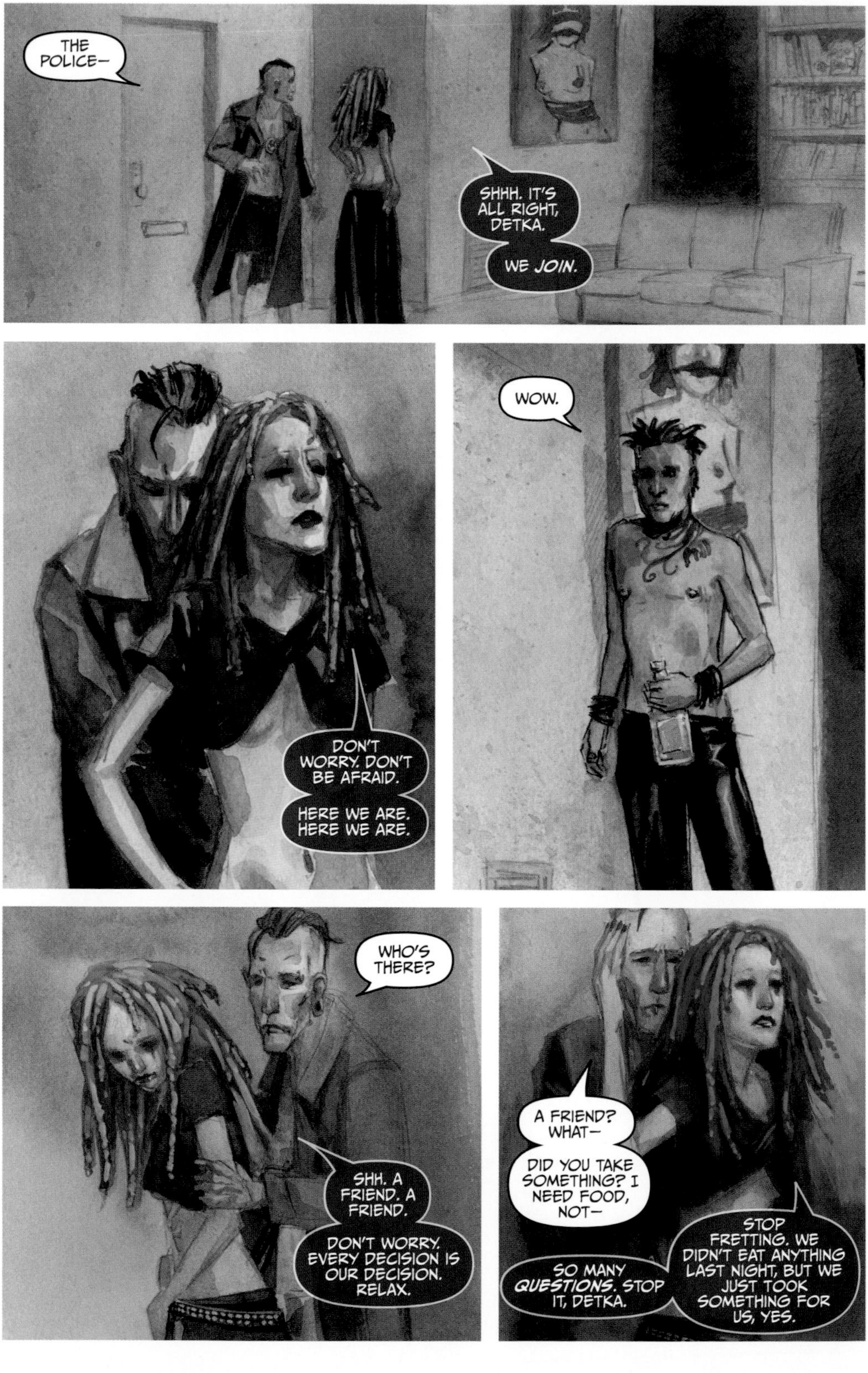
THE POLICE—
SHHH. IT'S ALL RIGHT, DETKA.
WE *JOIN*.
DON'T WORRY. DON'T BE AFRAID.
HERE WE ARE. HERE WE ARE.
WOW.
WHO'S THERE?
SHH. A FRIEND. A FRIEND.
DON'T WORRY. EVERY DECISION IS OUR DECISION. RELAX.
A FRIEND? WHAT—
DID YOU TAKE SOMETHING? I NEED FOOD, NOT—
STOP FRETTING. WE DIDN'T EAT ANYTHING LAST NIGHT, BUT WE JUST TOOK SOMETHING FOR US, YES.
SO MANY *QUESTIONS*. STOP IT, DETKA.

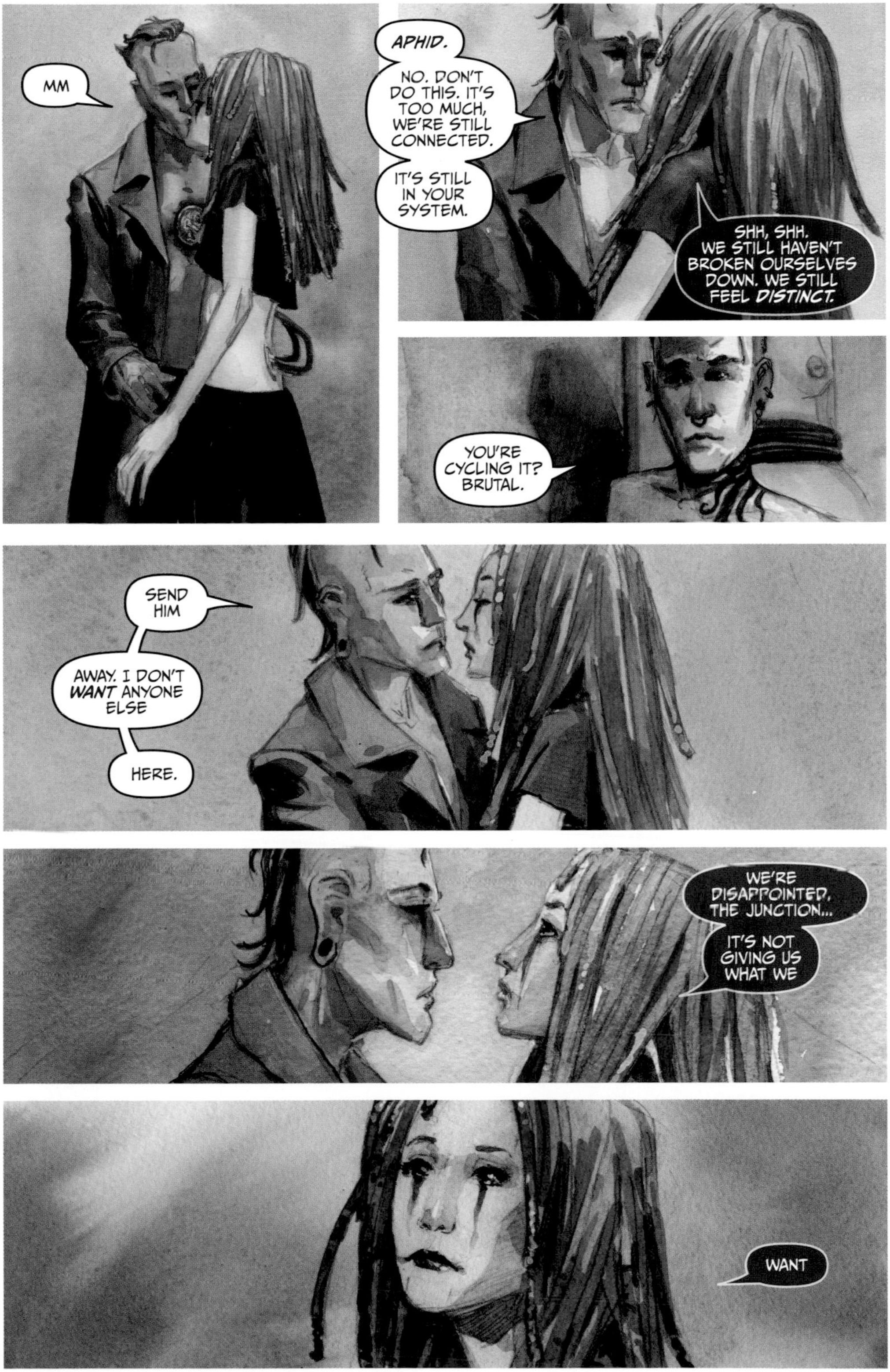
MM
APHID.
NO. DON'T DO THIS. IT'S TOO MUCH, WE'RE STILL CONNECTED.
IT'S STILL IN YOUR SYSTEM.
SHH, SHH. WE STILL HAVEN'T BROKEN OURSELVES DOWN. WE STILL FEEL *DISTINCT.*
YOU'RE CYCLING IT? BRUTAL.
SEND HIM
AWAY. I DON'T *WANT* ANYONE ELSE
HERE.
WE'RE DISAPPOINTED, THE JUNCTION...
IT'S NOT GIVING US WHAT WE
WANT

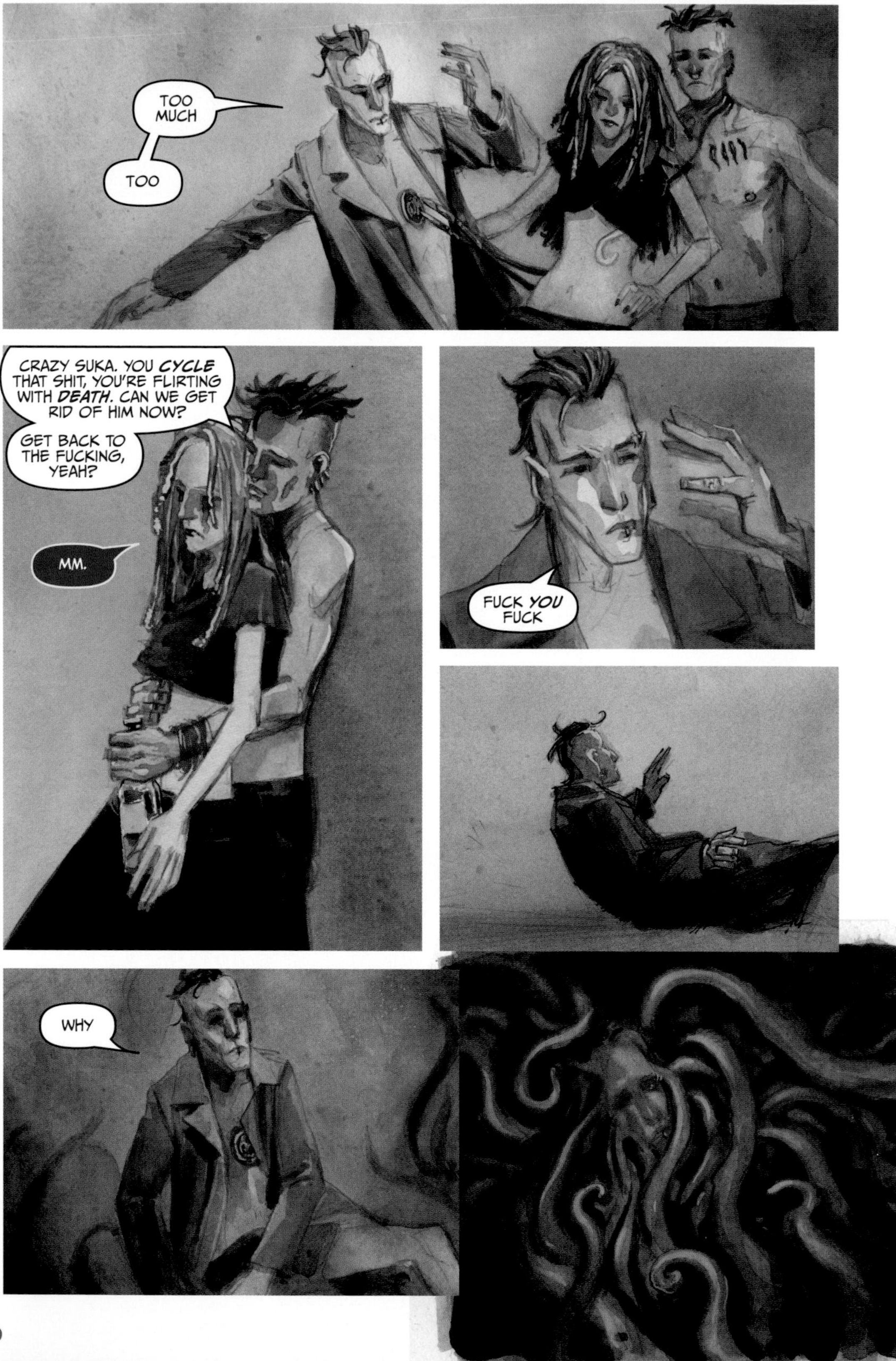
TOO MUCH
TOO
CRAZY SUKA. YOU CYCLE THAT SHIT, YOU'RE FLIRTING WITH DEATH. CAN WE GET RID OF HIM NOW?
GET BACK TO THE FUCKING, YEAH?
MM.
FUCK YOU FUCK
WHY

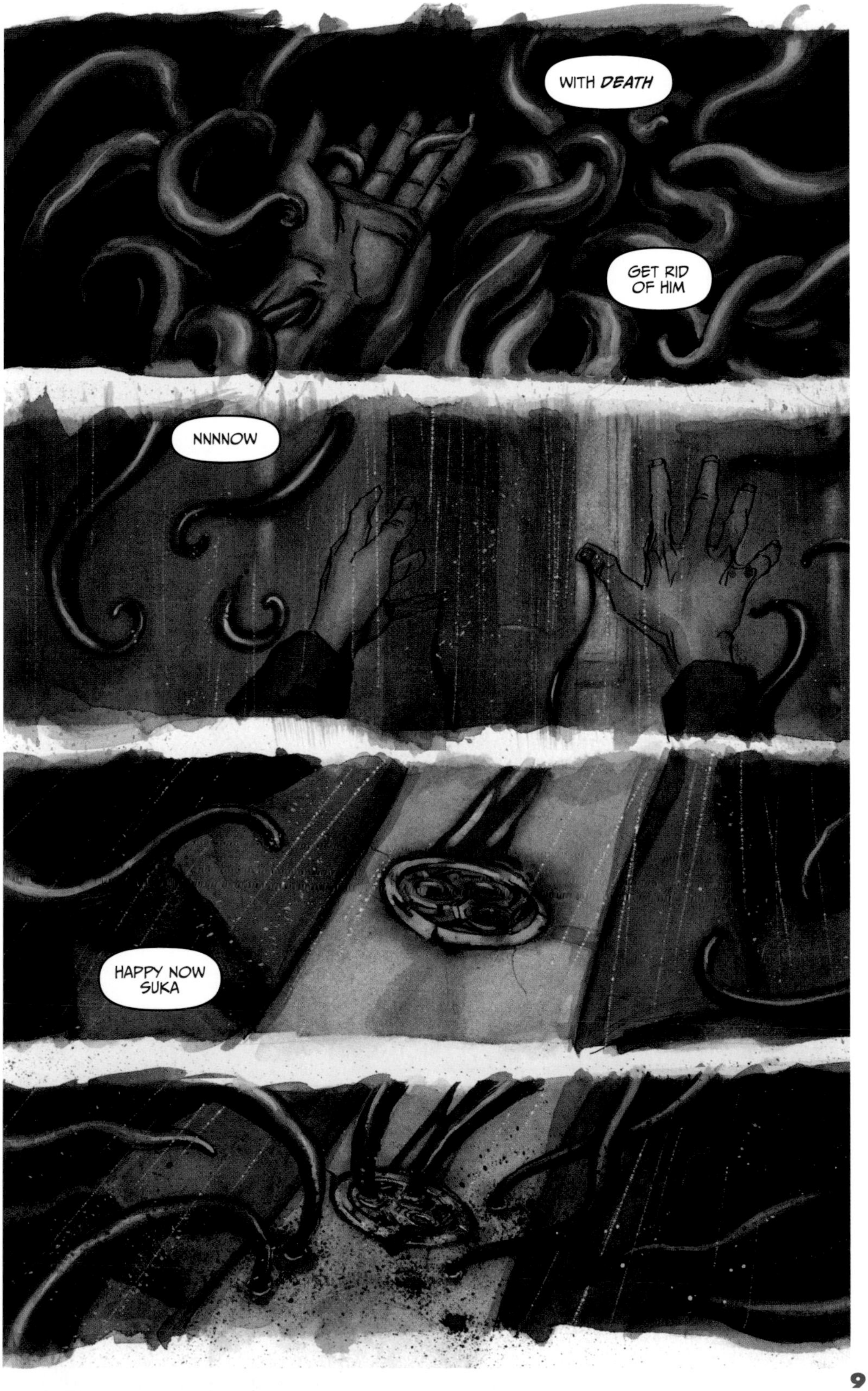
WITH *DEATH*
GET RID OF HIM
NNNNOW
HAPPY NOW SUKA

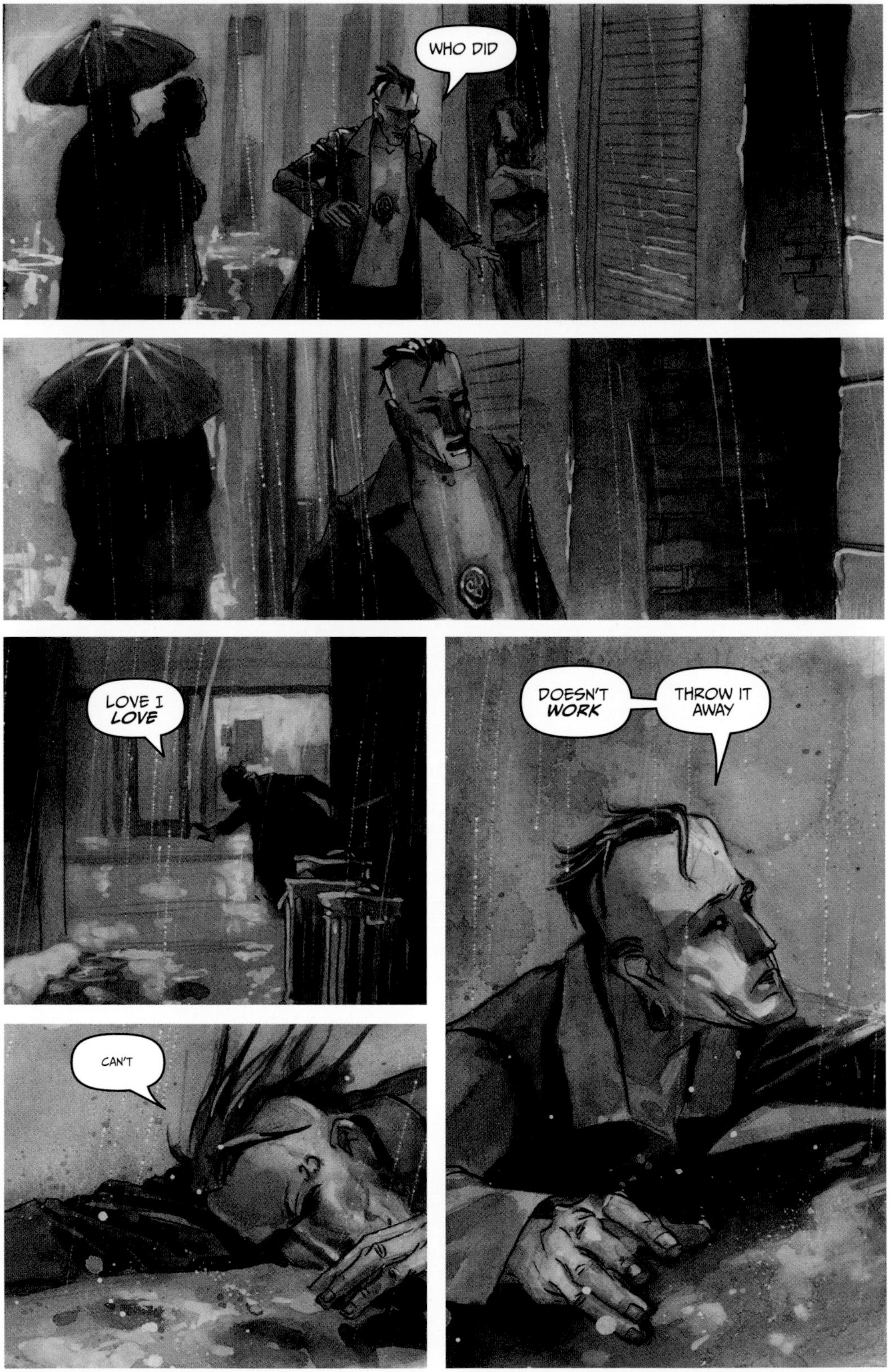
WHO DID
LOVE I LOVE
CAN'T
DOESN'T WORK
THROW IT AWAY

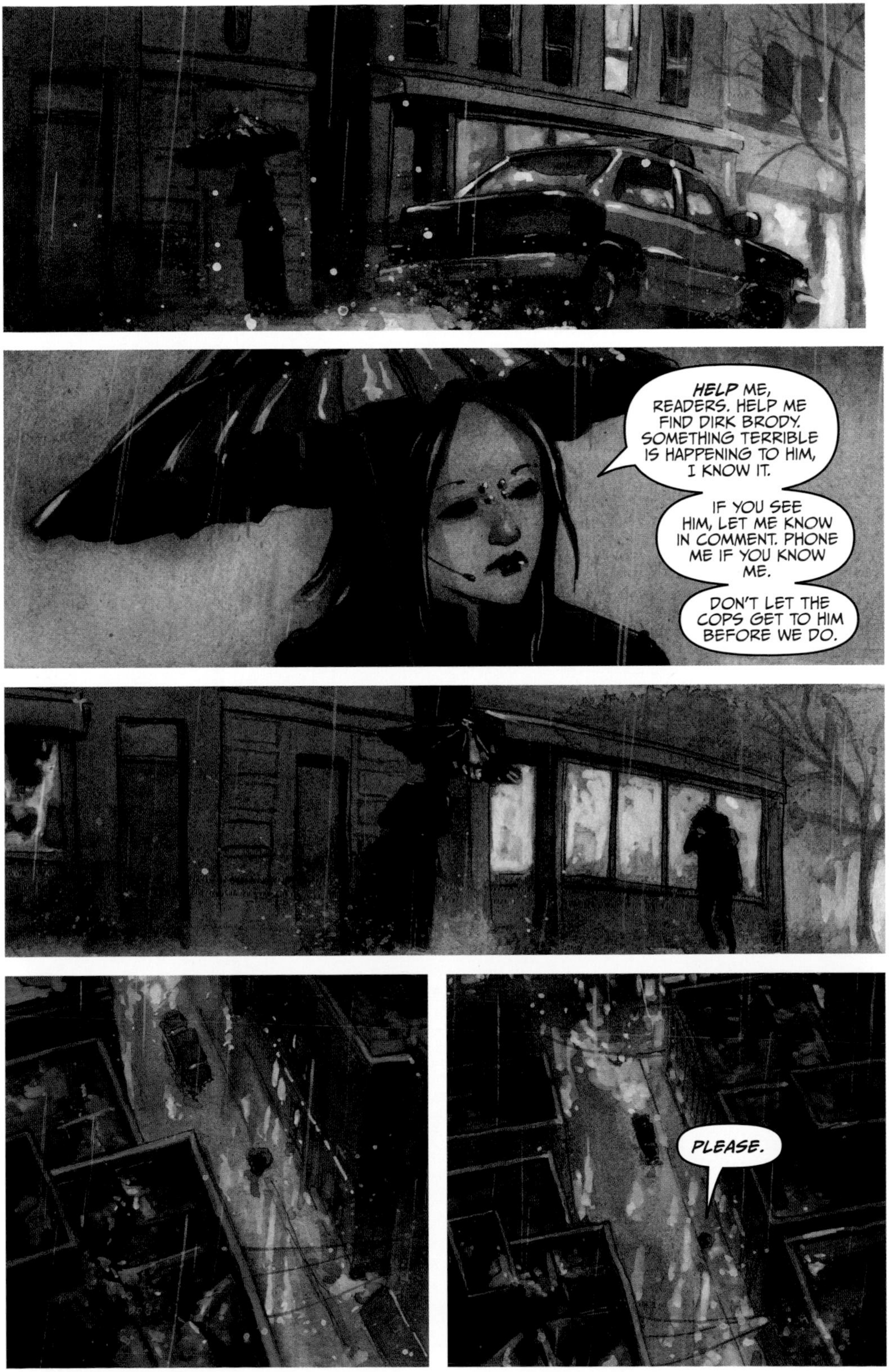

HELP ME, READERS. HELP ME FIND DIRK BRODY. SOMETHING TERRIBLE IS HAPPENING TO HIM, I KNOW IT.
IF YOU SEE HIM, LET ME KNOW IN COMMENT. PHONE ME IF YOU KNOW ME.
DON'T LET THE COPS GET TO HIM BEFORE WE DO.
PLEASE.

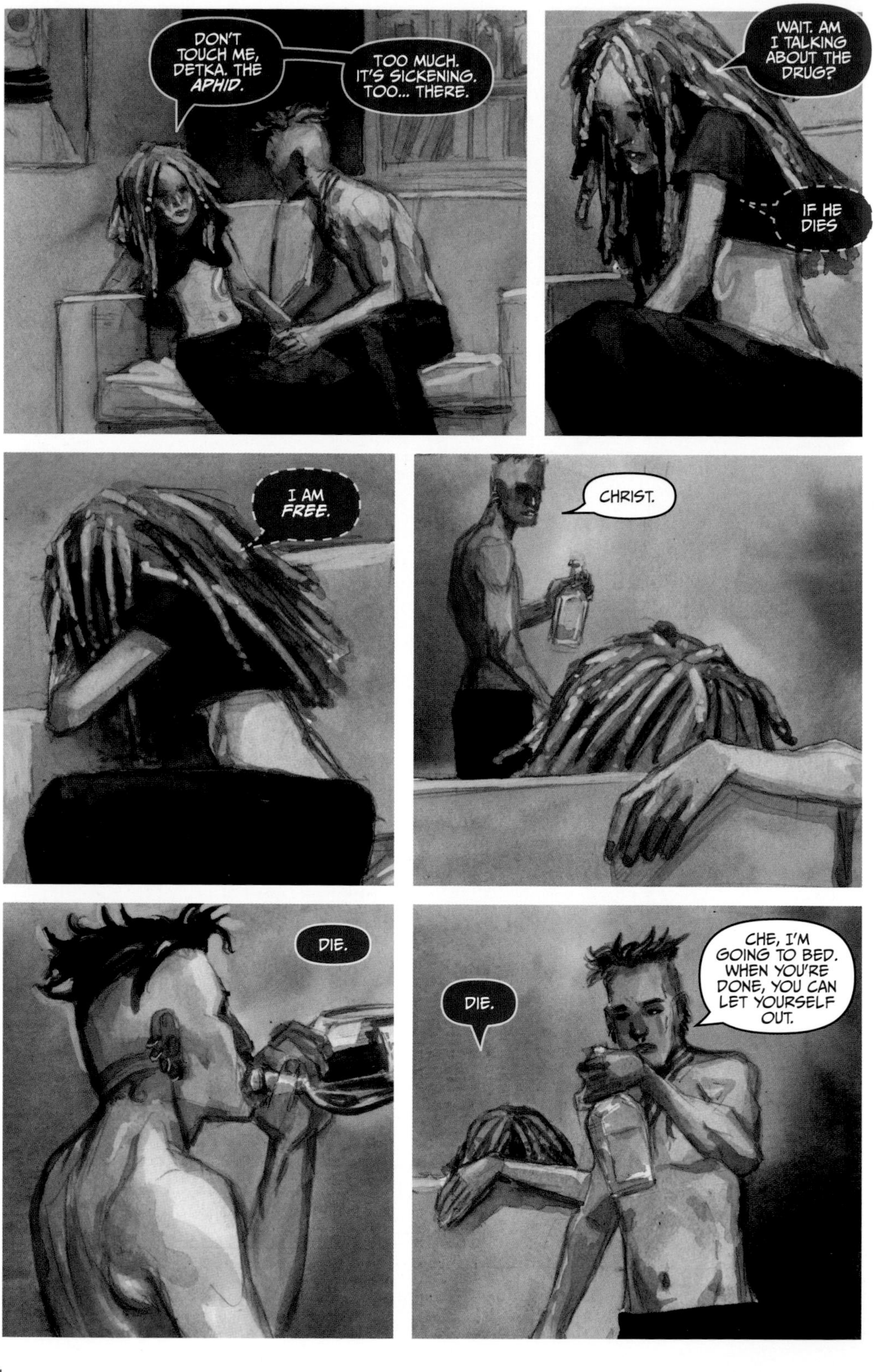
DON'T TOUCH ME, DETKA. THE *APHID*.
TOO MUCH. IT'S SICKENING. TOO... THERE.
WAIT. AM I TALKING ABOUT THE DRUG?
IF HE DIES
I AM *FREE*.
CHRIST.
DIE.
DIE.
CHE, I'M GOING TO BED. WHEN YOU'RE DONE, YOU CAN LET YOURSELF OUT.

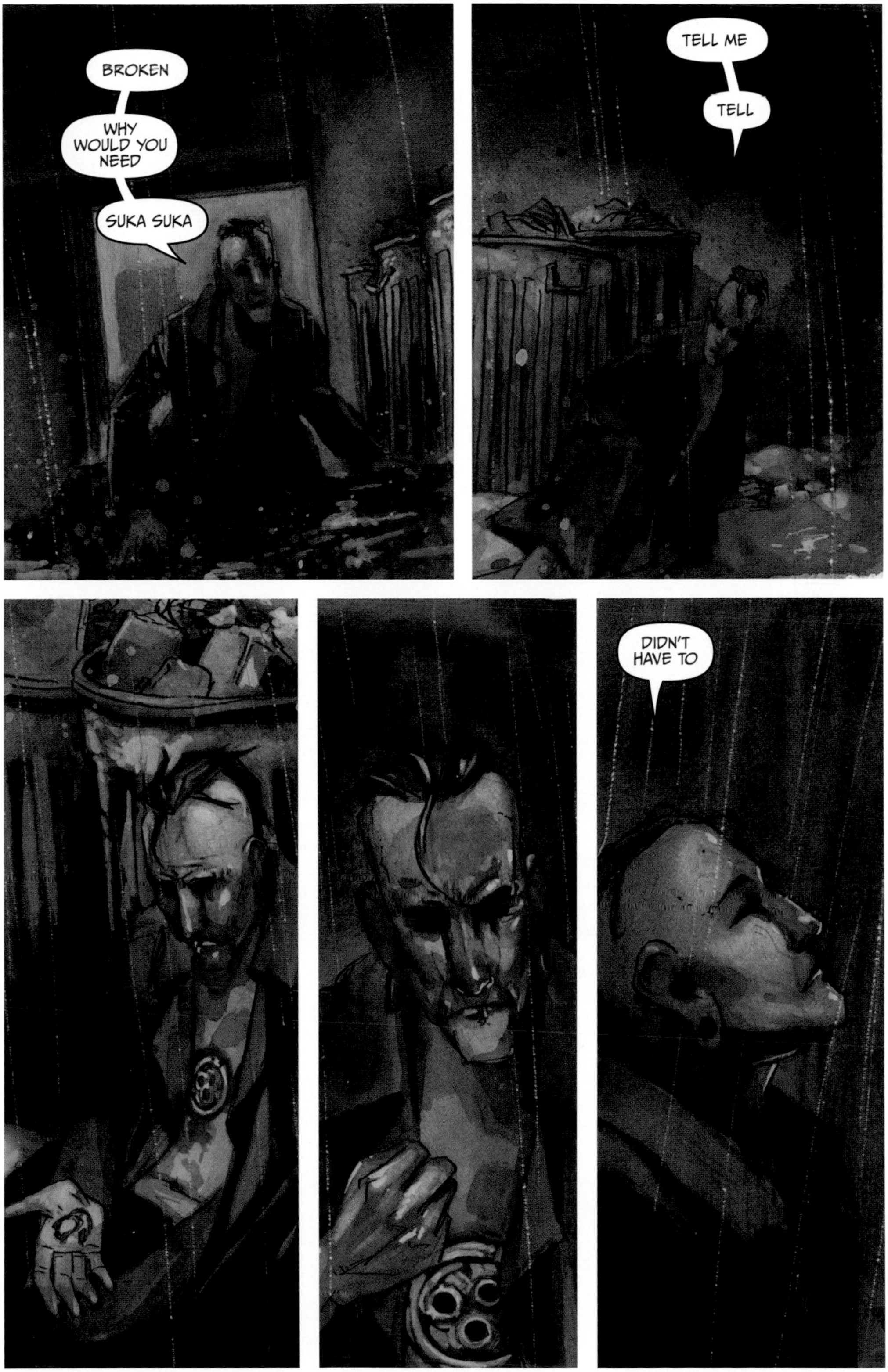
BROKEN
WHY WOULD YOU NEED
SUKA SUKA
TELL ME
TELL
DIDN'T HAVE TO

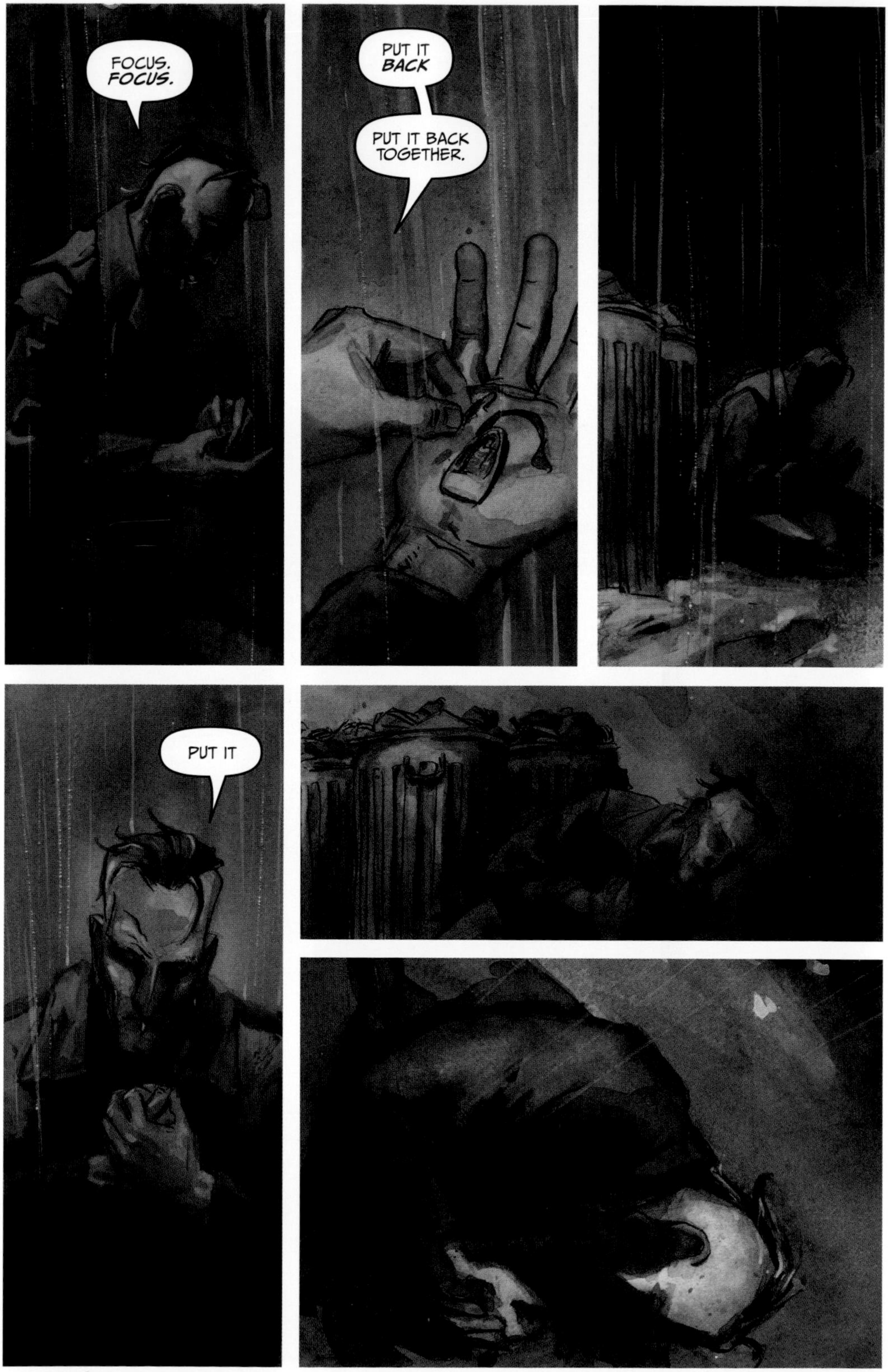
FOCUS. *FOCUS.*
PUT IT *BACK*
PUT IT BACK TOGETHER.
PUT IT

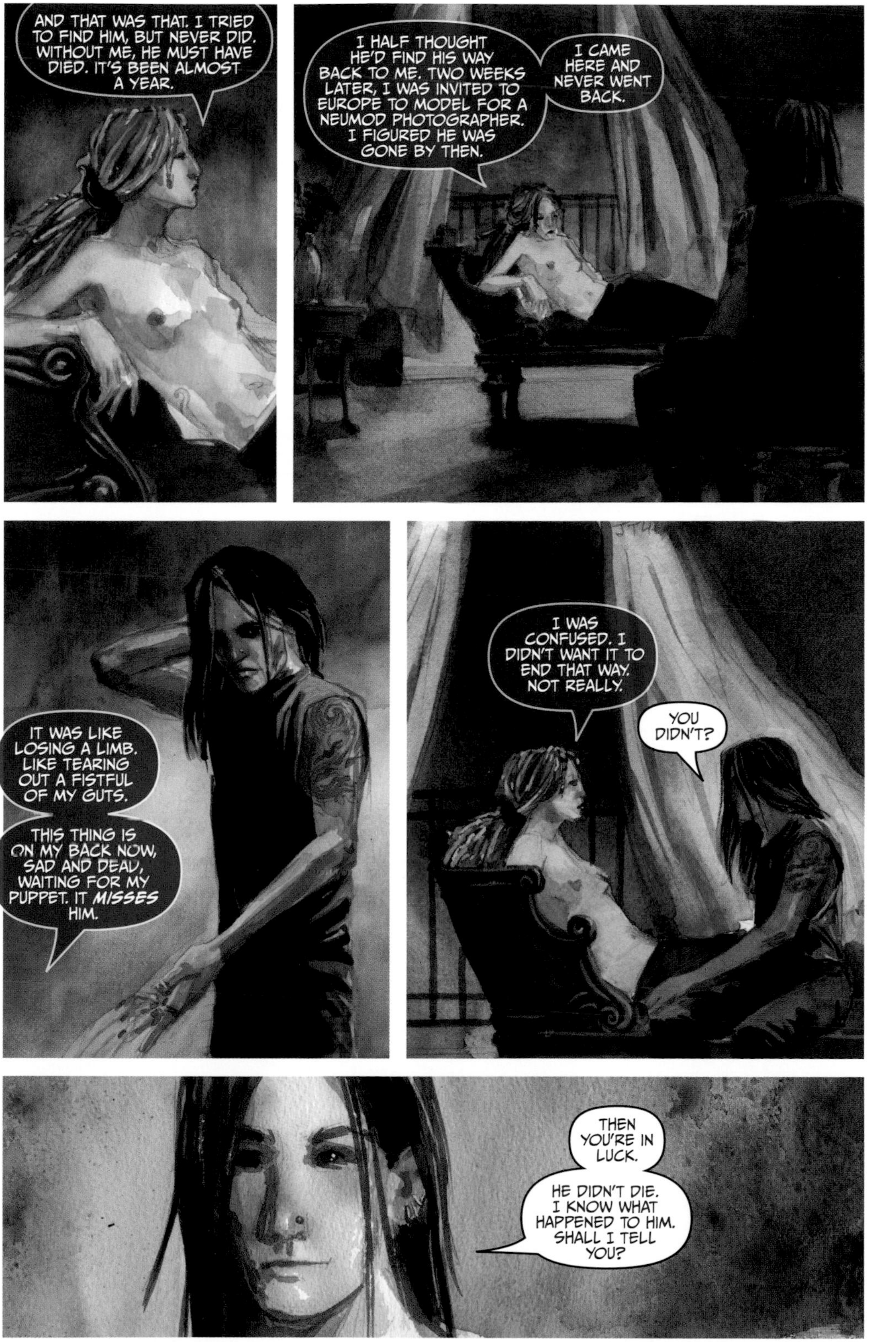
AND THAT WAS THAT. I TRIED TO FIND HIM, BUT NEVER DID. WITHOUT ME, HE MUST HAVE DIED. IT'S BEEN ALMOST A YEAR.
I HALF THOUGHT HE'D FIND HIS WAY BACK TO ME. TWO WEEKS LATER, I WAS INVITED TO EUROPE TO MODEL FOR A NEUMOD PHOTOGRAPHER. I FIGURED HE WAS GONE BY THEN.
I CAME HERE AND NEVER WENT BACK.
IT WAS LIKE LOSING A LIMB. LIKE TEARING OUT A FISTFUL OF MY GUTS.
THIS THING IS ON MY BACK NOW, SAD AND DEAD, WAITING FOR MY PUPPET. IT *MISSES* HIM.
I WAS CONFUSED. I DIDN'T WANT IT TO END THAT WAY. NOT REALLY.
YOU DIDN'T?
THEN YOU'RE IN LUCK.
HE DIDN'T DIE. I KNOW WHAT HAPPENED TO HIM. SHALL I TELL YOU?

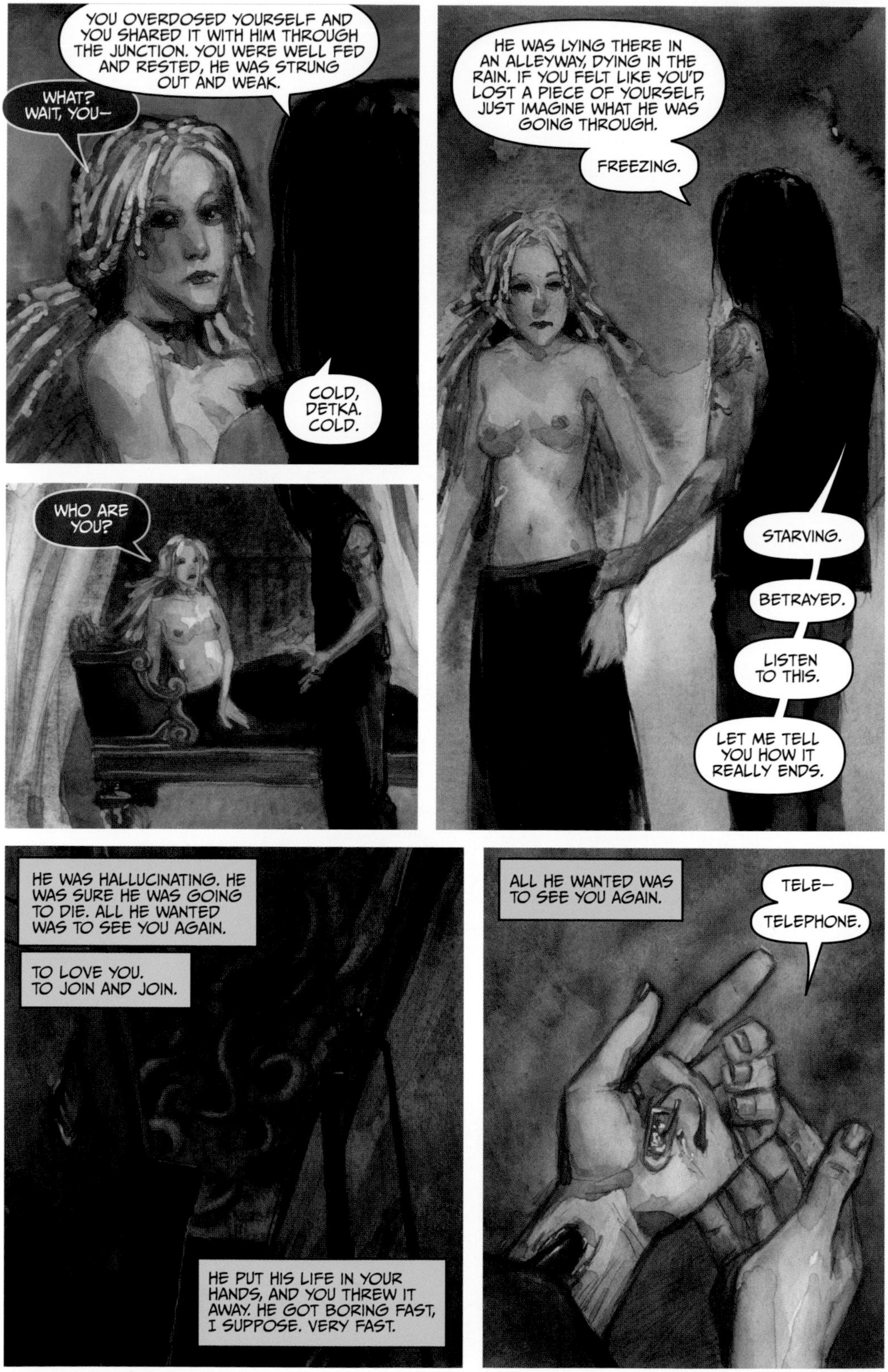

YOU OVERDOSED YOURSELF AND YOU SHARED IT WITH HIM THROUGH THE JUNCTION. YOU WERE WELL FED AND RESTED, HE WAS STRUNG OUT AND WEAK.
WHAT? WAIT, YOU—
COLD, DETKA. COLD.
WHO ARE YOU?
HE WAS LYING THERE IN AN ALLEYWAY, DYING IN THE RAIN. IF YOU FELT LIKE YOU'D LOST A PIECE OF YOURSELF, JUST IMAGINE WHAT HE WAS GOING THROUGH.
FREEZING.
STARVING.
BETRAYED.
LISTEN TO THIS.
LET ME TELL YOU HOW IT REALLY ENDS.
HE WAS HALLUCINATING. HE WAS SURE HE WAS GOING TO DIE. ALL HE WANTED WAS TO SEE YOU AGAIN.
TO LOVE YOU. TO JOIN AND JOIN.
HE PUT HIS LIFE IN YOUR HANDS, AND YOU THREW IT AWAY. HE GOT BORING FAST, I SUPPOSE. VERY FAST.
ALL HE WANTED WAS TO SEE YOU AGAIN.
TELE—
TELEPHONE.

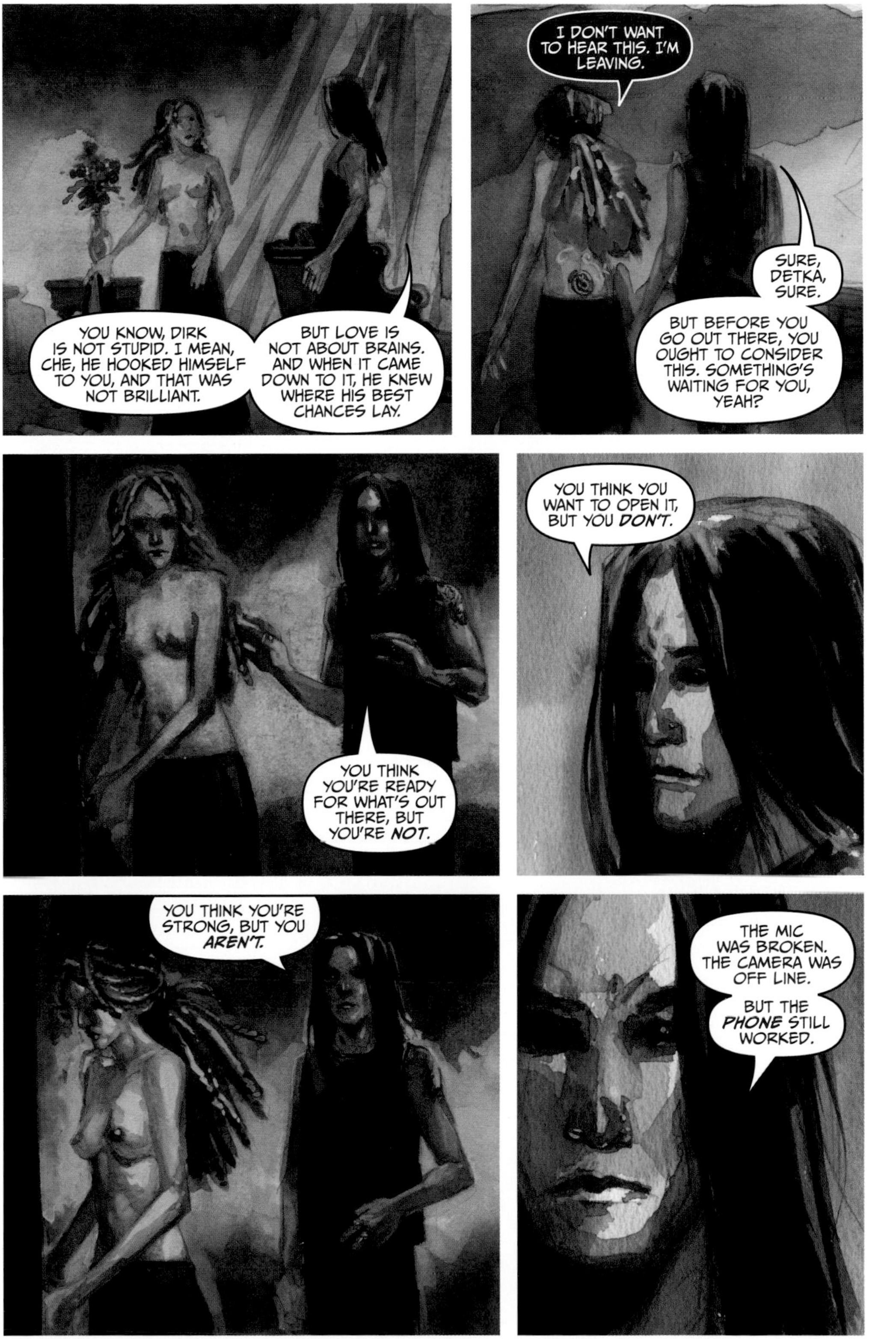
YOU KNOW, DIRK IS NOT STUPID. I MEAN, CHE, HE HOOKED HIMSELF TO YOU, AND THAT WAS NOT BRILLIANT.
BUT LOVE IS NOT ABOUT BRAINS. AND WHEN IT CAME DOWN TO IT, HE KNEW WHERE HIS BEST CHANCES LAY.
I DON'T WANT TO HEAR THIS. I'M LEAVING.
SURE, DETKA, SURE.
BUT BEFORE YOU GO OUT THERE, YOU OUGHT TO CONSIDER THIS. SOMETHING'S WAITING FOR YOU, YEAH?
YOU THINK YOU'RE READY FOR WHAT'S OUT THERE, BUT YOU'RE *NOT*.
YOU THINK YOU WANT TO OPEN IT, BUT YOU *DON'T*.
YOU THINK YOU'RE STRONG, BUT YOU *AREN'T*.
THE MIC WAS BROKEN. THE CAMERA WAS OFF LINE.
BUT THE *PHONE* STILL WORKED.

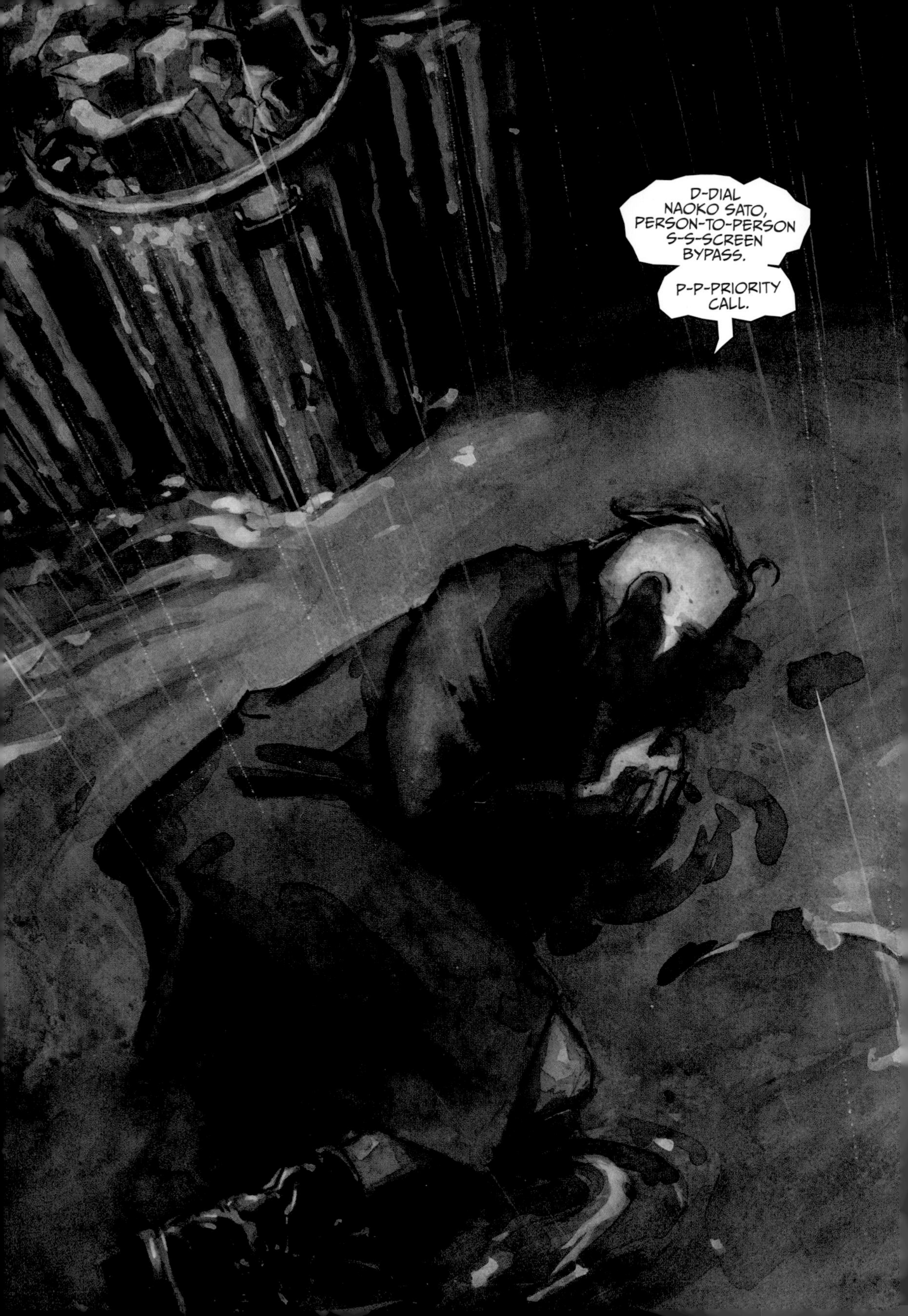

D-DIAL NAOKO SATO, PERSON-TO-PERSON S-S-SCREEN BYPASS.
P-P-PRIORITY CALL.

CHAPTER FIVE

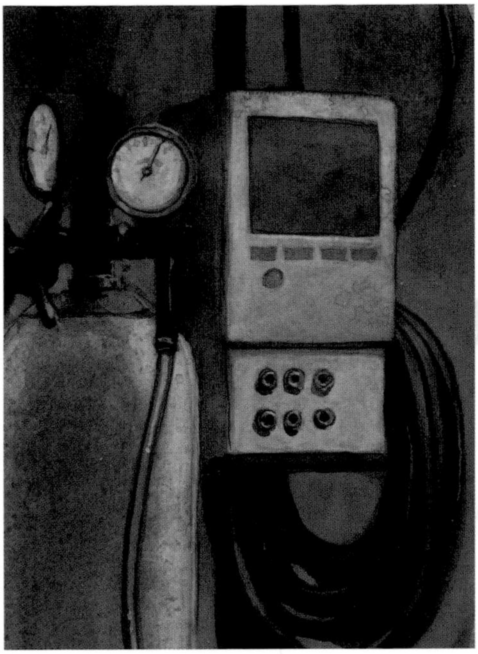

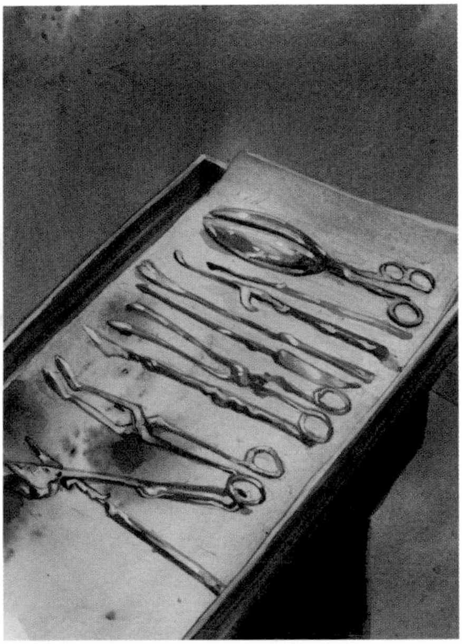

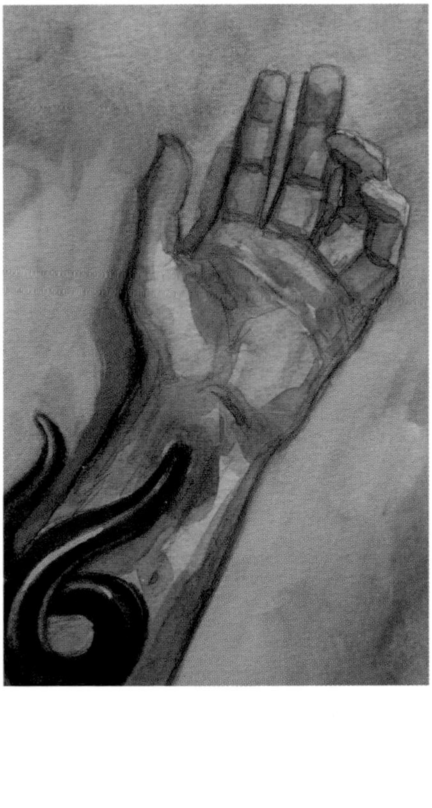

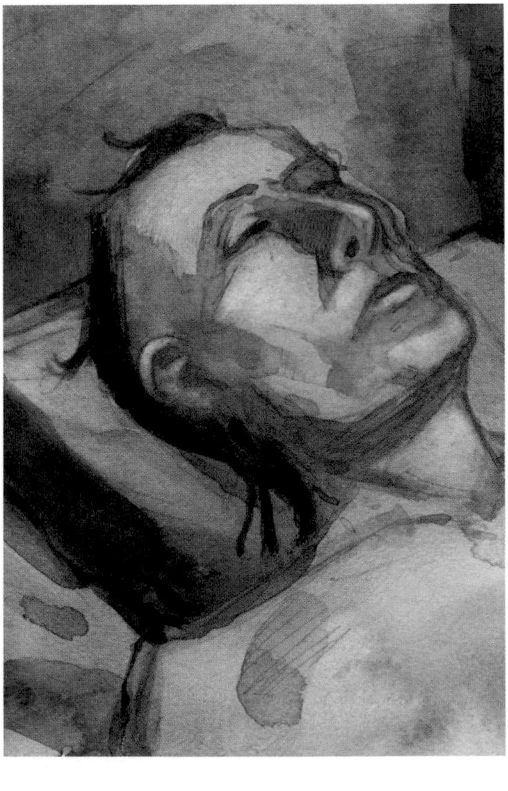

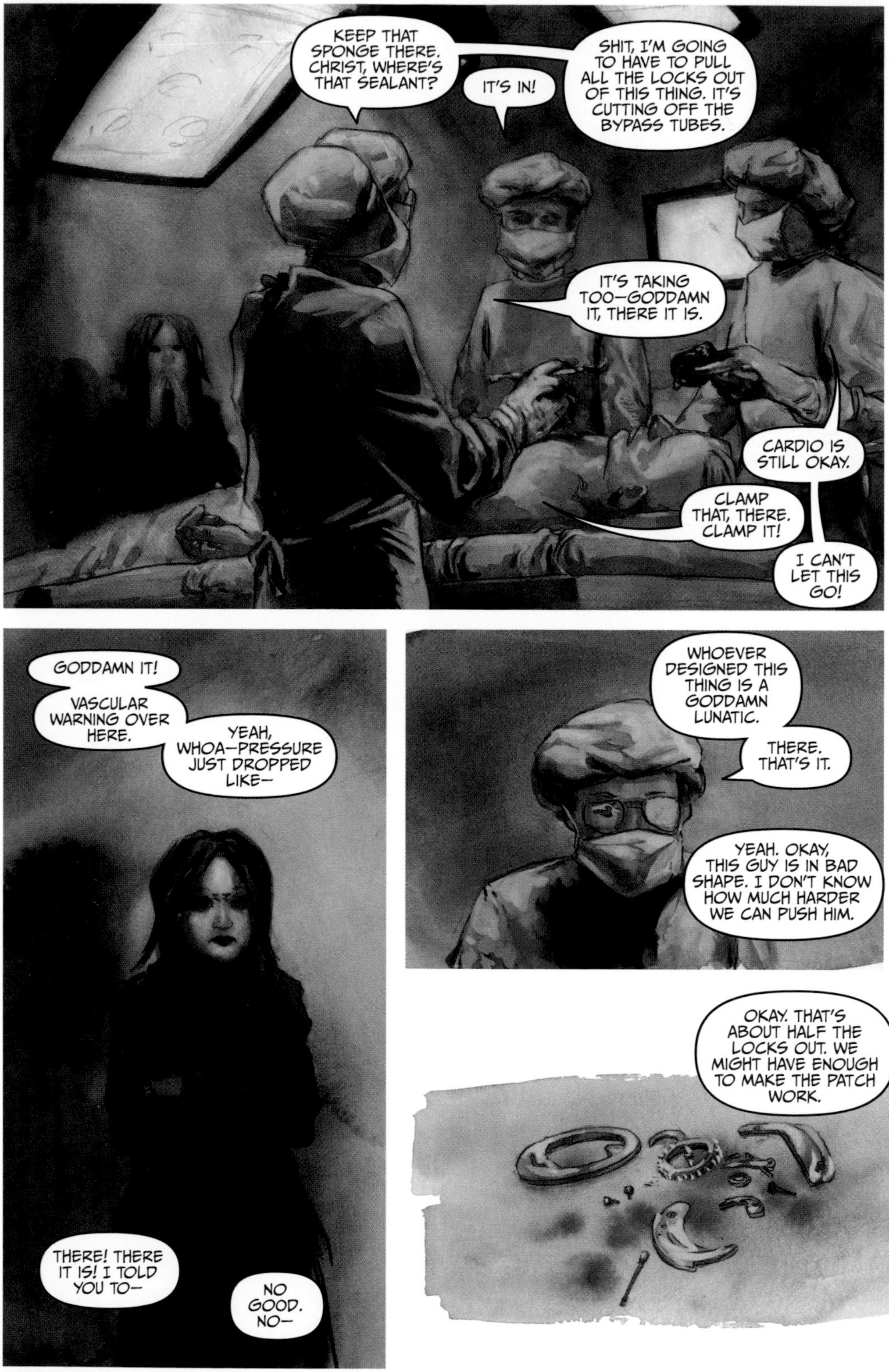
KEEP THAT SPONGE THERE. CHRIST, WHERE'S THAT SEALANT?
SHIT, I'M GOING TO HAVE TO PULL ALL THE LOCKS OUT OF THIS THING. IT'S CUTTING OFF THE BYPASS TUBES.
IT'S IN!
IT'S TAKING TOO—GODDAMN IT, THERE IT IS.
CARDIO IS STILL OKAY.
CLAMP THAT, THERE. CLAMP IT!
I CAN'T LET THIS GO!
GODDAMN IT!
VASCULAR WARNING OVER HERE.
YEAH, WHOA—PRESSURE JUST DROPPED LIKE—
THERE! THERE IT IS! I TOLD YOU TO—
NO GOOD. NO—
WHOEVER DESIGNED THIS THING IS A GODDAMN LUNATIC.
THERE. THAT'S IT.
YEAH. OKAY, THIS GUY IS IN BAD SHAPE. I DON'T KNOW HOW MUCH HARDER WE CAN PUSH HIM.
OKAY. THAT'S ABOUT HALF THE LOCKS OUT. WE MIGHT HAVE ENOUGH TO MAKE THE PATCH WORK.

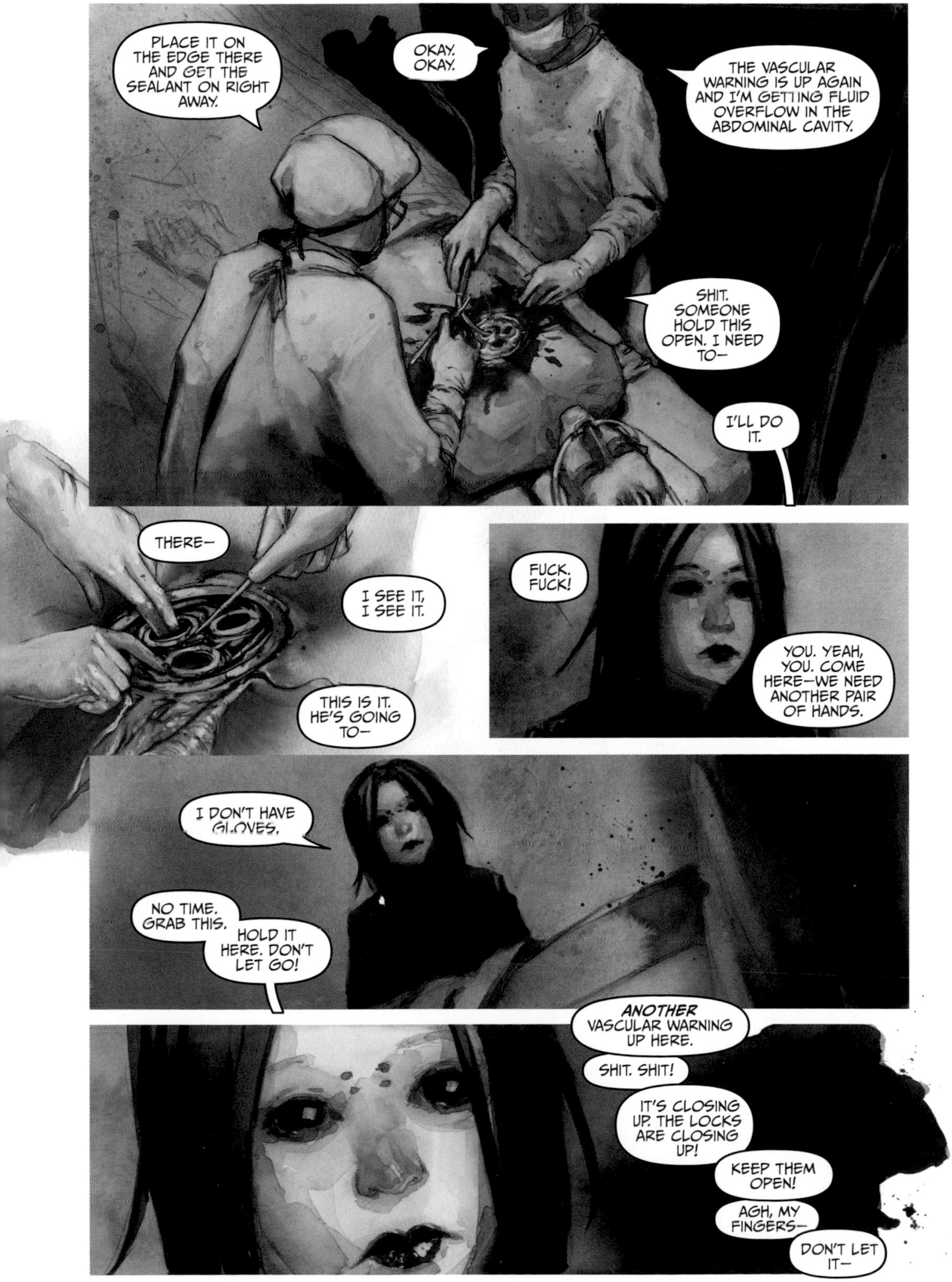
PLACE IT ON THE EDGE THERE AND GET THE SEALANT ON RIGHT AWAY.
OKAY. OKAY.
THE VASCULAR WARNING IS UP AGAIN AND I'M GETTING FLUID OVERFLOW IN THE ABDOMINAL CAVITY.
SHIT. SOMEONE HOLD THIS OPEN. I NEED TO—
I'LL DO IT.
THERE—
I SEE IT, I SEE IT.
THIS IS IT. HE'S GOING TO—
FUCK. FUCK!
YOU. YEAH, YOU. COME HERE—WE NEED ANOTHER PAIR OF HANDS.
I DON'T HAVE GLOVES.
NO TIME. GRAB THIS.
HOLD IT HERE. DON'T LET GO!
ANOTHER VASCULAR WARNING UP HERE.
SHIT. SHIT!
IT'S CLOSING UP. THE LOCKS ARE CLOSING UP!
KEEP THEM OPEN!
AGH, MY FINGERS—
DON'T LET IT—

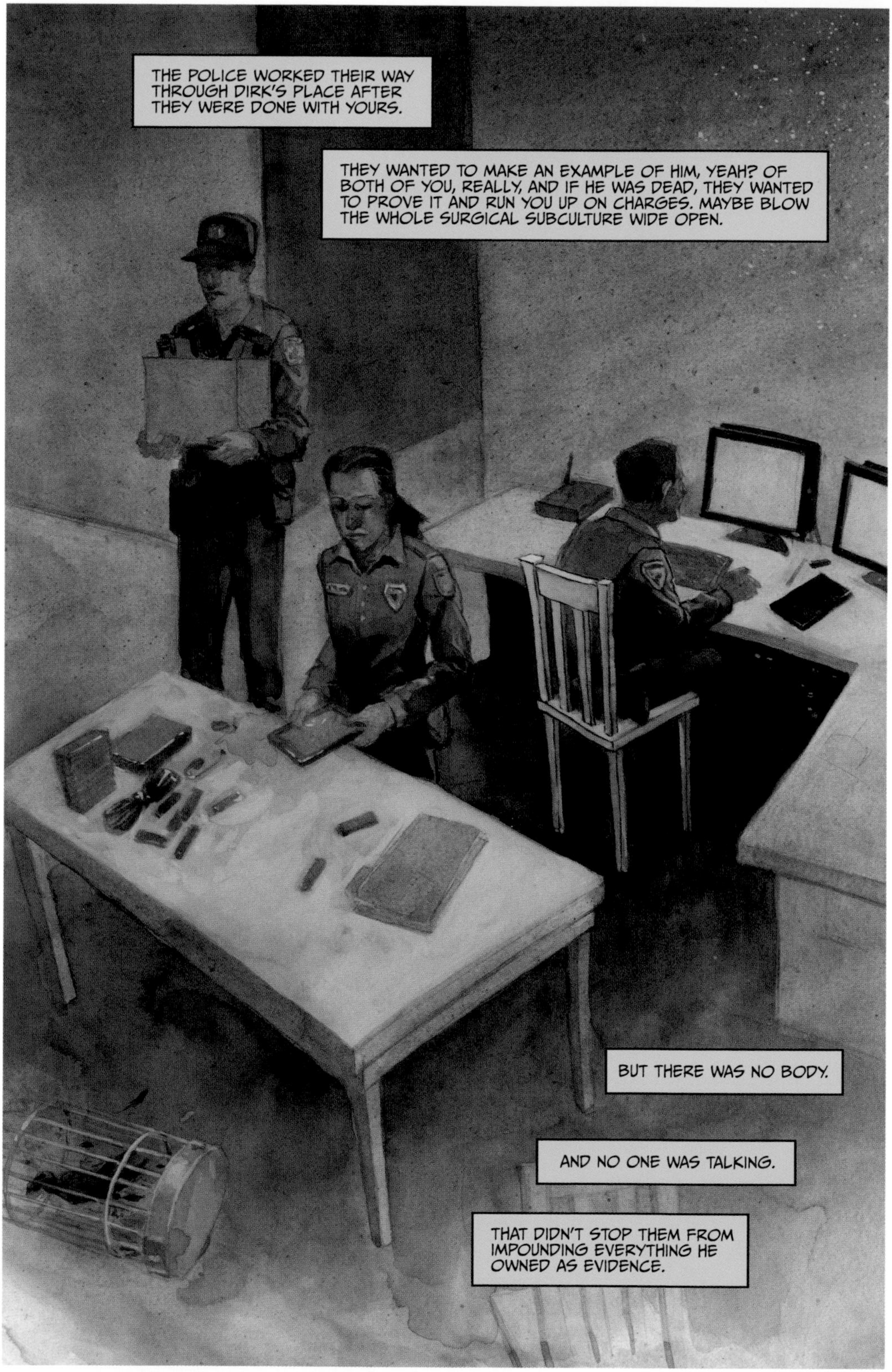
THE POLICE WORKED THEIR WAY THROUGH DIRK'S PLACE AFTER THEY WERE DONE WITH YOURS.
THEY WANTED TO MAKE AN EXAMPLE OF HIM, YEAH? OF BOTH OF YOU, REALLY, AND IF HE WAS DEAD, THEY WANTED TO PROVE IT AND RUN YOU UP ON CHARGES. MAYBE BLOW THE WHOLE SURGICAL SUBCULTURE WIDE OPEN.
BUT THERE WAS NO BODY.
AND NO ONE WAS TALKING.
THAT DIDN'T STOP THEM FROM IMPOUNDING EVERYTHING HE OWNED AS EVIDENCE.

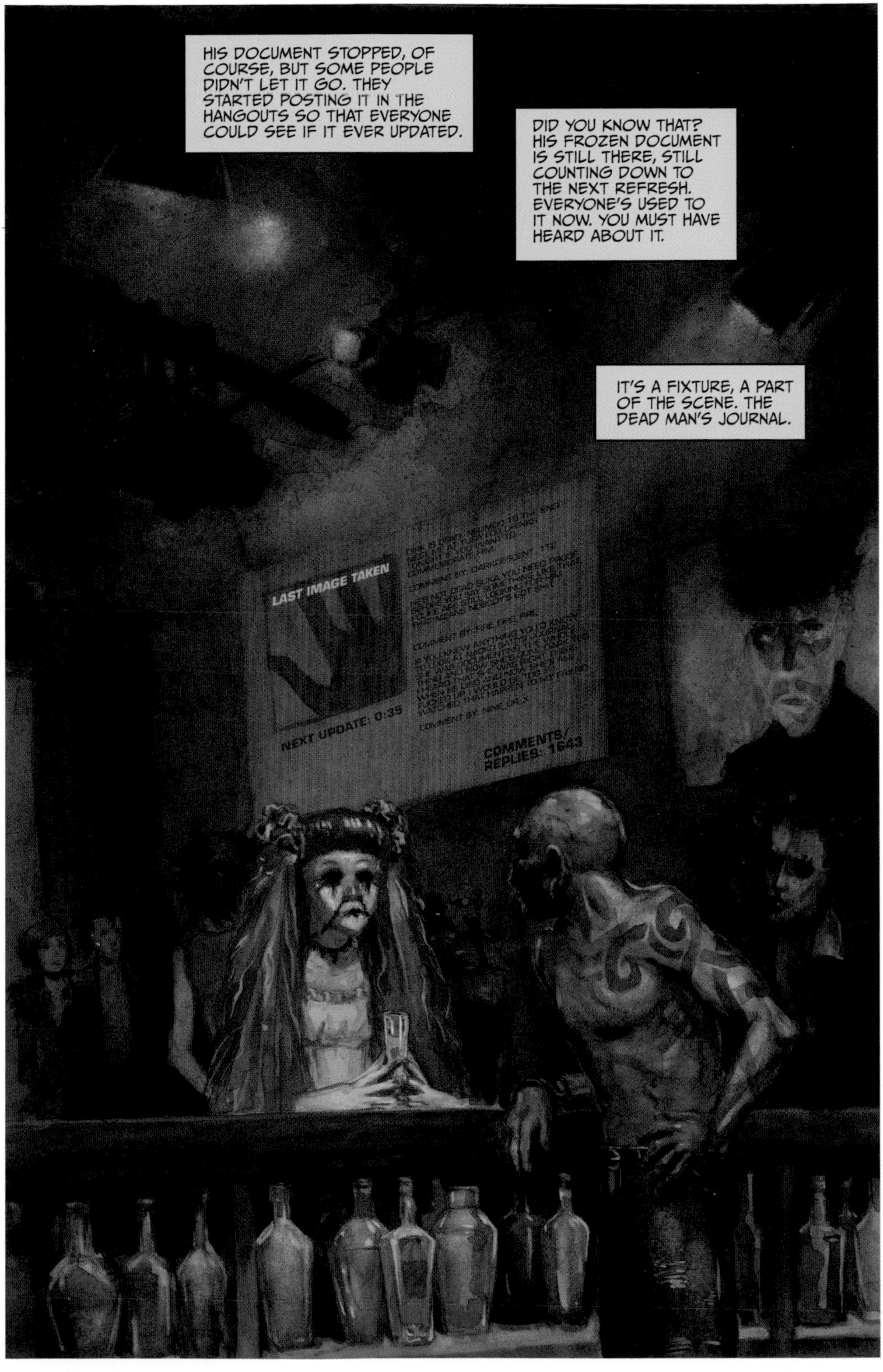
HIS DOCUMENT STOPPED, OF COURSE, BUT SOME PEOPLE DIDN'T LET IT GO. THEY STARTED POSTING IT IN THE HANGOUTS SO THAT EVERYONE COULD SEE IF IT EVER UPDATED.
DID YOU KNOW THAT? HIS FROZEN DOCUMENT IS STILL THERE, STILL COUNTING DOWN TO THE NEXT REFRESH. EVERYONE'S USED TO IT NOW. YOU MUST HAVE HEARD ABOUT IT.
IT'S A FIXTURE, A PART OF THE SCENE. THE DEAD MAN'S JOURNAL.
LAST IMAGE TAKEN
NEXT UPDATE: 0:35
COMMENTS/
REPLIES: 1643

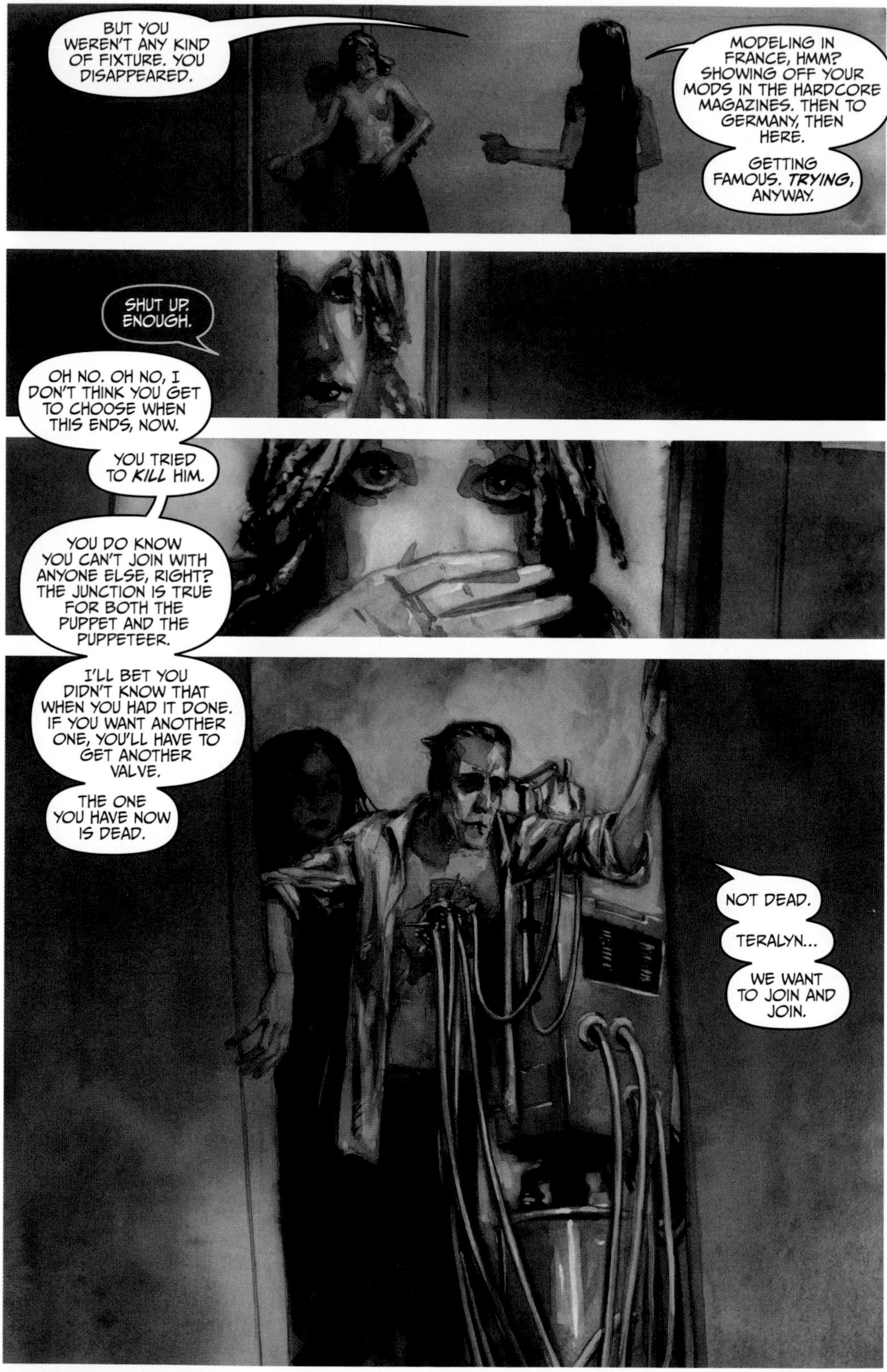
BUT YOU WEREN'T ANY KIND OF FIXTURE. YOU DISAPPEARED.
MODELING IN FRANCE, HMM? SHOWING OFF YOUR MODS IN THE HARDCORE MAGAZINES. THEN TO GERMANY, THEN HERE.
GETTING FAMOUS. *TRYING*, ANYWAY.
SHUT UP. ENOUGH.
OH NO. OH NO, I DON'T THINK YOU GET TO CHOOSE WHEN THIS ENDS, NOW.
YOU TRIED TO *KILL* HIM.
YOU DO KNOW YOU CAN'T JOIN WITH ANYONE ELSE, RIGHT? THE JUNCTION IS TRUE FOR BOTH THE PUPPET AND THE PUPPETEER.
I'LL BET YOU DIDN'T KNOW THAT WHEN YOU HAD IT DONE. IF YOU WANT ANOTHER ONE, YOU'LL HAVE TO GET ANOTHER VALVE.
THE ONE YOU HAVE NOW IS DEAD.
NOT DEAD.
TERALYN...
WE WANT TO JOIN AND JOIN.

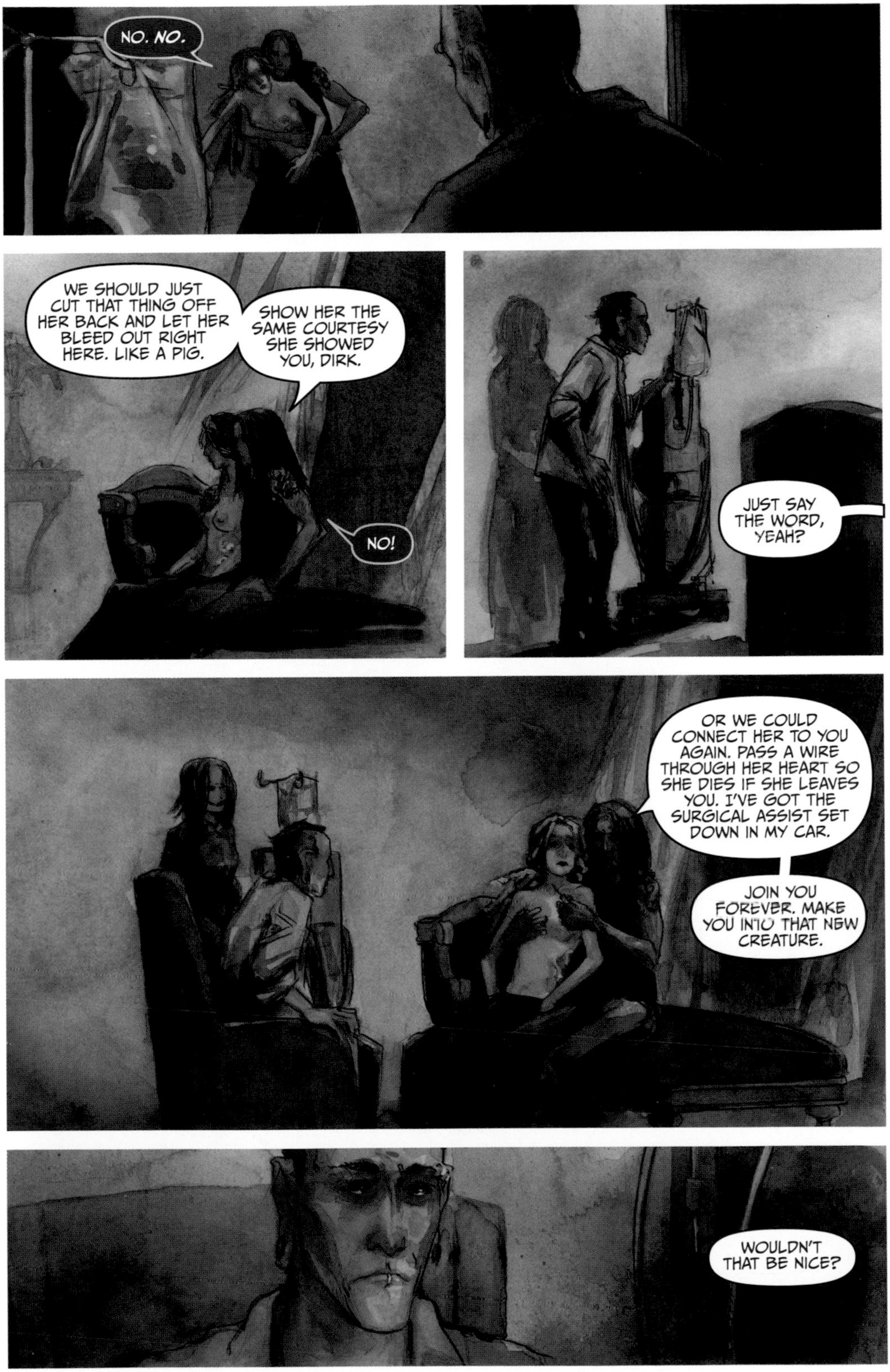
NO. NO.
WE SHOULD JUST CUT THAT THING OFF HER BACK AND LET HER BLEED OUT RIGHT HERE. LIKE A PIG.
SHOW HER THE SAME COURTESY SHE SHOWED YOU, DIRK.
NO!
JUST SAY THE WORD, YEAH?
OR WE COULD CONNECT HER TO YOU AGAIN. PASS A WIRE THROUGH HER HEART SO SHE DIES IF SHE LEAVES YOU. I'VE GOT THE SURGICAL ASSIST SET DOWN IN MY CAR.
JOIN YOU FOREVER. MAKE YOU INTO THAT NEW CREATURE.
WOULDN'T THAT BE NICE?

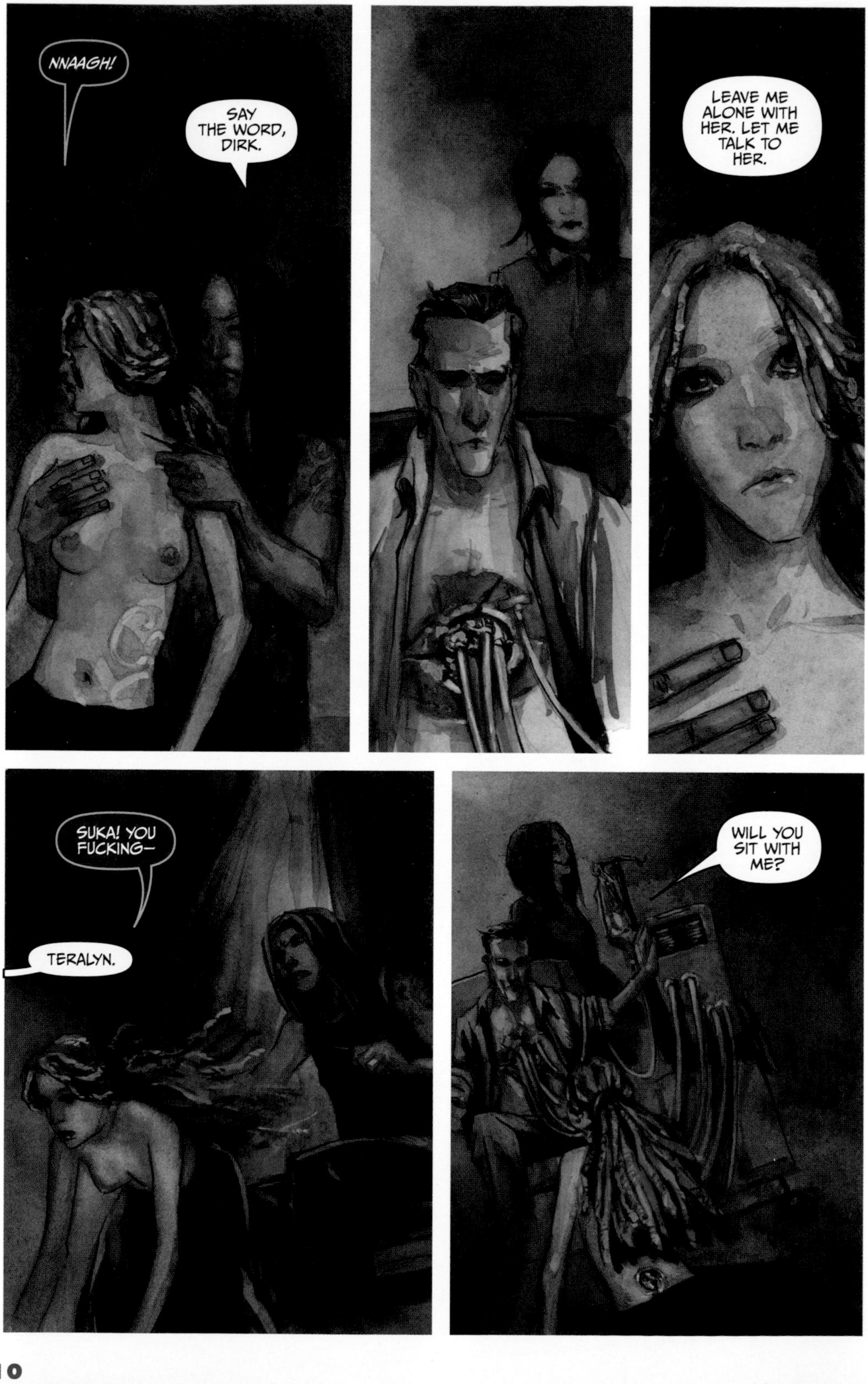
NNAAGH!
SAY THE WORD, DIRK.
LEAVE ME ALONE WITH HER. LET ME TALK TO HER.
SUKA! YOU FUCKING—
TERALYN.
WILL YOU SIT WITH ME?

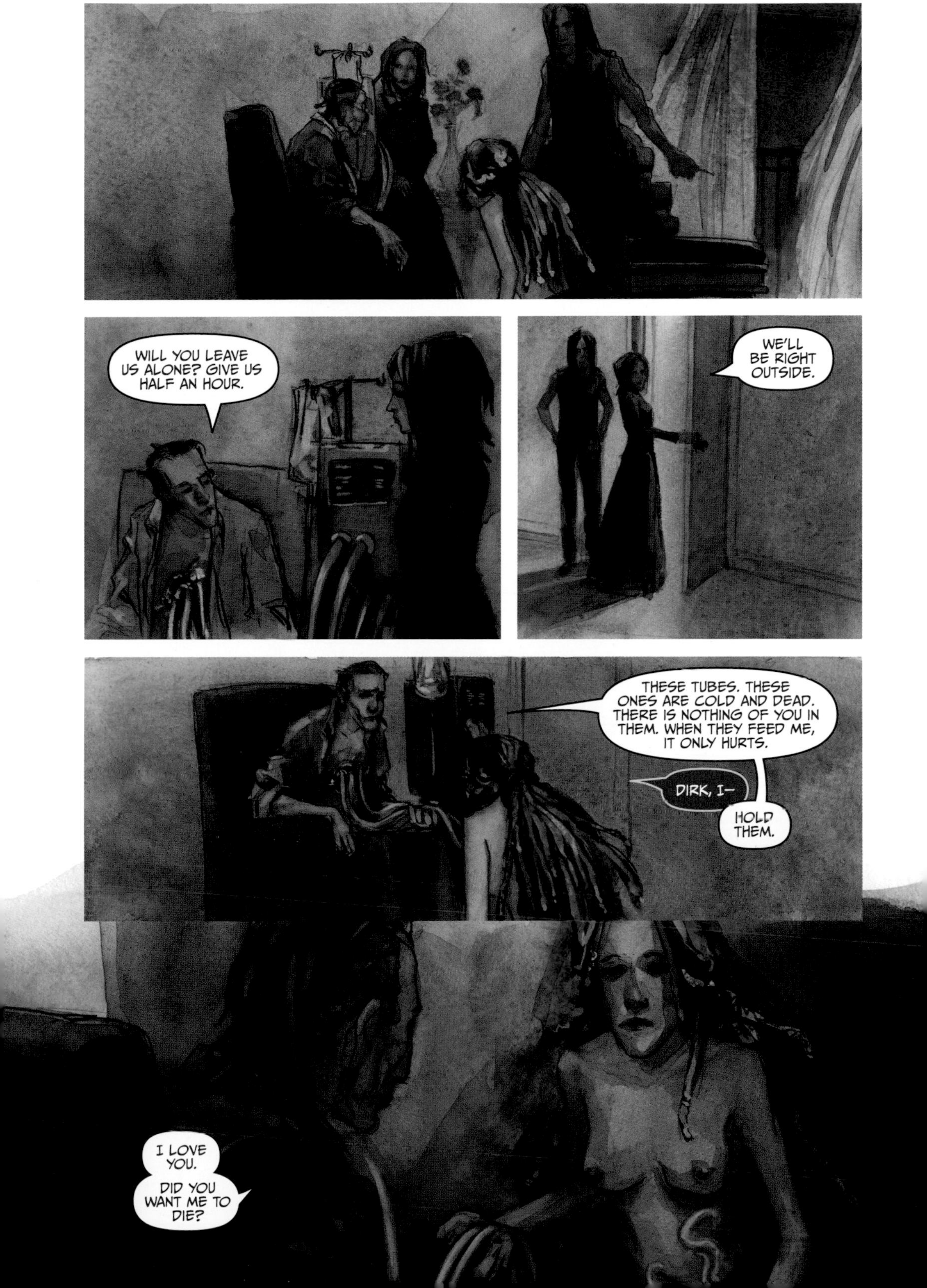
WILL YOU LEAVE US ALONE? GIVE US HALF AN HOUR.
WE'LL BE RIGHT OUTSIDE.
THESE TUBES. THESE ONES ARE COLD AND DEAD. THERE IS NOTHING OF YOU IN THEM. WHEN THEY FEED ME, IT ONLY HURTS.
DIRK, I—
HOLD THEM.
I LOVE YOU.
DID YOU WANT ME TO DIE?

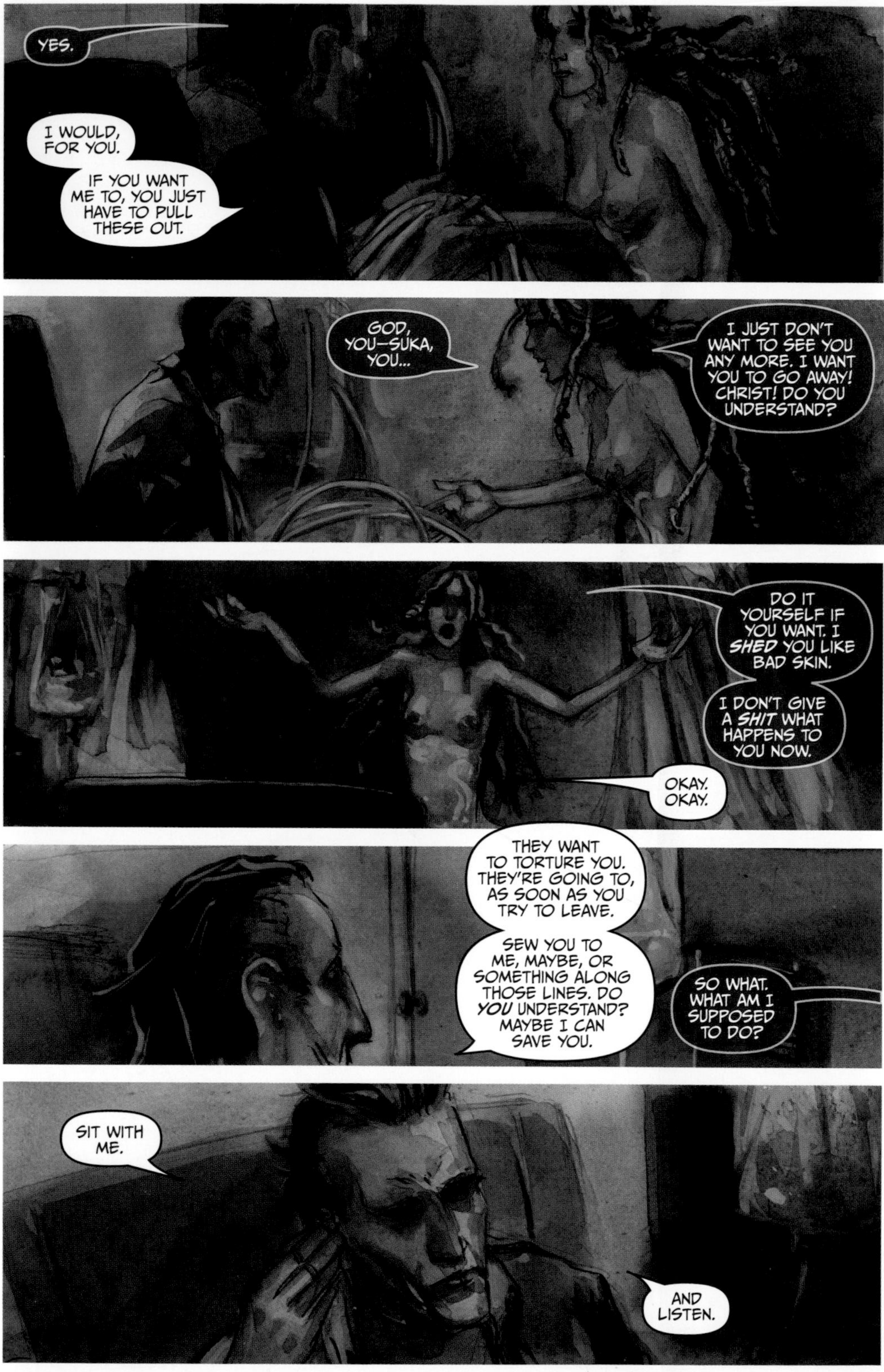
YES.
I WOULD, FOR YOU.
IF YOU WANT ME TO, YOU JUST HAVE TO PULL THESE OUT.
GOD, YOU—SUKA, YOU...
I JUST DON'T WANT TO SEE YOU ANY MORE. I WANT YOU TO GO AWAY! CHRIST! DO YOU UNDERSTAND?
DO IT YOURSELF IF YOU WANT. I *SHED* YOU LIKE BAD SKIN.
I DON'T GIVE A *SHIT* WHAT HAPPENS TO YOU NOW.
OKAY. OKAY.
THEY WANT TO TORTURE YOU. THEY'RE GOING TO, AS SOON AS YOU TRY TO LEAVE.
SEW YOU TO ME, MAYBE, OR SOMETHING ALONG THOSE LINES. DO *YOU* UNDERSTAND? MAYBE I CAN SAVE YOU.
SO WHAT. WHAT AM I SUPPOSED TO DO?
SIT WITH ME.
AND LISTEN.

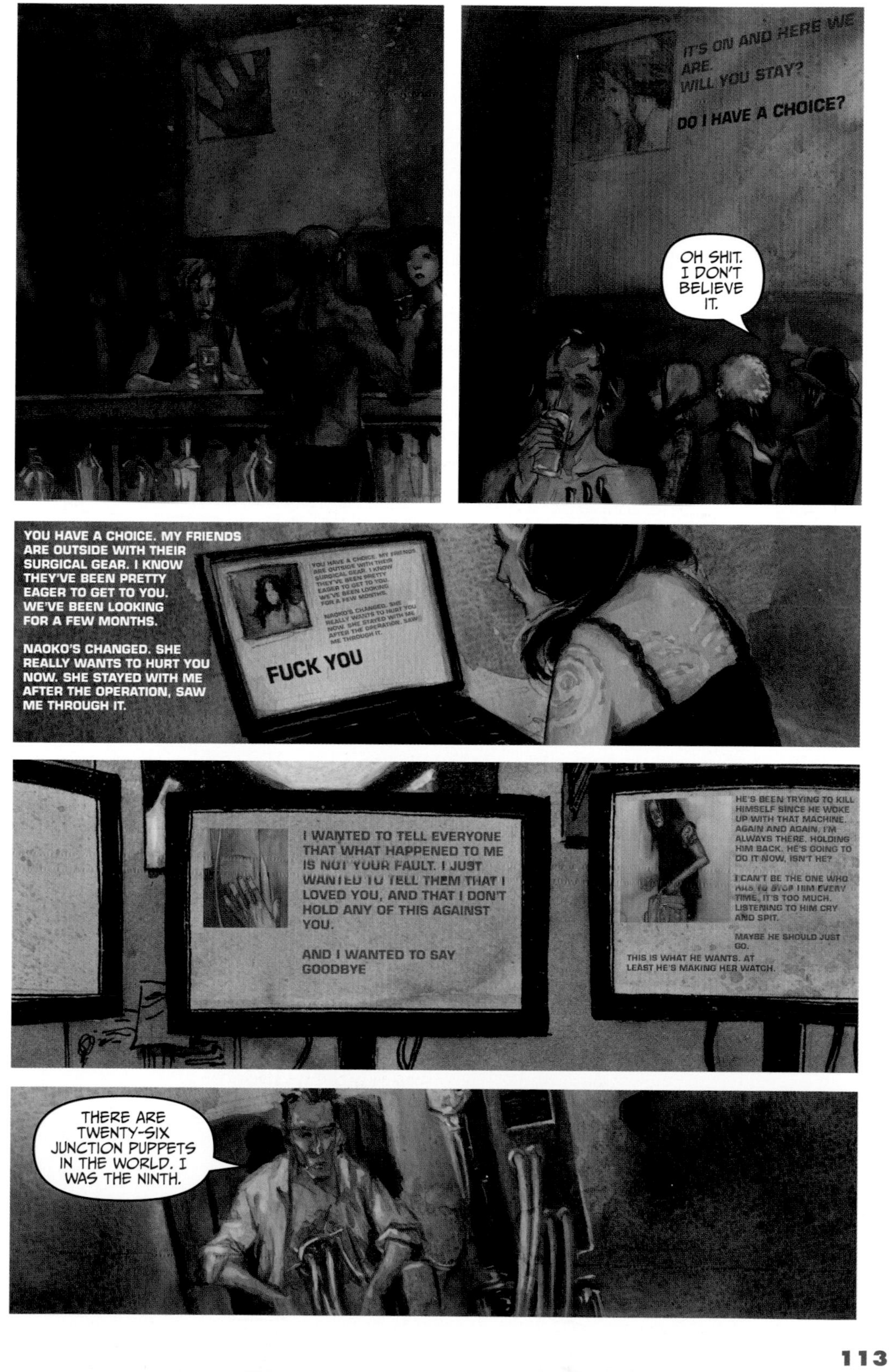
IT'S ON AND HERE WE ARE. WILL YOU STAY?
DO I HAVE A CHOICE?
OH SHIT. I DON'T BELIEVE IT.
YOU HAVE A CHOICE. MY FRIENDS ARE OUTSIDE WITH THEIR SURGICAL GEAR. I KNOW THEY'VE BEEN PRETTY EAGER TO GET TO YOU. WE'VE BEEN LOOKING FOR A FEW MONTHS.
NAOKO'S CHANGED. SHE REALLY WANTS TO HURT YOU NOW. SHE STAYED WITH ME AFTER THE OPERATION, SAW ME THROUGH IT.
FUCK YOU
I WANTED TO TELL EVERYONE THAT WHAT HAPPENED TO ME IS NOT YOUR FAULT. I JUST WANTED TO TELL THEM THAT I LOVED YOU, AND THAT I DON'T HOLD ANY OF THIS AGAINST YOU.
AND I WANTED TO SAY GOODBYE
HE'S BEEN TRYING TO KILL HIMSELF SINCE HE WOKE UP WITH THAT MACHINE. AGAIN AND AGAIN, I'M ALWAYS THERE, HOLDING HIM BACK. HE'S GOING TO DO IT NOW, ISN'T HE?
I CAN'T BE THE ONE WHO HAS TO STOP HIM EVERY TIME. IT'S TOO MUCH. LISTENING TO HIM CRY AND SPIT.
MAYBE HE SHOULD JUST GO.
THIS IS WHAT HE WANTS. AT LEAST HE'S MAKING HER WATCH.
THERE ARE TWENTY-SIX JUNCTION PUPPETS IN THE WORLD. I WAS THE NINTH.

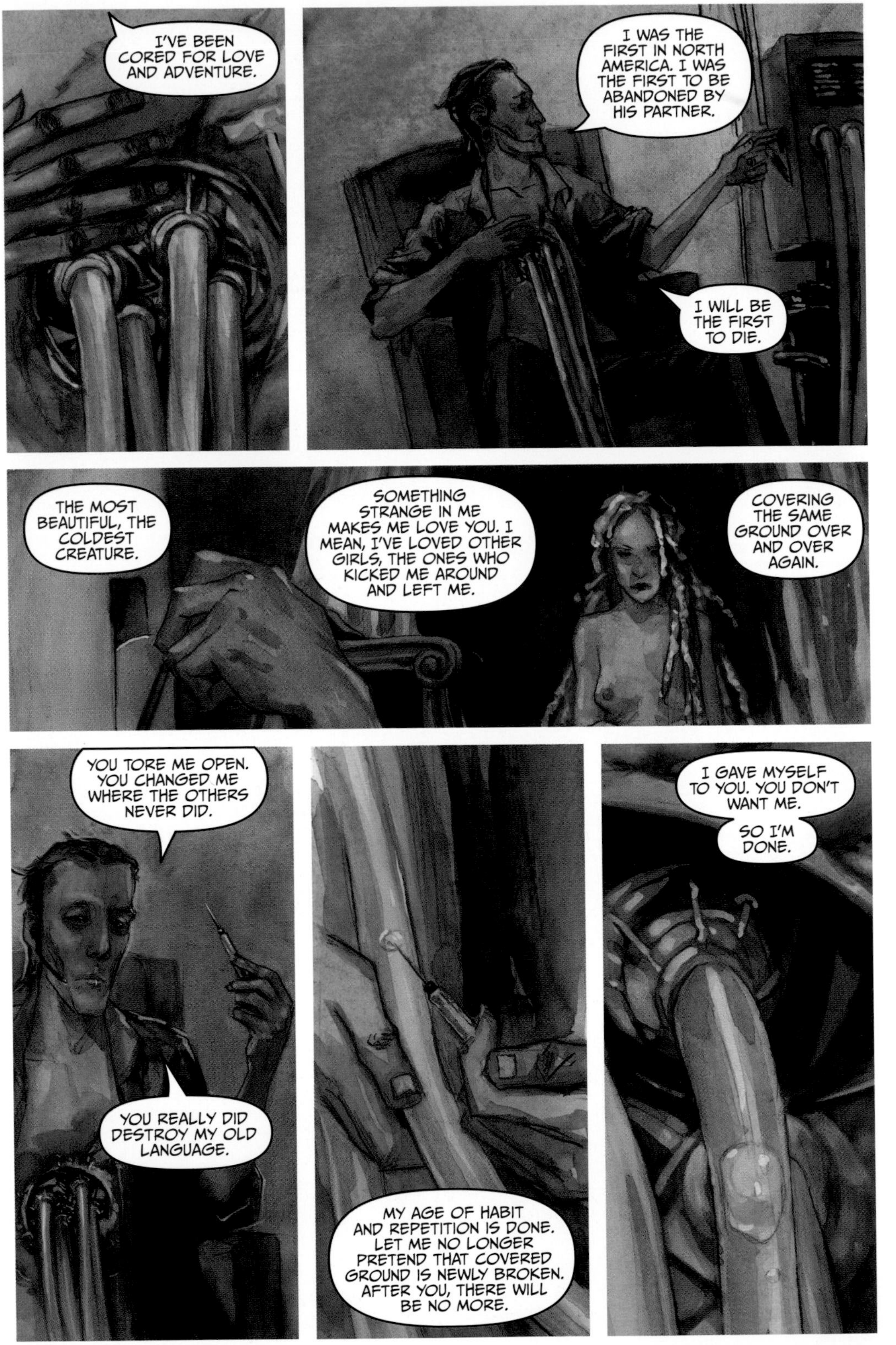
I'VE BEEN CORED FOR LOVE AND ADVENTURE.
I WAS THE FIRST IN NORTH AMERICA. I WAS THE FIRST TO BE ABANDONED BY HIS PARTNER.
I WILL BE THE FIRST TO DIE.
THE MOST BEAUTIFUL, THE COLDEST CREATURE.
SOMETHING STRANGE IN ME MAKES ME LOVE YOU. I MEAN, I'VE LOVED OTHER GIRLS, THE ONES WHO KICKED ME AROUND AND LEFT ME.
COVERING THE SAME GROUND OVER AND OVER AGAIN.
YOU TORE ME OPEN. YOU CHANGED ME WHERE THE OTHERS NEVER DID.
YOU REALLY DID DESTROY MY OLD LANGUAGE.
MY AGE OF HABIT AND REPETITION IS DONE. LET ME NO LONGER PRETEND THAT COVERED GROUND IS NEWLY BROKEN. AFTER YOU, THERE WILL BE NO MORE.
I GAVE MYSELF TO YOU. YOU DON'T WANT ME.
SO I'M DONE.

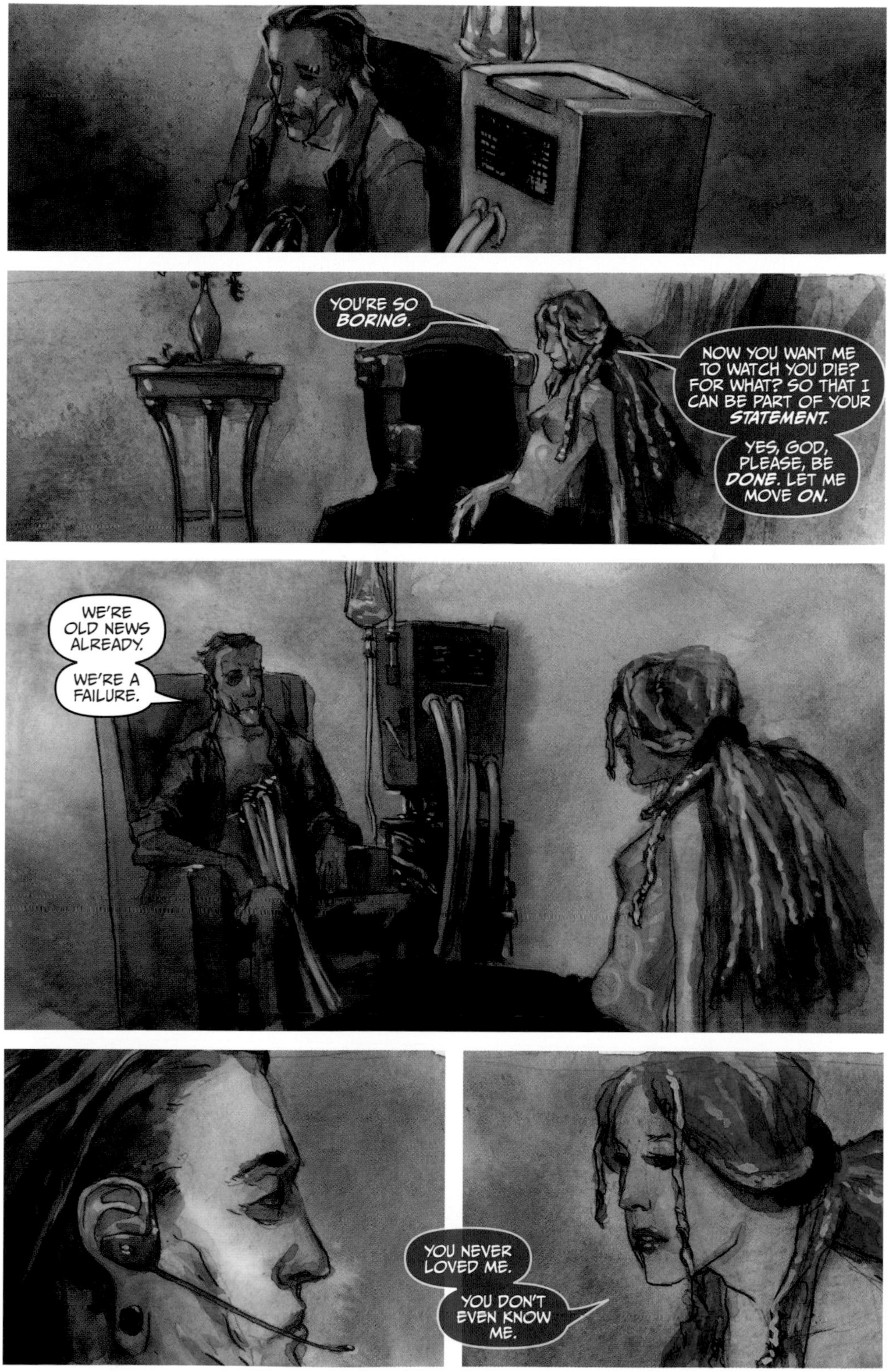
YOU'RE SO BORING.
NOW YOU WANT ME TO WATCH YOU DIE? FOR WHAT? SO THAT I CAN BE PART OF YOUR STATEMENT.
YES, GOD, PLEASE, BE DONE. LET ME MOVE ON.
WE'RE OLD NEWS ALREADY.
WE'RE A FAILURE.
YOU NEVER LOVED ME.
YOU DON'T EVEN KNOW ME.

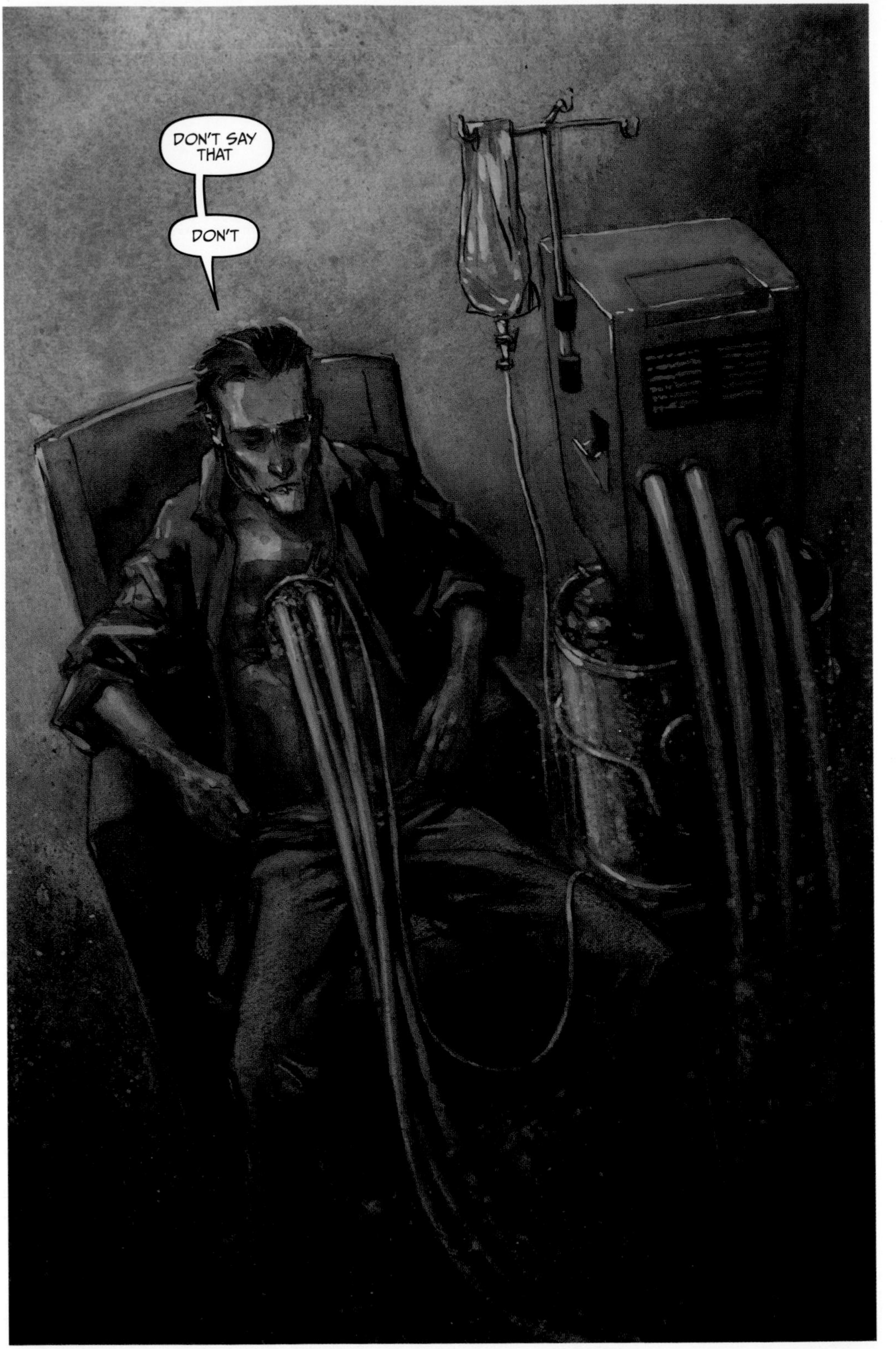
DON'T SAY THAT
DON'T

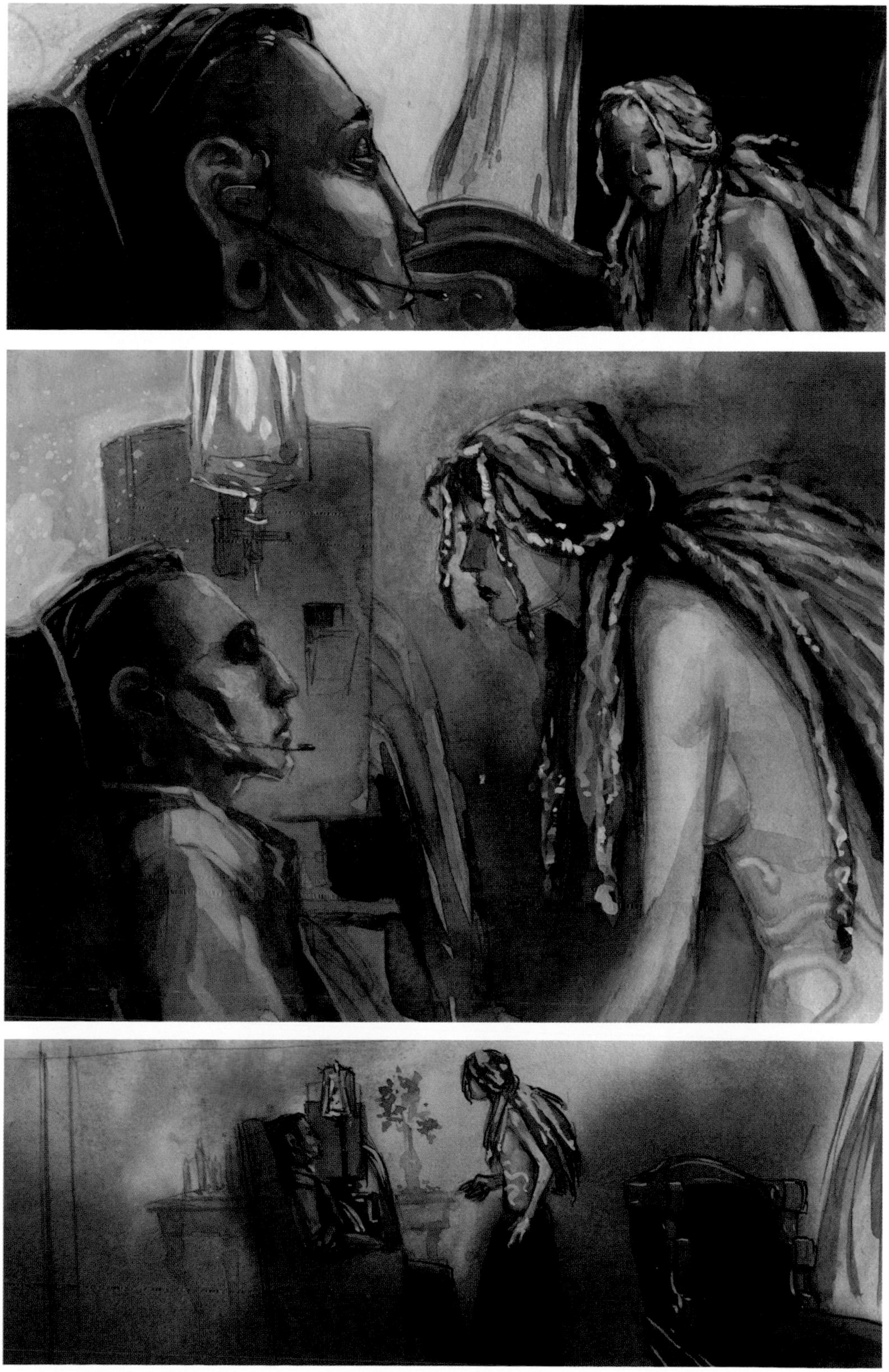

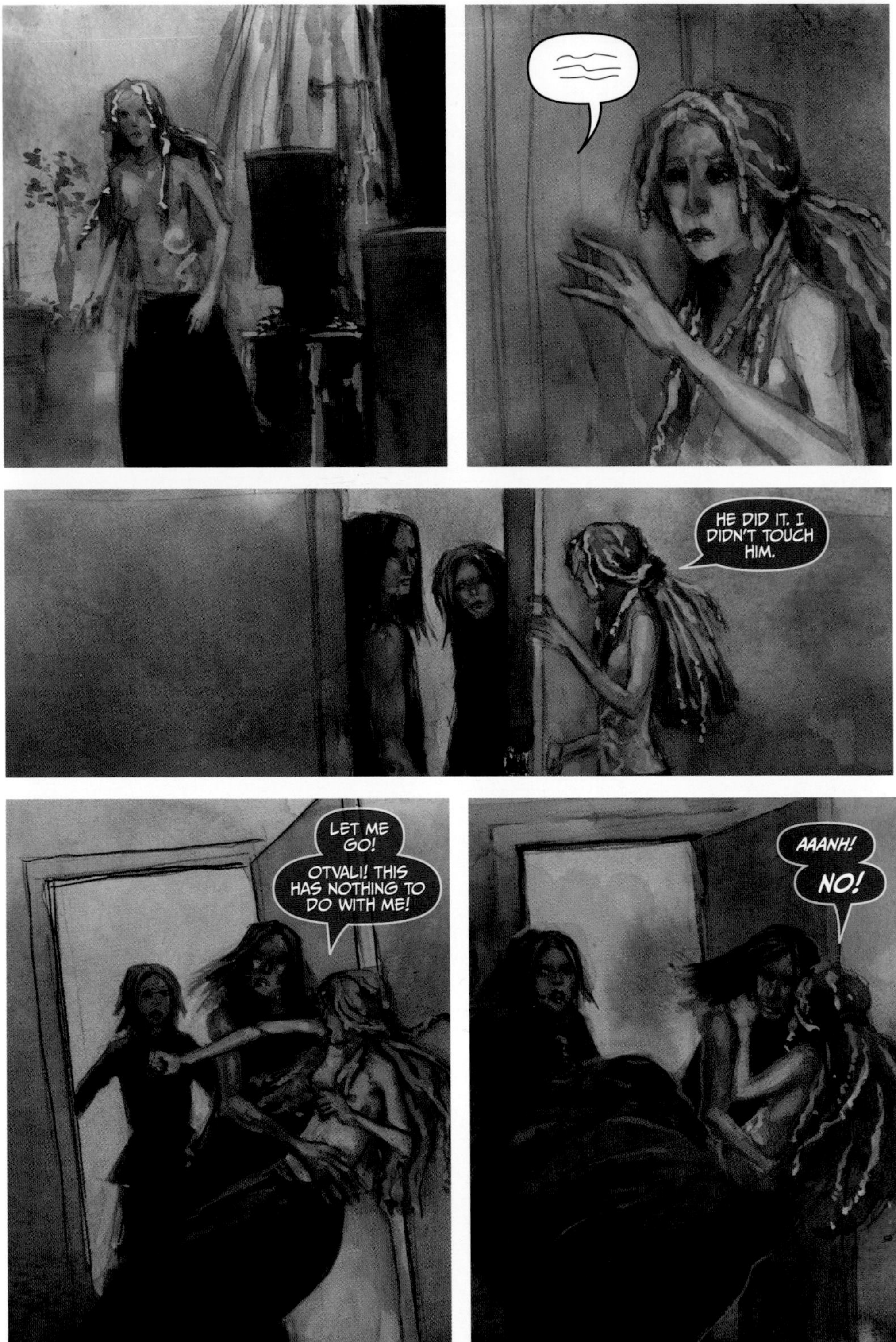
HE DID IT. I DIDN'T TOUCH HIM.
LET ME GO!
OTVALI! THIS HAS NOTHING TO DO WITH ME!
AAANH!
NO!

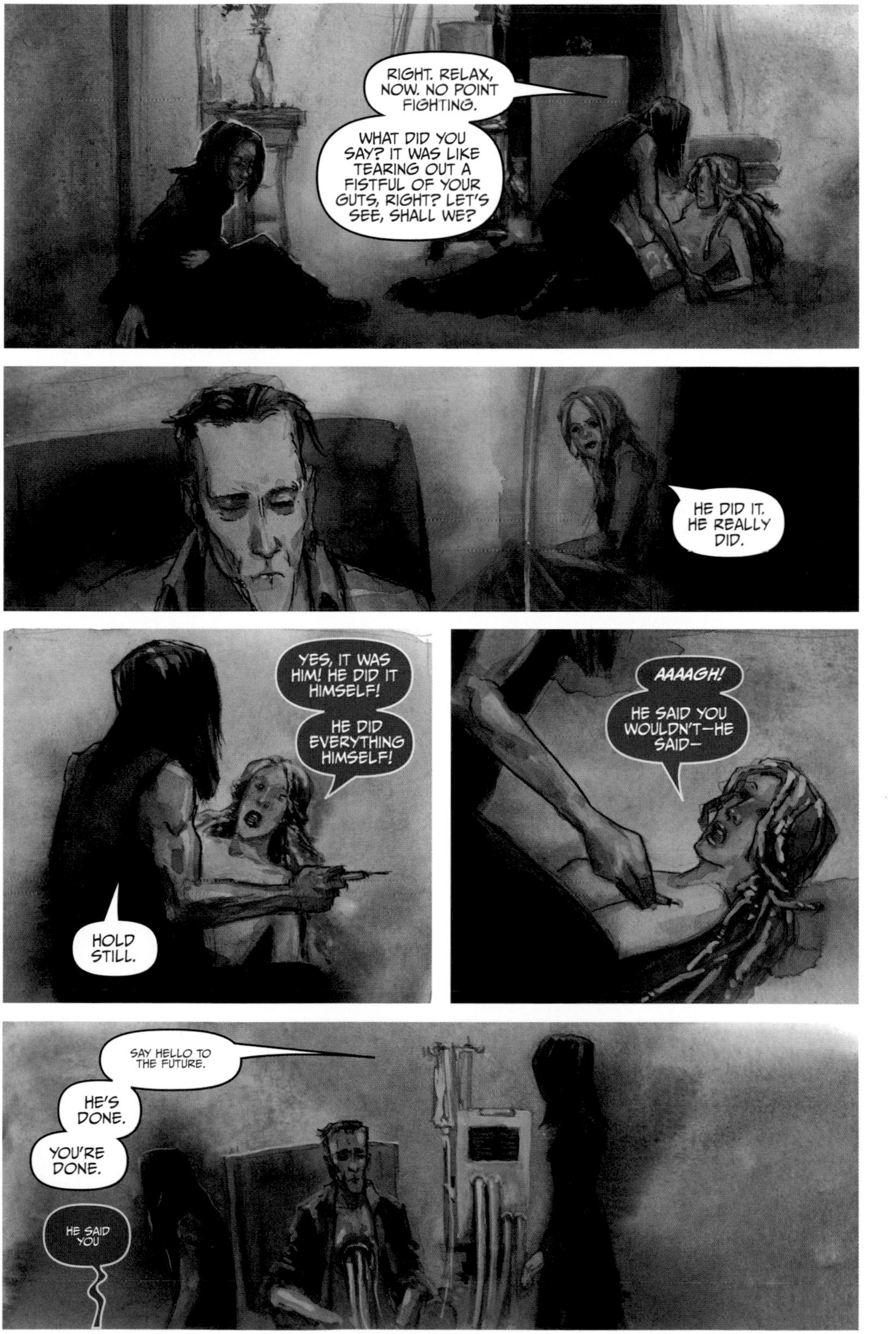
RIGHT. RELAX, NOW. NO POINT FIGHTING.
WHAT DID YOU SAY? IT WAS LIKE TEARING OUT A FISTFUL OF YOUR GUTS, RIGHT? LET'S SEE, SHALL WE?
HE DID IT. HE REALLY DID.
YES, IT WAS HIM! HE DID IT HIMSELF!
HE DID EVERYTHING HIMSELF!
HOLD STILL.
AAAAGH!
HE SAID YOU WOULDN'T—HE SAID—
SAY HELLO TO THE FUTURE.
HE'S DONE.
YOU'RE DONE.
HE SAID YOU

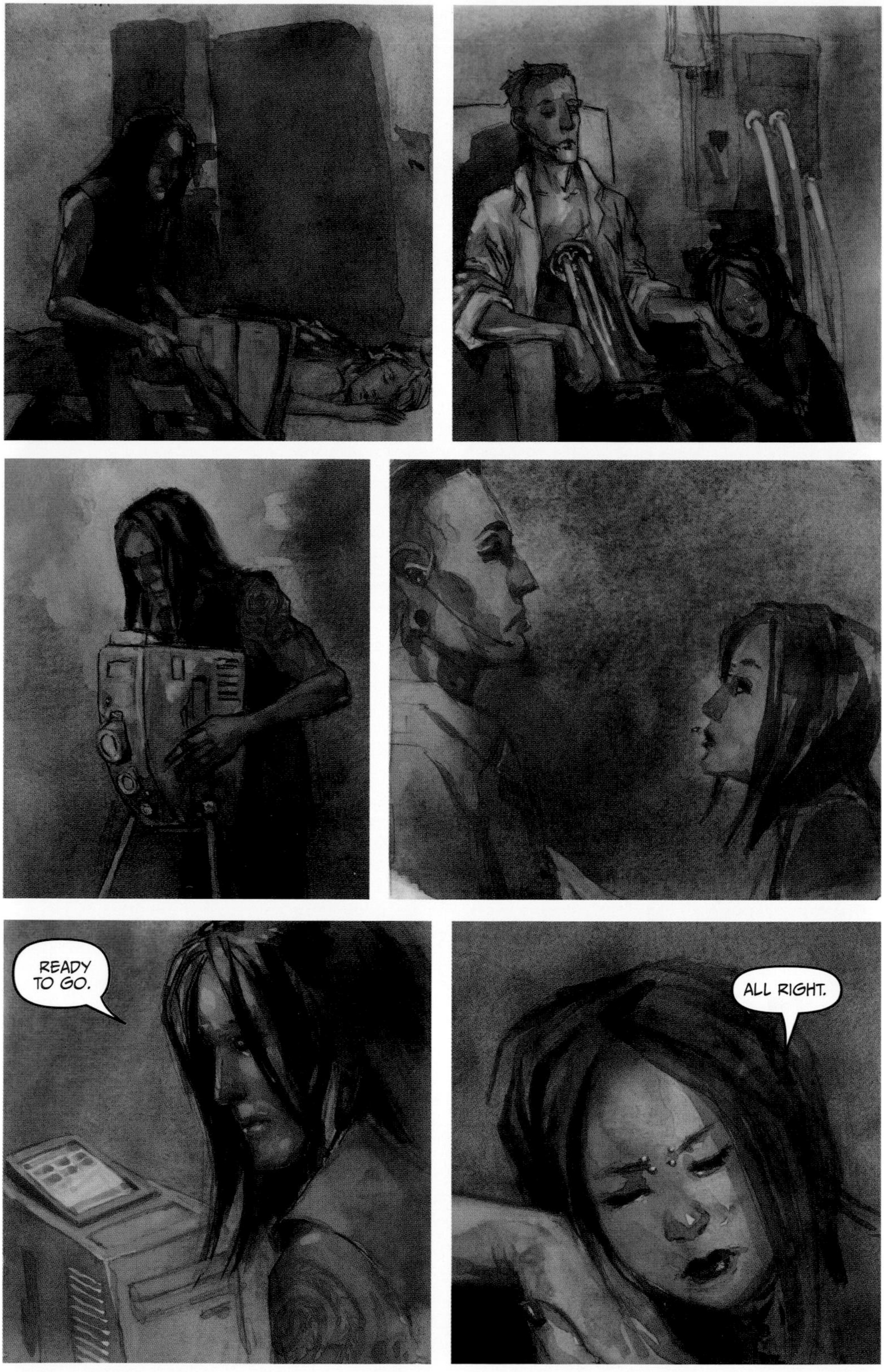
READY TO GO.
ALL RIGHT.

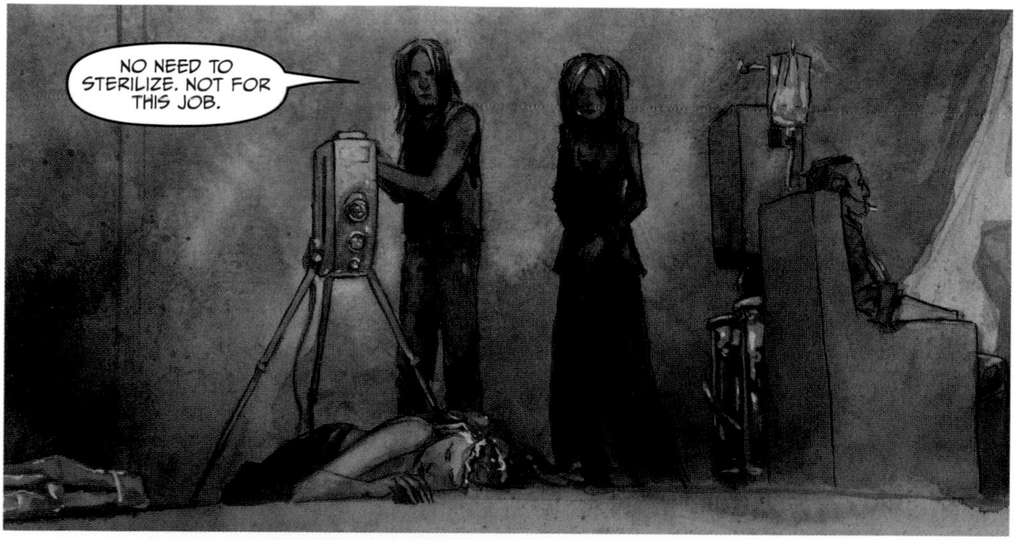
NO NEED TO STERILIZE. NOT FOR THIS JOB.

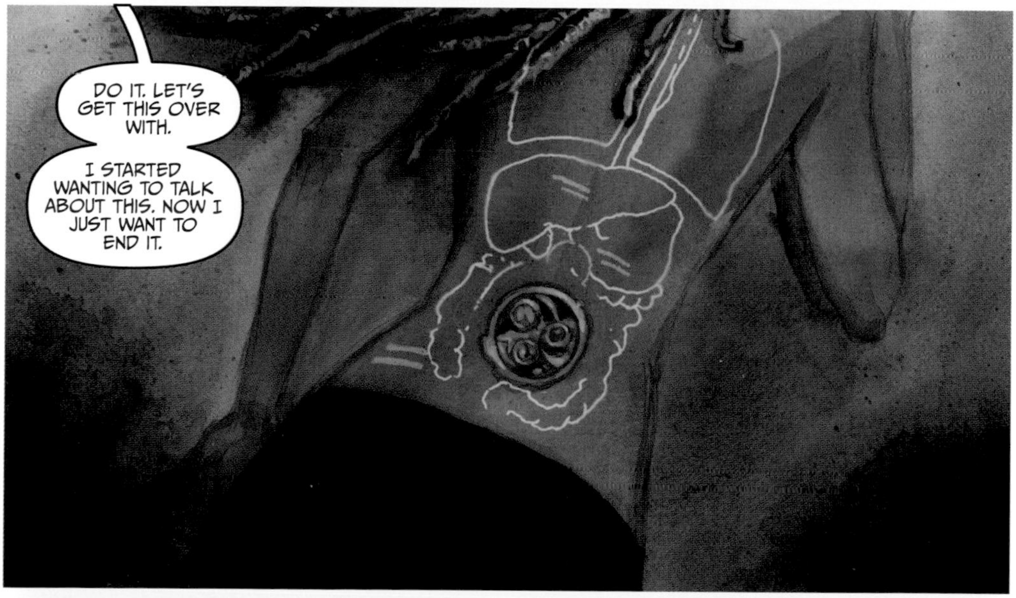
DO IT. LET'S GET THIS OVER WITH.
I STARTED WANTING TO TALK ABOUT THIS. NOW I JUST WANT TO END IT.

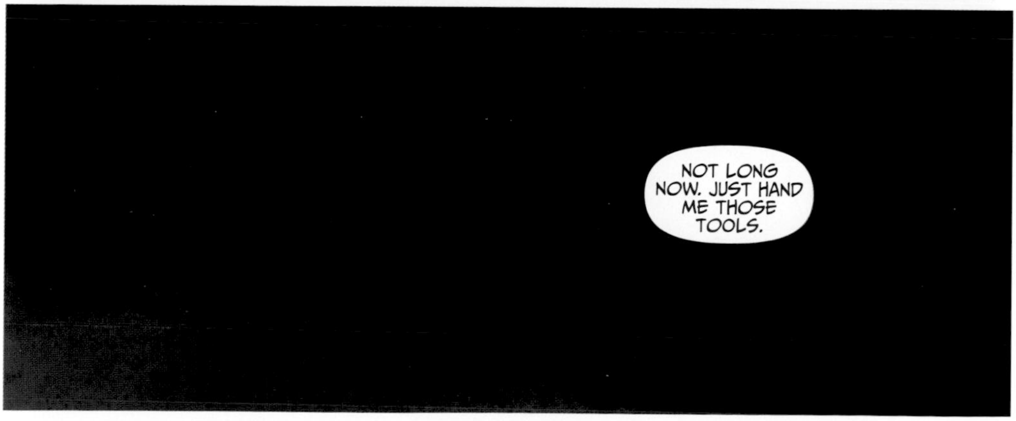
NOT LONG NOW. JUST HAND ME THOSE TOOLS.

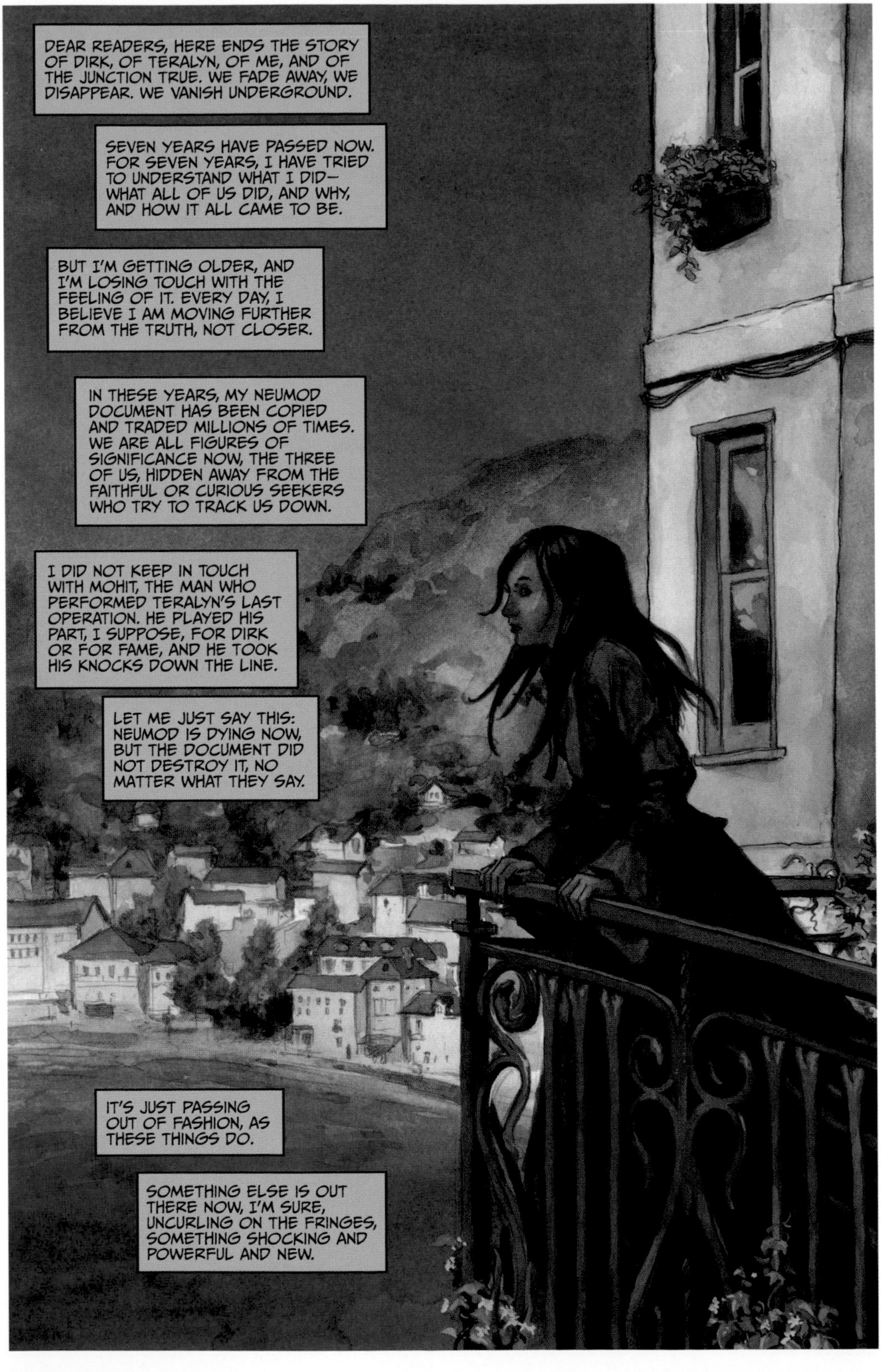
DEAR READERS, HERE ENDS THE STORY OF DIRK, OF TERALYN, OF ME, AND OF THE JUNCTION TRUE. WE FADE AWAY, WE DISAPPEAR. WE VANISH UNDERGROUND.
SEVEN YEARS HAVE PASSED NOW. FOR SEVEN YEARS, I HAVE TRIED TO UNDERSTAND WHAT I DID—WHAT ALL OF US DID, AND WHY, AND HOW IT ALL CAME TO BE.
BUT I'M GETTING OLDER, AND I'M LOSING TOUCH WITH THE FEELING OF IT. EVERY DAY, I BELIEVE I AM MOVING FURTHER FROM THE TRUTH, NOT CLOSER.
IN THESE YEARS, MY NEUMOD DOCUMENT HAS BEEN COPIED AND TRADED MILLIONS OF TIMES. WE ARE ALL FIGURES OF SIGNIFICANCE NOW, THE THREE OF US, HIDDEN AWAY FROM THE FAITHFUL OR CURIOUS SEEKERS WHO TRY TO TRACK US DOWN.
I DID NOT KEEP IN TOUCH WITH MOHIT, THE MAN WHO PERFORMED TERALYN'S LAST OPERATION. HE PLAYED HIS PART, I SUPPOSE, FOR DIRK OR FOR FAME, AND HE TOOK HIS KNOCKS DOWN THE LINE.
LET ME JUST SAY THIS: NEUMOD IS DYING NOW, BUT THE DOCUMENT DID NOT DESTROY IT, NO MATTER WHAT THEY SAY.
IT'S JUST PASSING OUT OF FASHION, AS THESE THINGS DO.
SOMETHING ELSE IS OUT THERE NOW, I'M SURE, UNCURLING ON THE FRINGES, SOMETHING SHOCKING AND POWERFUL AND NEW.

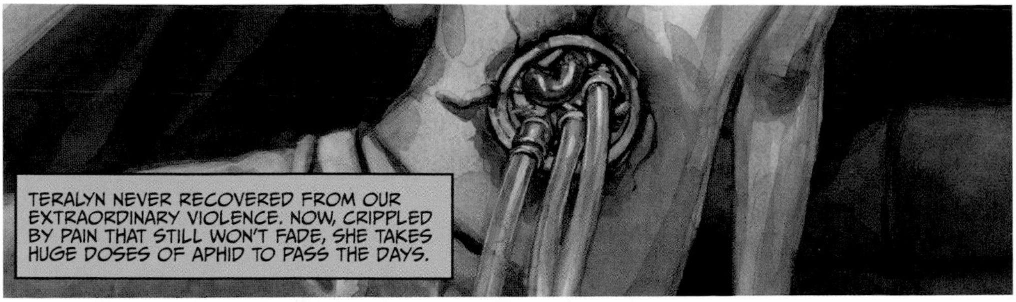
TERALYN NEVER RECOVERED FROM OUR EXTRAORDINARY VIOLENCE. NOW, CRIPPLED BY PAIN THAT STILL WON'T FADE, SHE TAKES HUGE DOSES OF APHID TO PASS THE DAYS.

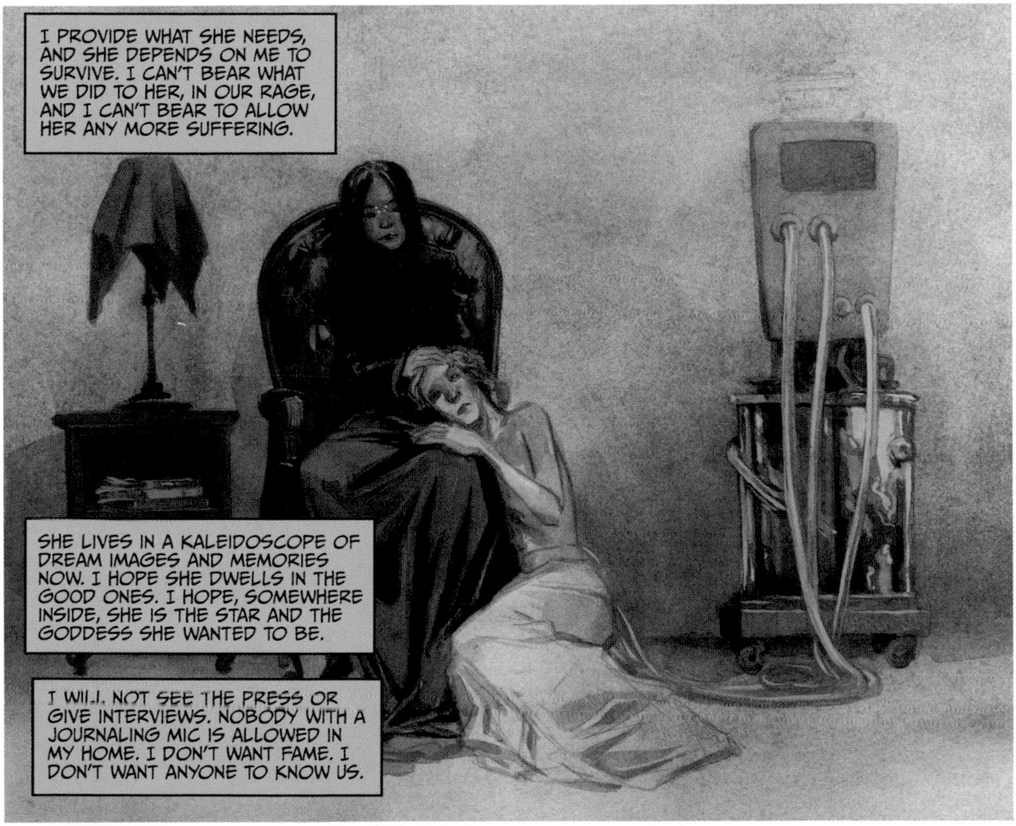
I PROVIDE WHAT SHE NEEDS, AND SHE DEPENDS ON ME TO SURVIVE. I CAN'T BEAR WHAT WE DID TO HER, IN OUR RAGE, AND I CAN'T BEAR TO ALLOW HER ANY MORE SUFFERING.
SHE LIVES IN A KALEIDOSCOPE OF DREAM IMAGES AND MEMORIES NOW. I HOPE SHE DWELLS IN THE GOOD ONES. I HOPE, SOMEWHERE INSIDE, SHE IS THE STAR AND THE GODDESS SHE WANTED TO BE.
I WILL NOT SEE THE PRESS OR GIVE INTERVIEWS. NOBODY WITH A JOURNALING MIC IS ALLOWED IN MY HOME. I DON'T WANT FAME. I DON'T WANT ANYONE TO KNOW US.

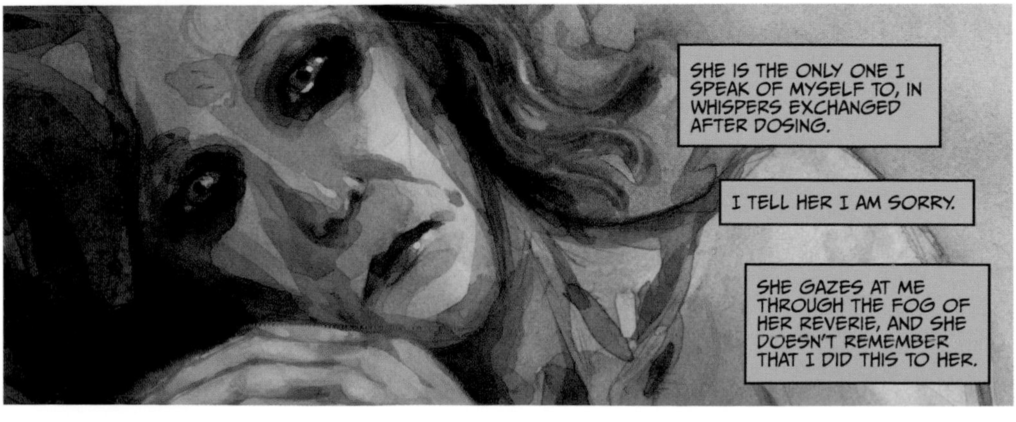
SHE IS THE ONLY ONE I SPEAK OF MYSELF TO, IN WHISPERS EXCHANGED AFTER DOSING.
I TELL HER I AM SORRY.
SHE GAZES AT ME THROUGH THE FOG OF HER REVERIE, AND SHE DOESN'T REMEMBER THAT I DID THIS TO HER.

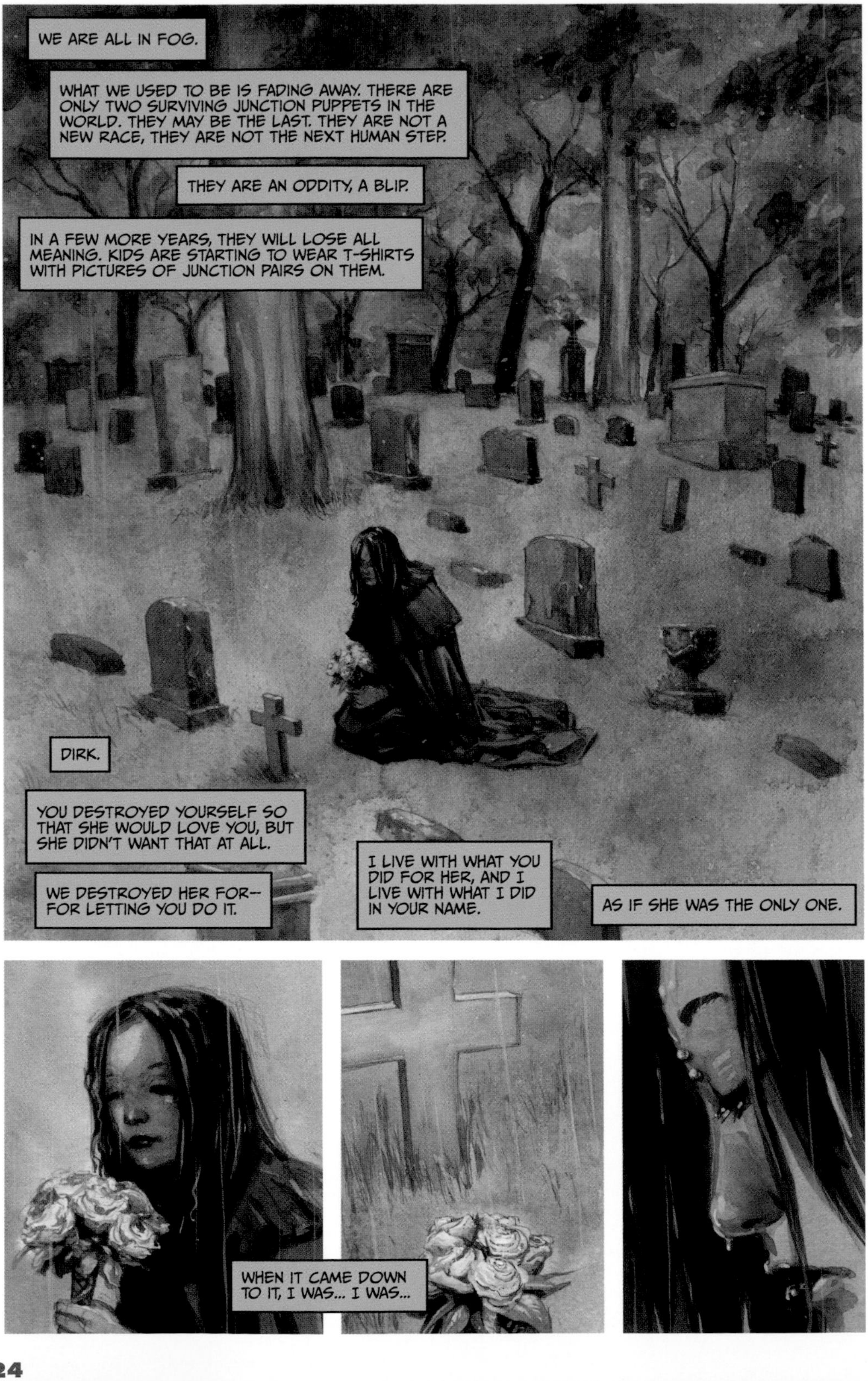
WE ARE ALL IN FOG.
WHAT WE USED TO BE IS FADING AWAY. THERE ARE ONLY TWO SURVIVING JUNCTION PUPPETS IN THE WORLD. THEY MAY BE THE LAST. THEY ARE NOT A NEW RACE, THEY ARE NOT THE NEXT HUMAN STEP.
THEY ARE AN ODDITY, A BLIP.
IN A FEW MORE YEARS, THEY WILL LOSE ALL MEANING. KIDS ARE STARTING TO WEAR T-SHIRTS WITH PICTURES OF JUNCTION PAIRS ON THEM.
DIRK.
YOU DESTROYED YOURSELF SO THAT SHE WOULD LOVE YOU, BUT SHE DIDN'T WANT THAT AT ALL.
WE DESTROYED HER FOR-- FOR LETTING YOU DO IT.
I LIVE WITH WHAT YOU DID FOR HER, AND I LIVE WITH WHAT I DID IN YOUR NAME.
AS IF SHE WAS THE ONLY ONE.
WHEN IT CAME DOWN TO IT, I WAS... I WAS...

Ray Fawkes is a Toronto-based author and illustrator. He is an Eisner, Harvey, Shuster, and Doug Wright Award nominee for his work on various graphic novels and comic book titles, and is a YALSA award winner for his "Possessions" series. His work for DC and Marvel comics includes such titles as *Batman: Eternal*, *Constantine*, *Justice League Dark*, and *Wolverines*, and he is the creator of the critically acclaimed graphic novels *One Soul* and *The People Inside*.

Vince Locke began his career as an artist in 1986 drawing *Deadworld*, a zombie horror comic that soon became an underground hit. Since then, his comics work has included *The Sandman, American Freak, Batman, Witchcraft: La Terreur, The Spectre, Judge Dredd, The Unwritten,* and *A History of Violence,* which was later adapted into a movie directed by David Cronenberg. Locke has also painted over a dozen album covers for the death metal band Cannibal Corpse, illustrated work by the dark-fantasy author Caitlín R. Kiernan, and supplied paintings for *Aqua Teen Hunger Force* on Cartoon Network. He lives with his wife and three sons in Michigan.

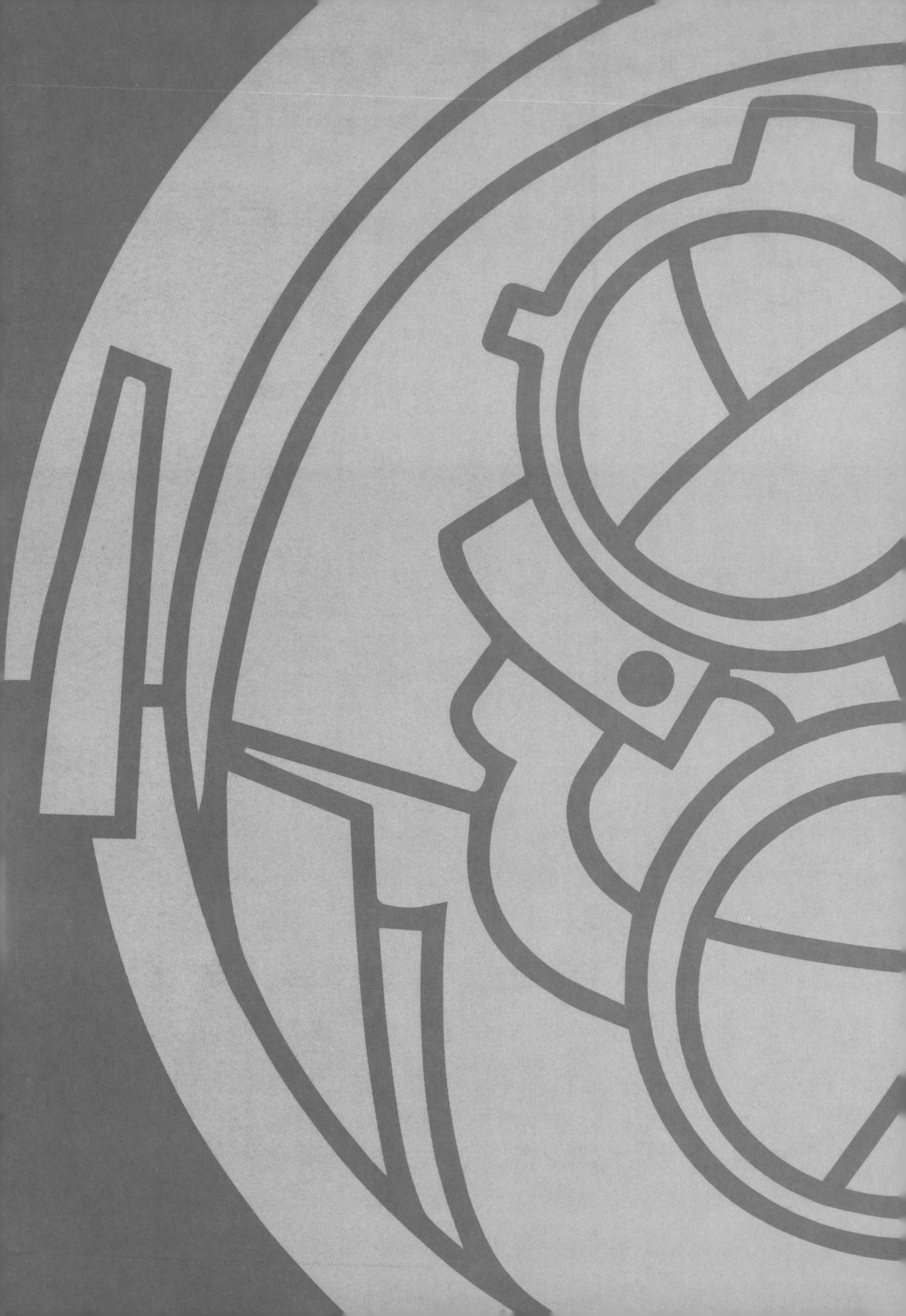